S0-BHU-949

DICTIONARY OF SCIENCE & CREATIONISM

DICTIONARY OF SCIENCE & CREATIONISM

RONALD L. ECKER

FOREWORD BY MARTIN GARDNER

PROMETHEUS BOOKS
BUFFALO, NEW YORK

Library of Congress Catalog Card Number 89-63832

For my parents,
Roy and Lucille Ecker,
two special creationists

Foreword
by Martin Gardner

Many excellent books, listed in this volume's bibliography, deal with the monstrous scientific ignorance of today's creationists. This book, however, is the first to be organized as a dictionary to make it easy to look up information on specific topics. If, for instance, you want to know how creationists distort the simple laws of thermodynamics, you don't have to consult scattered pages cited in the index. Just turn to the entry on thermodynamics.

Ronald Ecker has done a splendid job of pulling together vast amounts of relevant data and presenting them in concise, readable, accurate ways. The book is also more up to date than other books covering similar ground. For example, you may read somewhere that the Seventh-Day Adventist Robert Gentry has recently claimed that polonium halos prove that God created our entire galaxy, including the earth, about 10,000 years ago. What are polonium halos? Turn to the book's entry and you will quickly find out.

Will this book alter the mind-set of any creationist? Probably not, but among conservative Christians with more open minds it may do some good. Most of all, it can be a valuable aid to politicians and educators, as well as journalists of the print and electronic media, when they face pressures to alter state laws about teaching evolution or to force textbook publishers to meet creationist demands.

One of the saddest, in some ways most frightening, consequences of the steady decline in the quality of American education is the surprising upsurge of fundamentalism. Battles thought to have been won fifty years ago are now being fought all over again, just as bitterly, and certainly with less humor. (Mencken, how we miss you!) I recall an occasion in the 1930s when I mentioned to a college professor that a book blasting Protestant liberalism had just been published by a Presbyterian fundamentalist. The professor, feigning great surprise, said, "I though he died!" Fifty years ago it did indeed seem as if fundamentalism, though not totally dead, was at least expiring in mainstream denominations. I know of no social scientist who predicted it would ever be revived.

No longer content with proclaiming that evolution is in conflict with the Bible, creationists now boldly assert that science supports the Genesis account as strongly as it does evolution—some would say *more* strongly. Such contentions can be made only by someone who knows almost nothing about geology. True, there are conflicting views among experts on exactly *how* the process of evolution works, but that evolution *has* been taking place, over a few billion years, is as well established as Copernican astronomy. Only a person willfully ignorant can think otherwise.

When a theory becomes strongly confirmed, scientists customarily call it a fact. At one time the notion that the earth and its sister planets go around the sun was called a theory. Who today, even among fundamentalists, say this? There were reasons in Darwin's day for calling evolution a theory. It has since become a fact, supported to the hilt by overwhelming empirical evidence. Henry Morris and Duane Gish, the two creationists most often cited in this book, are today's equivalents of the willfully ignorant Christians of past ages who, like Martin Luther, insisted that the earth is flat. This was bad science even in ancient Greece, when good evidence for the earth's roundness was well known to Aristotle. Luther's sole reason for opposing such evidence was that it contradicted Holy Writ. Even Saint Augustine knew the earth was round, but he argued that its other side could not be inhabited because it would violate the Bible's statement that every eye would see Jesus when he returned.

Today, the Roman Catholic church, having finally learned from its blunder with Galileo, no longer opposes evolution, or even modern biblical criticism. Evolution is taken as God's method of creation by the majority of educated Catholics around the world, and by almost all Catholic theologians. The church permits evolution to be taught in Catholic schools, adding only the caveat that at some point in history God infused immortal souls into the minds of the first humans, whose bodies had evolved from apelike primates. Liberal Anglo-Catholics and Protestants have also learned the folly of rejecting well-established science.

Of the most popular televangelists—Jimmy Swaggart, Oral and Richard Roberts, Pat Robertson, Jerry Falwell, and that curious couple Jim and Tammy Bakker—not one accepts evolution. (As for Robert Schuller, who knows what he thinks about any controversial doctrine?) It would be hard to find a Pentecostal or conservative Southern Baptist, or a member of such fundamentalist cults as the Seventh-Day Adventists, Jehovah's Witnesses, and the Worldwide Church of God, who does not believe that evolution was inspired by Satan.

Although they are apparently blind to the fact, creationist leaders are guilty of what they themselves call the sin of pride. When they read in 2 Timothy 2:15 that one should "study to shew thyself approved unto God, a workman that needeth not to be ashamed, rightly dividing the word of truth," they think this means to study the Bible, even though the Bible did not exist in Paul's day and the Gospels had not yet been written. What Paul meant was this: Learn as much as you can about matters bearing on your faith. That is what the leaders of creationism refuse to do. They remain convinced, in their vast pride, that already they have rightly divided the truth.

If Swaggart would take a few years off from his bellowing, weeping, babbling in the Unknown Tongue, and begging for money, and get a bachelor's degree from a college not run by other fundamentalists, those who know so much more than he might not think him such a fool. After getting passing grades in elementary geology and biology, would he continue to attack evolution? We will never know, because there is not a chance in Hades that Swaggart is capable of such humility. Has not God told him that evolution is the Devil's work? Why should he waste precious time—think of the millions of lost souls he could save from eternal torment!—studying anything except the Bible and books by other Pentecostals?

It is, I fear, utterly beyond the comprehension of fundamentalist preachers and evangelists that maybe, just maybe, the God they pray to might actually want them to stop preaching long enough to learn some basic science—long enough to become workmen that needeth not to be ashamed.

Preface

"A nation at risk." That is what the National Commission on Excellence in Education (1983) called the United States in 1983, citing a "rising tide of mediocrity" in American educational performance. Our nation, the commission report warned, was raising a new generation that was "technologically and scientifically illiterate." Six years later Lauro F. Cavazos, the U.S. Secretary of Education, could report little improvement in this dismal state of affairs. "This situation scares me," Cavazos told the American people, "and I hope it scares you" (Ordovensky 1989). A 1989 report by the Educational Testing Service on American students' math and science achievement was described by a spokesman for the National Science Foundation as "nothing short of frightening" (Byrne 1989). The report ranked American schoolchildren near the bottom among schoolchildren of several countries studied. "These results," the report concluded, "pose a serious challenge to our position in the world community" (Meisler 1989).

Such bleak assessments of American learning led to a summit meeting in October, 1989, at which President Bush and the nation's governors agreed to set national performance standards and goals for America's schools. But as former education secretary William Bennett asks (quoted in Goodgame 1989), "What happens if we don't reach the goals?"

It is bad enough that most adult Americans—94 percent, according to one recent study (Culliton 1989)—are scientifically illiterate. In a democracy, Isaac Asimov (1989) has cogently stated, a scientifically illiterate citizenry cannot make intelligent decisions about science or pressure its leaders in sensible directions. "We live in a society exquisitely dependent on science and technology," notes Carl Sagan (1989), "in which hardly anyone knows anything about science and technology. This is a clear prescription for disaster."

We do not need, nor should we tolerate, public school teachers presenting sectarian religious beliefs as science to schoolchildren who are not learning enough science as it is. (There is also the matter of the First Amendment of the U.S. Constitution, which prohibits any governmental "establishment of religion.") Yet such classroom presentation of religion-as-science is in effect what the creation "science" movement is all about. I want to stress that this book is not "against" the concept of a Creator. The book has no "antireligious" ax to grind. A legitimate complaint of creationists and noncreationists alike is that many public school textbooks in recent years have avoided the subject of religion altogether. There is something wrong, for example, when a history textbook defines pilgrims simply as "people who make long trips" (Nord 1986). Students should learn something about religion and the important role it has played in the history of their nation and the world, as part of a basic education. What this book opposes is pseudoscience. The book's intent is to help combat a particularly insidious brand of pseudoscience, a sectarian creationism that calls itself "scientific" and is determined to impose itself on the American public school system. Ordinarily the term *creationist* would by definition apply to anyone who happens to believe in a Creator. It is important to note, therefore, that whenever the term *creationist(s)* appears in this book, it is intended, unless otherwise noted, to apply only to those who are participants in or supporters of the so-called creation "science" movement.

Modern American creationism has been characterized by its leading spokesman, Henry M. Morris of the Institute for Creation Research (ICR), as a Christian movement that seeks "to reach a generation brainwashed in evolutionary humanism—a generation standing urgently in need of the foundational truth of special creation" (Morris 1987a, 4). The theory of evolution, say the creationists (ICR 1987, iv), is contrary to "the Word of God" as well as "to all the real facts of science." It is, in Morris's words (1970, 71), "the anti-God conspiracy of Satan himself!" The creationists argue, of course, that the purpose of teaching creation "science" in the public schools is only to present "the scientific evidences for creation" (see Zetterberg 1983, 395), not to teach any religion. Yet ICR vice president Duane Gish (1973, 266), in discussing "creation theory," refers specifically to "the acts of a preexisting Being." The ICR textbook *Scientific Creationism* describes this Being with a litany of adjectives: "infinite, eternal, omnipotent, omnipresent, omniscient, moral, spiritual, volitional, truthful, loving, living" (Morris 1985b, 20). The ICR knows perfectly well that this is a religious, not a scientific, concept. It must be remembered that the ICR, the creation "science" movement's flagship organization, is a Christian fundamentalist institution. It is described by Morris (1987d), its founder and president, as a "God-called ministry" whose mission is that of "creation evangelism."

From the late 1970s through 1981, creationists succeeded in getting bill after bill introduced in state legislatures that would require the teaching of creation "science" in any public schools where evolutionary theory also was taught. (Laws simply banning the teaching of evolution were ruled unconstitutional by the Supreme Court in 1968.) One such "balanced treatment" law was enacted by Arkansas in 1981, only to be struck down by U.S. District Court Judge William Overton as being "simply and purely an effort to introduce the Biblical version of creation into the public school curricula" (Overton 1982, 315). A similar 1981 law passed by Louisiana was ruled unconstitutional by the U.S. Supreme Court in 1987, bringing to an end creationist attempts to have creationism taught by law in America's public schools.

But the creationists have retreated only from the legislatures, not from their ongoing war in general against the so-called religion of humanism. They see evolution as a tenet of the "humanist religion," which for all practical purposes, says Morris (1985b, iii), is "the official state religion promoted in the public schools." Creationists have been effective in the past in pressuring teachers and school boards to include their brand of "science" in the classroom, and such local-level impact is once again the main creationist strategy. While the 1987 Supreme

Court decision precludes *forcing* public school teachers to teach creationism, the Court did not rule that teaching "scientific" creationism per se in public schools is unconstitutional. And the creationists now argue that teachers have a "right," as a matter of "academic freedom" (see Fezer 1988), to teach various "theories" of origins and to sue if that right is interfered with (Bird 1987, ii). A creationist legal defense fund is available to lend its support (see *Creation/Evolution Newsletter* 8[5]:8).

As for teachers who do not wish to teach creationism, many can be pressured by creationists into simply not teaching evolution (see Mayer 1984). Most creationists, if they had the choice, would probably prefer the nonteaching of evolution to equal time for "scientific" creationism (a fundamentalist invention of the sixties to combat reintroduction of evolution to the classroom). Silence on the subject of evolution was standard in America's public schools for some forty years after the 1925 Scopes trial. "We would really be satisfied," says the Creation-Science Research Center's Robert Kofahl (quoted in Edwords 1980, 10-11), "to see the subject of origins removed entirely from public school science. . . . Let's *forget* about origins." (It should be noted that evolution is not a theory of "origins," it is a theory of change. It is also the most important unifying concept in modern biology [National Academy of Sciences 1984, 221].)

No one should underestimate the amount of grassroots support for the creationist cause. Polls indicate that about half of the American people reject the idea of human evolution (Culliton 1989; Gallant 1984, 290; Russell 1986). A 1987 study in Ohio (Zimmerman 1987) found that almost 40 percent of that state's high-school biology teachers favor teaching creationism in the public schools. Robert L. Simonds, headquartered in Costa Mesa, California, heads a nationwide coalition of creationist teachers and parents called the National Association of Christian Educators and Citizens for Excellence in Education (NACE/CEE), whose aim is to take over all the school boards, thereby to control public education and so also, in Simond's words, "public opinion and this nation" (Hechinger 1986). Combating such creationist efforts at both the national and local levels is the National Center for Science Education (NCSE). Headquartered in Berkeley, California, the NCSE coordinates a network of activist groups called Committees of Correspondence located in all fifty states. Devoted to enhancing the integrity of science education, the NCSE is "the only national organization," says its president John R. Cole (1989), "specializing in the creation-evolution controversy."

Meanwhile the ICR creationists have urged that more parental home schooling and private Christian/creationist schools be developed (ICR 1987, iii; for an incisive look at the fundamentalist Christian-school movement, see *Free Inquiry* 7[4]), and it can even be argued that if creationists had their way they would abolish the public school system altogether. Take, for example, the position of the Reverend Jerry Falwell, who preaches weekly to millions on television and has boasted of the creationist biology teachers turned out by his Liberty University ("Of course, they'll be teaching evolution," says Falwell [*Creation/Evolution* 8:44], "but teaching why it's invalid and why it's foolish"). Falwell (quoted in Bollier 1984, 18) has a dream: "I hope I live to see the day when, as in the early days of our country, we won't have any public schools. The churches will have taken them over again and Christians will be running them. What a happy day that will be!"

There are a number of books available that deal with the scientific invalidity of "scientific" creationist claims. What is different about this one? The *Dictionary of Science and Creationism* was written to fill the need for a creation/evolution reference work in dictionary form. It is designed as a concise, nontechnical, ready-reference source of information, providing overviews of all major scientific areas that relate to evolutionary theory and using that information to show the pseudo-scientific nature of "scientific" creationism. All articles are cross-referenced—words in CAPITAL LETTERS in the body of an article indicate related entries—and there is a comprehensive index to help the reader find subjects that do not have their own entries. The dictionary will hopefully be of benefit to teachers and school board members who must deal with local creationist pressure, indeed to all defenders of the integrity of science education in countering creationist tactics. It should be of benefit to the interested casual reader as well. Even those with no particular concern about the creationist movement may find a few things about science that they did not know before. And maybe in the process they will become more concerned about what the creationists would like to contribute to the already lamentable condition of science education in America. Since evolutionary theory is supported by evidence from virtually all branches of the natural sciences, it is necessary to attack or revise much of modern science in order to attack evolution. And that is just what the creationists do.

I wish to thank the following individuals for kindly agreeing to read those portions of the manuscript that relate to their respective fields and for their critical comments and suggestions: Heinrich K. Eichhorn, professor of astronomy, and Richard H. Hiers, professor of religion, at the University of Florida; and Martin Roeder, professor of biological science, and Steven S. Winters, professor of geology, at Florida State University. I also wish to thank the staffs of the University of Florida libraries and the State Library of Florida for their help in obtaining the necessary materials for this project. I am grateful also to William J. Bennetta in San Francisco and Eugene J. Crook of Florida State University for their assistance.

Fanning Springs, Florida
November 1989

ABIOGENESIS

The theory that LIFE arose from nonliving matter, the word meaning literally "not arising from life." Numerous laboratory experiments (see Chang et al. 1983; Miller and Orgel 1974) have shown that *amino acids* and *nucleotide bases*—the building blocks of *proteins* and *nucleic acids*, in turn the building blocks of life—form by natural CHEMISTRY under a variety of simulated primitive-EARTH conditions. What is yet to be determined is the chemical process by which these essential organic ingredients were forged into the first molecules capable of self-replication (see GENETICS), at which point NATURAL SELECTION or biological EVOLUTION could begin.

The earth's atmosphere around four billion years ago, when life is believed to have arisen, probably contained approximately the same amount of nitrogen, water, and carbon dioxide as today's atmosphere, but with about one percent hydrogen and no free oxygen (Walker 1977, 246, 277). The oxidizing effect of free oxygen would have inhibited life's generation (Schopf, Hayes, and Walter 1983, 375). (Ironically, free oxygen arose as a result of life through green-PLANT *photosynthesis*, providing new sources of energy for organisms that were able to adapt [Walker 1977, 248]). This explains why abiogenesis, known also as *spontaneous generation*, could occur naturally on the primitive earth but does not occur now. Life cannot form today because it would be immediately destroyed by oxidation and by other organisms (McGowan 1984, 48; Van Andel 1985, 225).

Creationists argue that even the simplest protein molecule, containing just the right sequence of amino acids, is too complex to have arisen by chance (Morris 1984a, 234). But no scientist claims that such a molecule could have somehow arisen full blown. It was rather the product, over geologic time, of a step-by-step process, governed by natural laws of chemistry, with no particular amino-acid sequence required. The same holds true for nucleic acids. The first nucleic acid did not have to be composed of any particular nucleotide sequence—the probability of one particular sequence arising would certainly be low—but had only to be composed of *some* sequence, the probability of some sequence arising, over a period of millions of years, being high (Futuyma 1982, 184). (Creationists argue, of course, that such time has not been available, the earth in their view being only a few thousand years old, a biblically influenced argument that is scientifically untenable; see EARTH and RADIOACTIVE DATING.) It should also be noted that organic compounds have been identified in interstellar clouds, comets, and atmospheres of the outer planets (Chang et al. 1983, 91), and that amino acids and nucleotide bases have even landed on the earth in meteorites (Cloud 1988, 11, 230; Miller and Orgel 1974, 193-96; *Science News* 124:150). For all we know, life's building blocks may occur naturally throughout the cosmos. This has led some to speculate that the earth was originally seeded with life from space, in the form of radiation-blown spores (the *panspermia* theory of the Swedish scientist Svante Arrhenius), microorganisms living on comets (proposed by Fred Hoyle and Chandra Wickramasinghe), or even microorganisms brought by unmanned spaceship (the *directed panspermia* theory of biologists Francis Crick and Leslie Orgel) (Crick 1981; Jackson and Moore 1987, 28-33). Such ideas not only lack evidence, however, but do not answer the question of how life first arose. They simply move the problem farther away.

Creationists are absolutely right when they say that life has yet to be created in the laboratory (Moore 1976, 68; Morris 1985b, 49). They would surely agree with geneticist Carl Woese (1983, 211) that theoretical accounts of the transition from nonliving to living matter are "little more than *Just So Stories.*" But origin-of-life research is not even forty years old; Nature, as Carl Sagan (1980, 40) points out, "has had a four-billion-year head start." Today biochemist Sidney Fox (1988) makes "proteinoids," proteinlike substances that self-organize in water to form "microspheres," cell-like units that may closely approximate the first primordial protocells. Chemist Graham Cairns-Smith (1985) argues that clay minerals played a decisive role in the emergence of self-replicating forms. Some scientists have argued that abiogenesis may have begun around hot ocean-floor vents (McKean 1983, 42), sites offering ammonia, methane, water, and heat, a mixture that in the pioneering origin-of-life experiment of Stanley Miller (1953) and Harold Urey yielded a "surprising number" of organic compounds (Miller and Orgel 1974, 84). (Miller rejects the vent theory, citing organic instability at such high temperatures; he sees first the atmosphere and later lagoons, lakes, and cool parts of the ocean as more likely sites of early organic synthesis [Monastersky 1988].) The Nobel Prize–winning discovery by chemists Thomas Cech and Sidney Altman that the genetic material RNA (ribonucleic acid) can act as an enzyme has led many origin-of-life researchers to believe that a primitive form of RNA was the link between prebiotic synthesis and the first living cells (Waldrop 1989a and 1989b; Amato 1989b).

It is possible that all the facets of abiogenesis may never be fully understood. Moreover, creationists are right when they say that even if scientists someday synthesize life in the laboratory, it will not prove how life actually arose (Morris 1985b, 49). But what scientists seek at the least is "a plausible theory" (McKean 1983, 42) of life's origin. And all present evidence supports the view that the precursors of life arose naturally, and that life's subsequent emergence, "given millions of years and the whole earth as a laboratory" (K. Miller 1984, 57), was a probable if not inevitable event.

ABRUPT APPEARANCE

A term—more fully, "abrupt appearance in complex form"—often used by "scientific" creationists to refer to CREATION. The term originated in the literature of evolutionary SCIENCE, where it is used in reference to the scarcity of intermediate forms (hence the "abrupt appearance" of new forms) in the FOSSIL RECORD. Thus creationist leader Henry Morris (1977, 31), president of California's INSTITUTE FOR CREATION RESEARCH (ICR), quotes evolutionists Valentine and Campbell (1975, 673): "The abrupt appearance of higher taxa [groups or categories] in the fossil record has been a perennial puzzle." ICR vice president Duane Gish (1985, 57, 231-33, 236, 242) quotes Niles Eldredge (Raup and Stanley 1971, 306) on the "rather abrupt appearance" of marine phyla during the CAMBRIAN EXPLOSION; Everett C. Olson (1965, 94) on "the abrupt appearances of new groups" in the fossil record; Stephen Jay Gould (1980, 188) on those same "abrupt transitions"; and Ayala and Valentine (1979, 266), Raup and

Stanley (1971, 306), and George Gaylord Simpson (Tax 1960, 149), all agreeing that most groups in the fossil record "appear abruptly." Anthropologist Laurie R. Godfrey, paleontologist Norman D. Newell, and geologist Preston Cloud also speak of "abrupt appearances" (Godfrey 1983, 201) or forms that "appear abruptly" (Cloud 1983, 143; Newell 1985, 191). The concept in fact dates back to Charles Darwin, who wrote in *On the Origin of Species* (1859, 306) of "the sudden appearance" of new forms in the fossil record.

It is clear, in context, what Darwin and the others quoted above are talking about: the "extreme rarity" (Gould 1980, 181)—not, as creationists would have it, the "absence" (Morris 1974, 267)—of TRANSITIONAL FORMS between groups or taxa (see TAXONOMY) in the fossil record. This rarity of intermediates led Eldredge and Gould (1972) to propose their evolutionary theory of PUNCTUATED EQUILIBRIA, which is a theory of rapid speciation (the splitting of one species into two) in geographically isolated populations, and has nothing to do with creation. As early as 1983, however, creationist leader Luther Sunderland began urging creationists to adopt "the abrupt appearance of various life forms" as a concept of creation that could be seen as independent of religion (Bennetta 1988b, 20; Kane 1987, 17). The late Sunderland equated abrupt appearance with Eldredge and Gould's punctuated equilibria—minus, of course, the concept of common descent (Kane 1987, 17). Sunderland's urging bore fruit, for in 1985 several creationist affidavits defining "creation-science" as the "scientific" evidence for "abrupt appearance in complex form" abruptly appeared in the long legal wrangle over the constitutionality of a 1981 Louisiana CREATIONISM law. (The law required "balanced treatment" for "creation-science" in public school teaching; see *EDWARDS v. AGUILLARD*.) Creationist attorney Wendell Bird (quoted in Cornell 1987), who represented the Louisiana creationists before the U.S. Supreme Court, maintains that abrupt appearance "does not imply a Creator"; it is based "explicitly and totally on scientific evidence." But granted there is ample evidence of abrupt appearances in the fossil record, to what origin, if not a Creator, do Bird and other Sunderland-style creationists attribute the appearances? Evolutionary theories of rapid speciation offer a naturalistic explanation for species "abruptly" appearing; creation "science" does not. As seventy-two Nobel laureates and twenty-four scientific organizations pointed out in a friend-of-court brief filed in the *Edwards* case, the creationist "abrupt-appearance construct" simply "fails to define a concrete alternative to evolution" (Amici Curiae 1986, 17). (The Supreme Court ruled the Louisiana law unconstitutional by a 7-2 vote.)

The ICR's Gish is straightforward about the Creator connection. He states (1985, 250) that the "abrupt appearance" of complex life forms is a major prediction of the creation model of origins; that the fossil record reveals such abrupt appearance; and that the fossil record "thus provides excellent support for special creation." But Gish, like Morris and the ICR's other "scientific" creationists, is a biblical literalist (see BIBLE) who believes (1985, 35) that GOD created all "kinds" of ANIMALS and PLANTS, "a *finished* creation," during "the creation-week" as described in the biblical book of Genesis. All things must therefore have abruptly appeared in one week. That is certainly not supported by the fossil record, which spans millions of years of EARTH history (in a clear evolutionary pattern, from simpler to more complex forms) as determined by stratigraphy and RADIOACTIVE DATING (see GEOLOGY). Yes, most groups "appear abruptly"—but "abrupt" in the context of geologic time, the context used by evolutionary scientists, means "hundreds, even thousands of years" of EVOLUTION leading to any one species (Gould 1980, 184). And any two taxonomic groups, no matter how rapidly evolved, may be separated chronologically by millions of years. So if all groups abruptly appeared/were abruptly created, they must therefore have done so/been so in stages, in a long series of abrupt appearances/creations over geologic time. But that's "progressive creation," a concept firmly rejected by ICR creationists as unbiblical (Morris 1985b, 220-22). The strictures of biblical chronology and events, literally interpreted, thus force ICR-style creationists to reject the geologic ages and argue that the earth is only several thousand years old (Aardsma 1988, iv; Ackerman 1986; Morris 1985b, 158). They argue that all kinds of animals lived (and thus appeared/were created) contemporaneously, all then drowning (except for the animals on the ark) in a worldwide deluge (see ARK, NOAH'S and FLOOD, NOAH'S). But they can make this argument only by rejecting all the scientific evidence—offering pseudoscience in its place—from ASTRONOMY, GEOLOGY, and PHYSICS, that the age of the earth is about 4.6 billion years. They must also reject strong evidence from Mesopotamian mythology (Lambert 1965), archaeology (MacDonald 1988), and the biblical description itself (Moore 1983) that Noah's Flood (like the Babylonian Utnapishtim's) occurred only in ancient myth. These leaders of creation "science" must reject, in short, everything that doesn't fit into their fundamentalist belief system. That's a pretty far cry from scientific method as any competent scientist would define it (see SCIENCE).

"Abrupt appearance in complex form" has a good deal in common with the creationist APPEARANCE OF AGE argument, according to which the universe was created fully functioning—light in transit from STARS, the first MAN fully grown, etc.—and thus only *appears* to be several billion years old. We all could have abruptly appeared five minutes ago, "with holes in our socks and hair that needed cutting" (Russell 1961, 70). The proposition is untestable, neither provable nor disprovable, the kind that is scientifically meaningless. Any illusion of scientific meaning in the creationist concept of abrupt appearance—whether five eons ago or five minutes—abruptly disappears under the light of the overwhelming scientific evidence for cosmic and biological evolution.

ACQUIRED CHARACTERISTICS, INHERITANCE OF

See LAMARCKISM.

ADAM AND EVE

The first MAN (Hebrew *adam*) and woman ("Eve" in the Hebrew is *hawwah,* meaning "life") created by GOD according to the biblical book of Genesis. In the first CREATION account (Gen. 1:1-2:4a), man is created "male and female," that is, man and woman are created simultaneously; in the second account (2:4b-25), Adam is created alone, with Eve later fashioned from his rib. (For discussion of the hypothesis that Genesis contains multiple documents, see BIBLE.) Living in paradisal Eden, Adam and Eve fall from grace by eating forbidden fruit, causing God to curse the ground and banish the pair from Eden.

The Adam and Eve story appears to derive in part from the Sumerian myth of Enki and Ninhursag, gods in paradisal Dilmun (for text, see Kramer 1969, 37-41). A pain in Enki's rib, caused by a curse from Ninhursag for eating certain PLANTS, is cured by the goddess Ninti, whose name means both "lady of life" and "lady of the rib" (Hooke 1963, 115). Other mythological motifs in the biblical story include a "tree of life" (found in Assyrian and Cretan art [Miller and Miller 1973, 780] and in the heaven of the ancient Egyptians [Budge 1895, xxvil]), the *cherubim* (winged human-headed lions found in Canaanite art [Wright 1962, 95]), and a wily "serpent" that brings man to grief (found, like the Babylonian flood story [see FLOOD, NOAH'S], in the Babylonian epic of Gilgamesh [Speiser 1969, 96]).

The story of Adam and Eve and their fall has been aptly described by Catholic biblical scholar Bruce Vawter (1977, 90) as "a paradigm of human conduct in the face of temptation." Its moral—debatable though it may be psychologically (see SOCIAL SCIENCES)—is, in the words of John L. McKenzie (1980, 46), that "the human condition is the result of a decision made by man himself," that "man is the way he is because he chooses to be that way." The story is considered literally true only by fundamentalists (see BIBLE) who insist on a doctrine of biblical inerrancy. And the leaders of the so-called scientific creationist movement, such as Henry Morris and Duane Gish of the INSTITUTE FOR CREATION RESEARCH (ICR), are Christian fundamentalists (see CREATIONISM). As an example of their "science," the ICR creationists (Morris 1985b, 212) interpret God's curse "on the ground" for Adam and Eve's sin as a curse on the "basic physical elements" and "all flesh constructed from those elements," so that the curse may be expressed in "scientific" terms as the principle of entropy or the second law of THERMODYNAMICS.

The first two chapters of Genesis, says Gish (1985, 23-24), are not "parables or poetry" but "simple historical facts," thus the Adam and Eve story "cannot be reconciled with any possible evolutionary theory concerning the origin of man." This view reflects as clearly as any the true nature of "scientific" creationism: a preconceived belief system based not on any scientific evidence but on the unalterable conviction that Genesis contains, in the words of the ICR's Ken Ham (1989b), "the literal foundations of all true doctrine."

ADAPTATION

The evolutionary process by which species or individuals thereof become modified the better to function and survive in their *environment*. (The word can also refer to the particular feature that has undergone modification.) All organisms are to some extent adapted to their environment, but some are better adapted or (when the environment changes) more able to adapt than others. A frequently cited example of observed adaptation to a changing environment is the so-called *industrial melanism* that developed in many species of moths, particularly the peppered moth (*Biston betularia*), in industrial regions of nineteenth-century England. Light-colored moths resting on a light background of lichen-covered tree trunks were quite inconspicuous to INSECT-eating BIRDS until industrial air pollution began blackening the tree trunks, making the light-colored moths easy prey (Dobzhansky 1985, 745). In 1848, a melanic or dark-colored mutant of the peppered moth appeared, its protective coloring allowing it to survive and reproduce until by the end of the century, as more and more melanic moths had outlived and thus out-reproduced the light ones, the genes for melanism had become dominant in the moth population's gene pool, the dark-colored moths almost completely replacing the light ones (Newell 1985, 184-85). All those dark-colored moths on a dark background of blackened tree trunks thus looked as if they had been specially designed for that environment, when actually they had become naturally adapted by a process of differential reproduction—the process of NATURAL SELECTION.

When a species has become well adapted, and there is little or no subsequent change in the environment, there is little or no further EVOLUTION. This explains, at least in part, so-called *living fossils*—

for example, the coelecanth, "the fish that time forgot" (Fricke 1988), and the brachiopod *Lingula*, almost the same as it was over four hundred million years ago (Briggs 1979, 76)—as well as the perception that MAN, who has considerable control over his own environment, has stopped physically (though not socially or culturally) evolving. (Paleontologist Niles Eldredge [1985, 109] theorizes that living fossils are also explainable as species that are the most generalized ecologically; he calls them "jacks-of-all-trades" who have not put all of their "evolutionary eggs" in one basket as have their more specialized kin.)

Since the process of adaptation by natural selection involves only "the illusion of design and planning" (Dawkins 1986, 21), we would expect the results to be less than perfect—and that is exactly what we find in nature. Natural selection, a blind process, a "tinkerer" (Jacob 1977) with no preconceived plan, working only with what is at hand, is indifferent to perfect functioning; it is "only comparatively better functioning which counts" (Ruse 1986, 17). For creationists, who see adaptive change as occurring only within the limits of originally created kinds (Gish 1985, 35; Morris 1985b, 51-52), maladaptations and other imperfections of nature would seem to be a formidable problem. Being Christian fundamentalists, however, the creationists have a ready religious explanation for nature's imperfections: GOD's "Curse" upon the world—"reflected in the scientific realm," says creationist leader Henry Morris (1978, 74), "by the universal law of increasing entropy" (see THERMODYNAMICS)—for the sin of ADAM AND EVE. John Morris (1989b), son of Henry, speculates that God, in the process of administering his curse, "actually changed the genetic makeup of each 'kind' so that all their descendants would be different." Morris admits that he may be over-speculating, "but sin ruins everything."

AGE OF THE EARTH

See EARTH.

AMPHIBIAN

A creature that lives on both land and in water (from Greek *amphibios,* meaning "both ways of life"). There is disagreement as to whether the modern family Amphibia (frogs, toads, newts, salamanders, and the worm-like caecilia) evolved from the early amphibians or directly from FISHES. The early amphibians, all now extinct, evolved from fishes and were ancestral to REPTILES.

The fishes ancestral to the early amphibians were probably the *rhipidistian crossypterygians,* lobe-finned fishes of the Devonian period (from about 395 million to about 345 million years ago). The now extinct rhipidistians had lungs (as their cousins the lungfishes still do) and could crawl on land by virtue of two strong pairs of fins. Since PLANTS then comprised most of land life, the lobe-finned fishes found a bright new world before them with almost no competition. The earliest known amphibian to evolve from this venture onto land was *Ichthyostega* of the late Devonian (Dixon et al. 1988, 48). Amphibian forms proliferated during the Carboniferous period (from about 345 to 280 million years ago) but were eventually displaced by their reptilian descendants during the Permian (280 to 230 million years ago). The reptiles, in turn, were ancestral to BIRDS and MAMMALS.

The standard creationist argument that there are no TRANSITIONAL FORMS in the FOSSIL RECORD is belied, as far as amphibians are concerned, by *Ichthyostega,* intermediate between Devonian fish and Carboniferous amphibian, and by *Seymouria,* a transitional form between amphibian and reptile. Creationist leader Duane Gish (1985, 75) tries to make a case against *Ichthyostega* as a fish-amphibian intermediate by discussing fish and amphibian vertebrae, but since he gets his facts backwards it is no wonder, notes paleontologist Chris McGowan (1984, 154-55), that the argument is confusing. ("Arch" vertebrae in amphibians are "more primitive" than "husk" vertebrae, not vice versa [McGowan 1984, 155].) Gish's error is found in the original 1972 edition of his book (*Evolution? The Fossils Say No!*), and remains unchanged, three editions later, in the retitled 1985 edition (*Evolution: The Challenge of the Fossil Record*). For discussion of Gish's argument against *Seymouria* as an amphibian-reptile intermediate, see REPTILE.

ANATOMY

The structure of biological organisms. *Morphology* (from the Greek word for *form*) is synonymous. When anatomical similarities between species are due to common evolutionary descent, they are said to be *homologous* ("agreeing"). The paired fins of FISHES and the legs of AMPHIBIANS, REPTILES, and MAMMALS, for example, are homologous organs in spite of apparent differences (Dobzhansky 1985, 746). Flowering PLANTS are homologous structures, all anatomically "built on the same plan" though there are a quarter of a million different species, a similarity in spite of diversity that is easily explicable by common descent (Dodson 1985, 983). When structures do not correspond by common descent but have evolved to be similar in function (the wings of BIRDS and the wings of INSECTS, for example), they are merely *analagous*, not homologous, and are examples of *convergent evolution*.

Similarities among species are considered by creationists to be evidence of "a common plan of creation used by the Creator" (Moore 1976, 30). Such an explanation is not only a religious one, however, but fails to account for anatomical imperfections (a well-known example, thanks to Stephen Jay Gould [1980, 19-26], being the panda's thumb, anatomically not a digit at all but a bone normally found in the wrist). Evolutionary biologists consider (homologous) similarities to be evidence of "descent with modification through natural selection" from a common ancestor (Darwin 1859), a completely natural explanation for what is certainly less than perfect anatomical design (see DESIGN ARGUMENT).

ANIMAL

A member of the kingdom Animalia, being multicellular forms of LIFE that, unlike PLANTS (kingdom Plantae), lack chlorophyll and thus are unable to manufacture their own food. Having to search for nutrition, most animals have some degree of motility. *Zoology* is the study of animals.

MAN is by the above definition an animal. (Few in any case would call man a plant!) But to place man in any category (see TAXONOMY) that does not automatically set him apart from other living things goes to the very heart of the CREATION/EVOLUTION dispute. The creationist moral objection to an evolutionary kinship between man and nonhuman beings has been succinctly stated by creationist John N. Moore (1976, 81): "Personal dignity, value, and worth are lost in viewing a human being as simply a made-over animal, another 'evolved' member of a species." But while man is taxonomically an animal, evolutionists do not say, as creationists would imply that they do, that man is *nothing but* an animal. "The essence of (man's) unique nature," as the late paleontologist George Gaylord Simpson (1967, 283-284) expressed it, "lies precisely in those characteristics that are not shared with any other animal." Conceptual thought and verbal speech are faculties that have brought man both mastery of the globe and the threat of his own EXTINCTION (Lorenz 1966, 238). But they have also given man the ability to discern his biological kinship with earth's other creatures. Charles Darwin (1859, 128-130) called it "a truly wonderful fact" that all forms of life are related to each other "in group subordinate to group," resembling each other "in descending degrees," and he spoke of the resulting "Great Tree of Life . . . with its ever branching and beautiful ramifications." That seems to reflect a far more reverent attitude toward life than that of creationists who rail against the concept of man's "animal origins" (see Saladin 1980, 59).

The knowledge that all forms of life are related by common descent should not fail to have a salutary effect on man's feeling toward his fellow organisms (Mayr 1988, 262). The fact that humans and other creatures are biologically related, says sociobiologist E. O. Wilson (1984, 130), "does not diminish humanity—it raises the status of nonhuman creatures."

ANTHROPOLOGY

See SOCIAL SCIENCES.

APE

See PRIMATE.

APPEARANCE OF AGE

The creationist argument, called also "apparent age," that the UNIVERSE was created fully functioning from the very first instant, therefore all objects that the Creator made would have the appearance of having already been there, that is, everything would have an "appearance of age" (Morris 1984a, 175; 1985b, 210; Moore 1976, 61). ADAM AND EVE, for example, were created as mature individuals (Morris 1985b, 209); they had arms, legs, and so forth that ordinarily take time to mature but in this case were full grown at CREATION with only the appearance of a history of growth. In the same way, the universe at large, say the creationists, is younger than it appears, God having created it with "functioning completeness" (Morris and Parker 1987, 307). So the universe can be, just as the BIBLE tells us, only about ten thousand years old (Aardsma 1988, iv), even though there "appears" to be evidence from ASTRONOMY, GEOLOGY, and PHYSICS that the age of the EARTH alone is about 4.6 billion years!

The seminal work on this subject was a book by Philip Henry Gosse entitled *Omphalos*, published in 1857. The title is the Greek word for *navel*, Gosse's argument being that Adam, for appearance's sake, must have had one. Gosse even concluded that Adam was created with partially digested food in his system that he had never eaten (Strahler 1987, 81). Fossils, moreover, were created by God, said Gosse, to look like once-living creatures that never existed. That particular notion is rejected by modern creationists, who attribute the FOSSIL RECORD instead to the life-quenching biblical Deluge (see FLOOD, NOAH'S). Today's creationists rather use appearance of age to argue, for example, that the light from STARS could have been created already in transit, so that the stars, despite the millions of light-years that their light may seemingly have had to travel in order for us to see it, could still have been created only a few thousand

1984a, 175-176).

Appearance of age, allowing the universe to be as young as the creationists desire, is, of course, an untestable hypothesis. One can claim that the universe was created half an hour ago and no one can refute it. But creationists have no real defense—they simply counter with righteous indignation (see Whitcomb and Morris 1961, 238)—against the charge by evolutionists such as the late Christian geneticist Theodosius Dobzhansky (1973, 127) that appearance of age implies a deceitful Creator, a God who in effect has planted false evidence of a long evolutionary past as if "deliberately to mislead sincere seekers of truth."

ARCHAEOPTERYX

An extinct, REPTILE-like BIRD that lived about 150 million years ago. Though classed as a genus of bird because of its feathers, *Archaeopteryx* ("ancient wing") is predominantly reptilian in its features and is considered a TRANSITIONAL FORM between reptiles and birds. A claim that its feathers—known from impressions in the limestone in which fossil specimens of *Archaeopteryx* have been found—were a hoax, the impressions the work of a forger, was refuted in a 1986 study by a team of British Museum paleontologists (Charig et al 1986). This was followed by the discovery of a new *Archaeopteryx* fossil specimen, complete with feather impressions, in 1987 (Wellnhofer 1988).

It is a standard creationist argument that there are no transitional forms in the FOSSIL RECORD. Creationists therefore argue that *Archaeopteryx* was "an undoubted true bird" (Gish 1985, 117), but they cannot explain away the fact that were it not for this bird's one uniquely avian characteristic—feathers—it would be classed as a reptile (Futuyma 1982, 189). Dr. Duane Gish of the INSTITUTE FOR CREATION RESEARCH can be credited with the best creationist effort to deal with this creature. According to Gish (1985, 117), the fact, for example, that *Archaeopteryx* had teeth, unlike modern birds, does not mean that this bird was transitional, because Cretaceous birds still had teeth and they lived after *Archaeopteryx*. But this argument, says paleontologist

Chris McGowan (1984, 121), misses the point that "the possession of teeth is a primitive feature which *Archaeopteryx* and Cretaceous birds inherited from their reptilian ancestors." Gish (1985, 113-114) also argues that clawed fingers on the wings of *Archaeopteryx* prove nothing because "at least three birds very much alive and well today" have claws on their wings. Again the point is missed that such birds are revealing their "reptilian pedigree" (McGowan 1984, 124).

In 1986 a fossil bird (*Protoavis*) was discovered that according to Gish (1987, iv) "should now completely mute the claims for a transitional status for *Archaeopteryx*." *Protoavis* was 75 million years older than *Archaeopteryx*, yet described by its discoverer (quoted in Weisburd 1986) as "a much more advanced bird than the *Archaeopteryx* fossils." What Gish fails to mention in his enthusiasm over this "startling" find is that "*Protoavis*, like *Archaeopteryx*, has distinctly dinosaurian features, such as clawed fingers, a tail, and teeth" (Weisburd 1986). Gish in effect tries to discredit one transitional form (*Archaeopteryx*) by singing the praises of another (*Protovavis*).

It is evident in his arguments that Gish either lacks or does not wish to deal with a proper understanding of transitional forms. A transitional form does not have to be, as creationists seem to assume, in the direct line of descent from one type of organism to another. In the words of Stan Weinberg (1986, 22), *Archaeopteryx* (as *Protoavis* clearly shows) "is not the *direct* ancestor of birds, it is a *collateral* ancestor—their *uncle* not their *father*." The important question about intermediate forms is whether the fossil record contains organisms that have a mix of characteristics common to two different groups (Kitcher 1982, 114). The obvious inference from such mosaic fossil organisms is the existence in the past of transitional forms—fathers, uncles, cousins—between the two groups. And *Archaeopteryx*, as Gish himself observes (1985, 114), "although unquestionably a bird, was a mosaic which included some features that are usually termed 'reptilian.' " Asks biologist Kenneth Miller (1982, 9): "Just how much more intermediate does something have to be?"

ARGUMENT FROM DESIGN

See DESIGN ARGUMENT.

ARK, NOAH'S

The homemade wooden ship in which Noah, his family, and pairs of all kinds of ANIMALS survived the worldwide Flood in the biblical book of Genesis (see FLOOD, NOAH'S). The leaders of creation "science," being Christian fundamentalists who espouse biblical inerrancy (see BIBLE), consider the Genesis Flood to be factual history, notwithstanding three known parallels (Sumerian, Sumero-Babylonian, and Babylonian) in Mesopotamian mythology (see Lambert 1965). These creationists, moreover, consider the Flood to be vital to the CREATION model of origins (Morris 1985b, 251-252), such a worldwide Deluge being the only "scientific" creationist explanation for the FOSSIL RECORD (see also GEOLOGY). This heavy creationist dependence on the Flood's historicity accounts for what might otherwise strike an outsider as an undue amount of attention paid by intelligent, educated adults to such a storybook subject as Noah's ark with (to quote a creationist) its "captive zoo" (McQueen 1988).

The problems posed by the ark for biblical literalists are formidable indeed. It has been estimated, to begin with, that for Noah to save one pair of each species of creature, he would have to somehow gather from all over the EARTH from two to four million animals, some four-fifths of them INSECTS (Asimov 1981, 157). This tremendous horde would have to be suitably accommodated aboard the ark (as would Noah and his wife, three sons, and three daughters-in-law). Creationists seek to avoid the millions-of-animals problem by first excluding all marine creatures (Whitcomb and Morris 1961, 68-69)—based on the erroneous assumption (see R. Moore 1983, 10-11) that such creatures could have survived the Flood on their own—and then by chucking the taxonomic concept of species in favor of the broader, ill-defined biblical concept of "kinds" (see TAXONOMY). John C. Whitcomb and Henry M. Morris (1961, 69) thus conclude that Noah had to take no more than 35,000 critters aboard the ark. Could the DINOSAURS fit in? Yes, says John Morris (1989b), there was "plenty of room" for "the younger ones." But even so, creationists admit that the problems of gathering to the ark and, once aboard, managing, feeding, cleaning up after, and otherwise caring for such a vast collection of creatures, are insurmountable without the deity's miraculous assistance. The story of the biblical Flood, says creationist John N. Moore (1976, 57), "is consistently supernatural." The Creation-Science Research Center's Kelly L. Segraves (1975, 133) tells us that "God sent the animals to Noah," an assumption with which Moore (1976, 57), Morris (1986, 88), and Whitcomb (1973, 32) agree. Once the animals were aboard the ark, creationists further assume that God, in Whitcomb's words (1973, 32), "supernaturally imposed a year-long hibernation . . . and thus removed the burden of their care completely from the hands of Noah and his family." (This divinely induced hibernation also explains why the animals did not reproduce during the lengthy voyage, it being God's purpose, in Segraves's words [1975, 140], "to repopulate the earth, not the ark.") The supernaturalism of the story must also include the ark's biblically stated length—300 cubits (450 feet) being impossibly long, due to structural stresses, for a seaworthy wooden vessel—and the fact that no type of vessel could have long survived a flood of such a violent, cataclysmic nature as that envisioned by the proponents of flood geology (R. Moore 1983, 4, 22-24). The overall problem for "scientific" creationists with respect to Noah's ark has been well summarized by Robert Moore in his definitive study of the subject (1983, 1): "Despite ingenious efforts to lend a degree of plausibility to the tale, nothing can be salvaged without the direct and constant intervention of the deity." Such divine intervention on behalf of Noah and his "overloaded ark" (Diamond 1985b) may be easy for creationists to accept, but it is hardly the stuff of SCIENCE.

Over the years many adventurous believers have climbed Mount Ararat in Turkey to try to find the ark's remains. Specimens of hand-hewn wood brought from the mountain by French industrialist Fernand Navarra in 1955 and again in 1969 were found by radiocarbon analysis to date from around A.D. 600-800, making the wood old indeed but far too young to be from Noah's ark (Bailey 1978, 64-81; Moore 1981, 9). (Two of his climbing companions have accused Navarra of deliberate fraud [Moore 1981, 9], and creationist leaders give no credence to Navarra's wood [LaHaye and Morris 1976, 133]). On a 1982 expedition up the mountain, former astronaut and perennial ark-hunter James Irwin fell off a ridge and lost most of his teeth (*Creation/Evolution* 10:37). In June 1986 Irwin suffered a heart attack and was arrested in September as an alleged spy by the Turkish authorities. Irwin called it "a year of dramatic arrests" (*Florida Times-Union* April 4, 1987). During a 1987 expedition, John Morris of the INSTITUTE FOR CREATION RESEARCH examined a much publicized boat-shaped formation about ten miles south of the mountain. Morris (1988, ii) found it to be "merely an unusual geologic formation." During this expedition, Morris was able to take long-sought aerial photographs of Mount Ararat. They unfortunately captured "no hints of the Ark" (1988, iii). A 1988 expedition included more photography plus use of a sonar device to seek "anomalous shapes" under the ice cap (ICR 1988). The ark proved to be as elusive as ever.

Such "arkeology" expeditions continue despite the fact that (1) the Bible clearly states (as every literalist should know) that the ark landed "in the mountains of Ararat" (Gen. 8:4), naming no particular mountain; (2) there is no certainty as to what ancient region the biblical word *Ararat* refers; and (3) no one knows why Agri Dagi (the Turkish mountain called Mount Ararat) came to be singled out as the alleged landing site (see Bailey 1978). In sum, it is no surprise that "in many Turkish government offices," as John Morris complains (1988, iv), "the whole search has become a joke."

ARKANSAS CREATIONISM TRIAL

See *McLEAN v. ARKANSAS*.

ASTRONOMY

The study of the UNIVERSE beyond EARTH. It is the view of Henry Morris, president of the INSTITUTE FOR CREATION RESEARCH (ICR) and America's leading "scientific" creationist, that the earth is "the center of God's interest in the universe," the STARS being "only of incidental significance," serving as signs and giving light to the earth (Morris 1984a, 162; 1974, 234). But modern astronomy seems to tell us the opposite: It is the earth, not the stars, that is of incidental significance. Our sun is but an ordinary star among billions of stars in the Milky Way Galaxy that itself is only one of billions of *galaxies* or star systems in the observable universe. The distances between galaxies are so immense that they are expressed not in miles or kilometers but in *light-years* or *parsecs*. A light-year is the distance light travels in one year (about 6 trillion miles or 9.5 trillion kilometers); a parsec is 3.26 light-years. The universe, moreover, is apparently expanding: Astronomer Edwin Hubble discovered in the late 1920s that the galaxies are receding from each other at speeds roughly proportional to the distances between them. The evidence for this recession is the *cosmological redshift*, the shift toward the red end of the *electromagnetic spectrum* of the spectral line pattern in light from receding sources. An expanding universe is also a prediction of Einstein's general theory of RELATIVITY. Astronomers estimate that it has been between 10 and 20 billion years since the BIG BANG itself, the hypothetical primordial event to which most cosmologists attribute the universal expansion.

Morris and other fundamentalist leaders of so-called creation "science" dispute the generally accepted age and structure of the universe in the attempt to make SCIENCE conform to their literal interpretation of the BIBLE. Theirs is a static, nonevolutionary universe created only "about 10,000 years ago" (Aardsma 1988, iv). According to Morris, there is "no evidence" for cosmic evolution (1984a, 169), and the stars, which "must be only several thousand years old" (1978, 61), have "stayed absolutely the same" for as long as man has observed them (1974, 234). But the cosmological redshift is hardly the only astronomical evidence that the universe is old and evolving. The evidence that stars evolve based on changes in their chemical composition is clear from study of the various stages in which different stars can be observed, from newborn stars like those in the Orion Nebula, through *main-sequence* stars like our sun, to dying stars like the spectacular *supernova* of 1987 (see STAR).The present abundances of radioactive elements compared with their decay rates and calculated rates of production in stars and in the early universe show that element formation has occurred over billions of years (Hartmann 1985, 461). The RADIOACTIVE DATING of meteorites and lunar material indicates an age for the SOLAR SYSTEM alone of some 5 billion years. The discovery through *radio astronomy* in 1964 of the *cosmic background radiation*—a relic radiation whose existence was predicted nearly twenty years earlier based on the theory of a primordial explosion—is an impressive argument in favor of big bang cosmology (Wilson 1979). That we live in a nonstatic, indeed, violent universe is further evinced by the impact craters on the earth, moon, and other planets and moons of the solar system. Morris would have us believe that these scars from explosive impacts and other "apparent disturbances" in the cosmos result from the "continuing cosmic warfare" between the heavenly angels and SATAN (1984a, 182-184; 1978, 63-67).

If all else fails, however, the leaders of creation "science" still have one argument designed to end all dispute about age. The universe, they say, was necessarily created with an APPEARANCE OF AGE, so that starlight, for example, may appear to have traveled billions of light-years through space but could actually have been created en route (Morris 1984a, 175-176). So the universe, despite all appearances, could be very young. This argument cannot be logically refuted—one may as easily argue that the universe was created this morning or sometime last week—but such a deliberately deceptive CREATION, bearing all the earmarks of eons of evolution, seems a blasphemous notion, "accusing God of absurd deceitfulness" (Dobzhansky 1973, 126; see APPEARANCE OF AGE).

Modern astronomy does not contradict the concept of creation. Indeed astronomers point to a time, some 10 to 20 billion years ago, when the universe, at least in its present form, apparently had a beginning. But astronomy also tells us that MAN physically does not occupy much of a niche in the cosmos. Astronomy's legacy, in the words of astronomer Joseph Silk (1980, xiii), is "the knowledge that we are specks of dust in the great maelstrom of the universe." It is natural to wonder, then, how this "space-rock" the earth (Hartmann

1985, 52), this "insignificant mote in an incomprehensible vastness" (Simpson 1964, 5), could really be the center of a universal Creator's interest. Even the biblical Psalmist (8:3-4), long before telescopes and awareness of galaxies in the billions, had to ask God a question: "When I consider thy heavens, the work of thy fingers, the moon and the stars which thou hast ordained; / What is man that thou art mindful of him? and the son of man, that thou visitest him?" (See GOD and WORLD VIEW.)

AUSTRALOPITHECINES

Apemen (literally "southern apes") who lived in Africa from about 4 million to 1 million years ago. The australopithecines had large brains relative to body size, had humanlike dental features (reduced canines and flat-worn molars), and walked on two legs (Nickels 1986, 6-8). They are the first known hominids or members of MAN's family Hominidae and are considered TRANSITIONAL FORMS between ape and man (see PRIMATE).

The first evidence from the FOSSIL RECORD of these intermediate creatures was the so-called Taung child, the skull of a three-year-old male unearthed in South Africa in 1924. Discoverer Raymond Dart named the Taung child *Australopithecus africanus* ("southern ape of Africa"). A more robust fossil species, named appropriately *Australopithecus robustus,* was also found in South Africa, and a still more robust form, *Australopithecus boisei,* was found in East Africa by Louis Leakey. The more lightly built or gracile species *Australopithecus afarensis* includes the famous "Lucy" skeleton, discovered in 1973 in Ethiopia by Donald Johanson (1981). With a potassium-argon date (see RADIOACTIVE DATING) of over 3 million years, Lucy and other fossilized remains found with her represent the oldest known hominid species.

Experts disagree (see Lewin 1987) on exactly how these early hominids relate to each other and which named species, if any, was directly ancestral to man (genus *Homo* of the hominid family). Johanson's view (Johanson and White 1979) is that A. *afarensis* is the common ancestor of the other australopithecines (evolutionary dead-ends) and *Homo*. One dissenter is Richard Leakey, who believes *Homo* must go back as much as 5 million years (Leakey 1981, 70), in which case the australopithecines, though certainly outstanding examples of transitional forms (Brace 1983, 251; Gould 1987, 68; McGowan 1984, 171-177), were not directly ancestral to *Homo* but rather were collateral dead-ends, with man's direct ancestor yet to be found.

Creationists, who naturally do not accept the evolutionary implications of such fossils, consider the australopithecines to be "merely extinct species of apes" (Morris 1978, 46). Creationist leader Duane Gish (1986) thinks that it's "silly" to argue about whether or not the australopithecines were intermediate between ape and man, since "even evolutionists argue about that." But that misrepresents the nature of the argument. Most paleoanthropologists do not doubt that the australopithecines were transitional; the disagreement is over which, if any, of these species lay in the direct line of descent between ape and man. The australopithecines could all be collateral developments, evolutionary dead ends, and still share with man's direct ancestor the kinds of mosaic features that define intermediate forms. (See also *ARCHAEOPTERYX*. For an excellent discussion of creationist misrepresentation of evolutionists on the australopithecines, see Albert 1985.)

BABEL, TOWER OF

The tower that men, when "the whole earth was of one language," sought to build in "Shinar" (Sumer) to "reach unto heaven," according to the biblical book of Genesis (11:1-9). The project prompted GOD (Yahweh) to confuse the builders' language, thus scattering them with separate tongues over the face of the EARTH. Creationists accept this account of linguistic dispersal from Babylon (Hebrew *Babel*) as the literal truth about the origin of MAN's languages (Morris 1978, 47, 53; 1985b, 193; 1974, 273). Creationist leader Henry Morris (1982b, 71-76) hypothesizes that SATAN met with Babylonian ruler Nimrod and his priests at the tower of Babel where they hatched a plot called the theory of EVOLUTION.

Languages evolve. French, Italian, and Spanish, for example, are descendants of Latin. How language first arose is a subject of debate (see Lieberman 1984). Three early theories on the origin of speech were known jocularly as the bow-wow, pooh-pooh, and ding-dong theories (Richards 1987, 246-247). In any case, some historical linguists are studying the evolution of languages with the hope of tracing all languages back to a hypothetical mother tongue spoken as much as 100,000 years ago (Lewin 1988d). This is seen as a vain hope by most linguists because languages change constantly and the oldest fossils—writing—only go back about 5,000 years. Raiders of the lost tongue are nonetheless hard at work—but wherever else the historical trail may ultimately lead them, it will not lead to Babylon, which did not even exist when writing was invented (Oates 1979, 9). Most biblical scholars see the Babel story as an ancient myth about linguistic origins that was adapted by the biblical writers to illustrate God's judgment upon man's continuing wickedness following the Fall and the Flood (see ADAM AND EVE and FLOOD, NOAH'S). No historian worthy of the name considers the Babel story to be factual history (see SOCIAL SCIENCES). Even the origin or *etymology* of the word *Babel* is a problem for creationists who insist on interpreting the text literally. The statement in Genesis 11:9 that Babel is so called "because the Lord there confounded the language of all the earth" is based on a bad Hebrew pun (Babel and *balal*, "to confuse"). If taken literally, the statement is simply not true. *Babel* is the Hebrew name for Babylon (Akkadian *Bab-ilani*, "gate of the gods") and means "gate of God" (Oates 1979, 60).

The city of Babylon had a great stepped temple-tower or *ziggurat* called Etemenanki ("the Temple Foundation of Heaven and Earth") that likely served as a model for the tower in the biblical story (Roux 1966, 358-59). Significantly there is also a known Sumerian myth about a divine confusion of man's original language into many (Vawter 1977, 152). Whatever its ultimate origin, the Babel story reflects the typically anthropomorphic deity of the biblical J source (see BIBLE), a deity of limited powers who must come down to earth to see the city and tower (Gen. 11:5) and who apparently fears that the tower builders will attempt to storm heaven ("now nothing will be restrained from them") unless something is done right away (Asimov 1981,

211-212). Is this really a credible portrayal of the "omnipotent, omnisicient" Creator (Morris 1985b, 200) praised by creationists?

BIBLE

The sacred scriptures (Greek *biblia,* "books") of Christianity. The Christian Bible is comprised of the Old and New Testaments and, among Catholics, several books called the Apocrypha. The Old Testament (called by Jews the Tanakh) is the Jewish Bible or sacred scriptures of Judaism. Christians and Jews thus share the CREATION accounts (there are two) found in Genesis, the opening biblical book. A central issue in the creation/evolution dispute is the degree to which the Bible is to be considered divinely inspired and the Genesis creation accounts free of factual error. It must necessarily be the position of SCIENCE that any evidence for or against creation or EVOLUTION must come from the study of natural phenomena, not from the reading and interpretation of Judeo-Christian scriptures, however much many scientists may personally accept the meaning or significance of scriptural teachings. The scientific approach to the question of origins is thus irreconcilable with that of *fundamentalism,* an American conservative religious movement that believes in biblical inerrancy. This movement had its roots in the nineteenth-century orthodox reaction to the "higher" (historico-literary) criticism of the Bible that originated among European theologians and was accepted by American "modernists" (Noss 1980, 480). Fundamentalism owes its name to the "Five Fundamentals," a list of five beliefs that the Presbyterian General Assembly drew up in 1910 as being essential to the Christian faith (Kehoe 1983, 7). Among those Fundamentals was the doctrine of biblical inerrancy. This doctrine remains a source of conflict today between conservative and liberal Christians, not to mention between conservative Christians and scientists. In recent years the issue of biblical inerrancy has threatened to bring schism to the Southern Baptist Convention, the largest Protestant denomination in America (see Palen 1987; Warner 1987).

The leaders of the so-called creation "science" movement are dyedin-the-wool fundamentalists, believing that the Bible "must be accepted as absolutely inerrant and authoritative" (Morris 1984a, 47), its creation story providing "simple historical facts" that "directly contradict evolution theory" (Gish 1985, 23). Most Protestants, Catholics, and Jews in America do not share this fundamentalist view (Frye 1983a). In his 1953 encyclical *Humani generis*, Pope Pius XII (quoted in Flew 1982, 49) stated that "the teaching of the Church leaves the doctrine of evolution an open question" so long as it is recognized that "souls are immediately created by God." In 1982 the Vatican's Pontifical Academy of Sciences (quoted in McIver 1988a, 16) described the evidence for human evolution as "beyond serious dispute." Most mainline Protestant and Jewish leaders also seem willing to allow evolution (given the overwhelming scientific evidence that it has occurred) a place in the divine scheme of things, and believe that the validity of biblical faith does not depend upon interpreting Genesis or any other part of the Old Testament as literal history. Biblical scholar Richard H. Hiers (1988, 111; 1989) notes the ironic fact that the only biblical book that claims "plenary inspiration" of the Old Testament is the apocryphal 2 Esdras, which enjoys in Catholicism "only the most tenuous canonical status." In Protestantism and Judaism it enjoys no status at all.

Most biblical scholars accept the *documentary hypothesis* according to which the first four books of the Bible are not the work of one author (traditionally said to be Moses) but rather are a conflation of three main literary sources (Friedman 1987, 22-28, 52-61; Hiers 1988, 219-223). These are called by scholars the Yahwist (J), Elohist (E), and Priestly (P) sources. (A fourth, the Deuteronomic [D] source, is found in Deuteronomy, which completes "the Five Books of Moses.") The first eleven chapters of Genesis, as is clear through comparison with nonbiblical texts, contain myths (see ADAM AND EVE; BABEL, TOWER OF; CREATION; and FLOOD, NOAH'S) that were adapted by the J and P sources from the common mythology of the ancient Near East (see Pritchard 1969). Such myths were *etiological*, that is, they were stories that dealt with causes, explaining the "why" of things, in the prescientific world. These stories were refined and used by the biblical sources to impart, not literal history or what today we call science (the ancient Hebrews knew nothing, after all, about atoms, microorganisms, or telescopes), but rather what the biblical authors held to be basic theological truths about the relationship between GOD and MAN. Literal interpretation of these myths is not only incompatible with modern science but dilutes their richness of theological meaning. Insisting that the Bible is infallible also sets the book above the message if not above God. Biblical scholar Bruce Vawter (1983), a Catholic priest, calls belief in biblical inerrancy "the superstition of bibliolatry," a "perversion of biblical religion" that "seriously misconstrues the meaning and purpose of the Bible."

Pope Pius XII (quoted in Frye 1983c, 199) expressed the belief that "man learns from two books: the universe for the human study of things created by God; and the Bible, for the study of God's superior will and truth. One belongs to reason, the other to faith. Between them there is no clash." Indeed the two books, reason and faith, science and the Bible, need never clash, but too often have done so because of unreasoning biblical literalism. Even the Protestant theocrat John Calvin (quoted in Frye 1983c, 202) understood this back in the sixteenth century, when he said that "the Holy Spirit had no intention to teach astronomy." Unfortunately the "scientific" creationists of the twentieth century have no such enlightened understanding.

BIG BANG

The theory that the present UNIVERSE began with the explosion of an indescribably hot, dense point of matter/energy. The theory is based on the observation that the universe is expanding, all its STAR systems or *galaxies* receding from each other at speeds roughly proportional to the distances between them (see ASTRONOMY). The recession naturally suggests that the galaxies were once much closer together, indeed that if we go back far enough in time we would find all the matter-energy in the universe squeezed into one "infinitesimal blob" (Davies 1983, 41)—what Belgian astronomer and Catholic priest Georges Lemaitre (1950), who first proposed the theory in 1927, called the "primordial atom."

The evidence for the recession of the galaxies is the *cosmological redshift,* the shift of the spectral line pattern toward the red end of the *electromagnetic spectrum* as a light source recedes from the observer. To find out how much time has elapsed since the primordial explosion, astronomers must estimate the distance and speed of recession of other galaxies from ours, as well as speculate on how long it took for the first galaxies to evolve from the first basic elements (hydrogen and helium). Current estimates of the time elapsed since the big bang range between 10 and 20 billion years (Eichhorn 1989). In 1964 striking evidence that such an explosion indeed occurred was discovered by radio astronomers Arno Penzias and Robert Wilson: They detected the *cosmic background radiation,* a microwave noise from all directions of space that is a relic of the radiation of the hot early universe (Wilson 1979). The existence of this radiation was predicted, based on big bang theory, almost twenty years before its detection. Its discovery won a Nobel Prize in PHYSICS for Penzias and Wilson. It also dealt a crippling blow to the rival *steady state theory,* according to which matter is continuously created in a universe that is infinite (Hoyle 1956). The big bang theory remains, with variations, today's standard cosmological model—"our best guess," in the words of astronomer William Hartmann (1985, 460), "about a grand mystery."

Creationist leader Henry Morris (1984a, 172) calls the big bang concept "improbable at best," and maintains that even if the universe is expanding it is "most plausible" to assume that GOD created it "at a certain ongoing stage" of expansion, that is, God created it to *look* like it's been expanding all the time (see APPEARANCE OF AGE). Committed to literal interpretation of the BIBLE, including its pre-scientific description of the universe, "scientific" creationists view the universe as young (about 10,000 years old) and static, the stars unchanging for as long as MAN has observed them (Morris 1974, 234). Such an antiquated view is contradicted not only by the cosmological redshift and cosmic background radiation but by the clear astronomical evidence for stellar evolution (see STAR).

But if the big bang theory is correct, then what, ask creationists, was the exact nature and origin of the "primordial atom"? The answer is that physics presently has no way to describe the infinitely dense point or *singularity* that exploded. Such a description must await a theory of *quantum gravity*, when and if theoretical physicists succeed in unifying RELATIVITY (dealing with gravity and large-scale structure) with *quantum mechanics* (dealing with subatomic particles) (see Hawking 1988). The earliest time for which theoretical physicists can presently even attempt to describe conditions in the universe is the so-called *Planck time:* a tenth of a thousandth of a millionth of a billionth of a trillionth of a trillionth of a second after the beginning of expansion and cooling (Gore 1983, 710). At Planck time, so physicists speculate, the *symmetry* of the single *superforce* that is believed to have existed at such high temperatures would already have been broken as *gravity* became a separate force. A fraction of a second after Planck time, the universe entered a split-second period of extraordinarily rapid *inflation* as energy congealed into elementary particles and the *strong* and *electroweak forces* separated (Guth and Steinhardt 1984, 116; Gore 1983, 740). As inflation ended, the universe, still less than one second after the explosion, continued to expand from the inflationary momentum, with the electroweak force separating into *electromagnetism* and the *weak force*, so that the four basic forces of nature had become established (Kutter 1987, 72). Not until the universe was three minutes old did it cool enough for the first atomic nuclei (*protons* and *neutrons*) to form, and it was 500,000 years before the temperature—down to 3,000 degrees Kelvin—was low enough for *electrons* to bind with the nuclei to form *atoms*. It was during this period that *photons*, the particles of light, were finally able to decouple from matter and travel through space. To quote Timothy Ferris (1988, 343), it was "the epoch of 'let there be light.' " And matter, to make a long story short, "has been clumping into stars, galaxies, and the like" ever since (Guth and Steinhardt 1984, 119).

Creationist leader Duane Gish (1986) argues that the big bang theory is a scenario of order arising from disorder, a violation of the second law of THERMODYNAMICS. But in fact the universe may be seen as more orderly in its early hot density than in its present lumpy state of dispersal. Physics professor Lawrence Staunton (1984) uses the example of a divided container, one part empty and one part filled with gas. Remove the division and the gas, expanding naturally, moves from a dense, highly ordered state to one of lower density and increased *entropy* (the measure of a system's disorder). In the case of the expanding universe, order may arise locally—LIFE itself is a prime example—but always at the expense of overall entropy increase. If the universe is "open"—that is, if there is not enough mass in the universe for gravity to stop the expansion and begin a contraction—it will expand to an eventual state of maximum entropy or *heat death*, all its energy expended (Barrow 1988, 224-226; Spielberg and Anderson 1985, 154-155).

Some scientists in their popular writings (e.g., Adair 1987; Jastrow 1978; Parker 1988; Silk 1980; Trefil 1983) identify the big bang with CREATION, though not (with the exception of Jastrow) in a religious sense. This practice can be misleading in that the big bang was not necessarily *the* beginning of the universe but only of its present form (Schafersman 1987, 6). It is possible, for example, that our present cosmos is but the latest bounce in a closed, *oscillating universe* that forever expands and contracts (Chaisson 1981, 27-28; Mallove 1987, 34; Weinberg 1977, 150-55). It must in any case be remembered that SCIENCE, which deals only with natural phenomena, cannot yet answer the question of ultimate origin and perhaps never will. (See UNIVERSE.)

BIOGENETIC LAW

See EMBRYOLOGY.

BIOGEOGRAPHY

The study of the geographical distribution of ANIMALS and PLANTS. Charles Darwin (1859, 397-399), in studying the LIFE forms of the Galápagos Islands off the South American coast, was struck by how closely the islands' species resembled, yet were different from, those of the mainland. Darwin saw no logical explanation for this in terms of "independent creation." He was led instead to the conclusion that life forms from the mainland had colonized the Galápagos where they were then "liable to modification" while still bearing through inheritance "the unmistakable stamp" of their mainland origin. Such was the beginning of Darwin's theory of EVOLUTION ("descent with modification") by NATURAL SELECTION. Biogeography, notes philosopher of SCIENCE Michael Ruse (1982, 309), "is *the* strongest point in the whole Darwinian story"—and its consideration, significantly, is almost nowhere to be found in the writings of so-called "scientific" creationists.

What was true of the Galápagos is true of other islands and of the continents as well. All regions have their distinctive species, and the closer they are geographically the more similar those species are (McGowan 1984, 5), while the farther regions are from each other the more different their species (Newell 1985, 131)—exactly the pattern we would expect to find as a result of migration and ADAPTATION of originally related animals to new environments. Thus migration and physical barriers, such as those created by CONTINENTAL DRIFT, and the resulting isolation are believed to play important roles in the evolution of new species (the theory of *allopatric speciation* [Mayr 1988, 173-174; Newell 1985, 187; see PUNCTUATED EQUILIBRIA]). One can attribute the great geographical diversity of similar forms to CREATION of each species only if one is willing to believe that the Creator was mimicking (to what purpose?) an evolutionary pattern.

The problem that biogeography poses for CREATIONISM is compounded by the fact that creation "scientists" consider the historicity of the biblical Flood and Noah's arkful of animals to be important to their case for creation (see ARK, NOAH'S; FLOOD, NOAH'S; and GEOLOGY). Thus "present-day animal distribution must be explained," state creationists John C. Whitcomb and Henry M. Morris (1961, 79), "on the basis of migrations from the mountains of Ararat" where Genesis says Noah's ark landed. Whitcomb and Morris attempt to make a case for land bridges as "the principal means" for getting all the world's animals from Ararat to their present habitats (1961, 79-88), but the problem is so formidable that they must finally resort to that old creationist standby, the miracle: "We see the hand of God guiding and directing these creatures in ways that man, with all his ingenuity, has never been able to fathom" (1961, 86). Since the work of Whitcomb and Morris, biogeography has virtually disappeared from creationist discussion. There is, however, a notable exception: A leading "scientific" creationist has actually admitted that the evidence of biogeography favors evolution over creation of species. "There is little doubt," says Dr. John Klotz (1985, 139), a seminary professor and member of the Creation Research Society board of directors, "that the facts of geographical distribution are easier to reconcile with the theory of evolution than they are with special creation." But Klotz, of course, does not concede. He lists what he considers some "exceptions"—the island of Java, for example, having few BIRD species that are peculiar to Java—that "warrant our reserving judgment at least for the time being" (1985, 139-140). But to biogeographers the evolutionary case, all "exceptions" considered, is simply overwhelming. Judgment has long since been rendered.

BIOLOGY

The study of living organisms (see LIFE). Biologists today commonly divide organisms into five broad categories or kingdoms: Monera (bacteria and blue-green algae), Protista (mostly single-celled microorganisms with cell nuclei), Fungi, Animalia (see ANIMAL), and Plantae (see PLANT) (Roeder 1989; see TAXONOMY). Biology includes the study of organic EVOLUTION, called by the National Academy of Sciences (1984, 22) "the most fundamental organizational concept in the biological sciences." Before Charles Darwin (1859) convinced the scientific world that all forms of life are related by common evolutionary descent (see NATURAL SELECTION), such things as the diversity of organisms and the similarities and differences between them were "merely a bewildering chaos of facts" (Mayr 1970, 1). This is why the late geneticist Theodosius Dobzhansky (1973)—a Christian who believed that evolution is GOD's method of CREATION—made his oft-quoted statement that "nothing in biology makes sense except in the light of evolution." The vast majority of biologists today consider it beyond dispute that evolution has occurred, though the mechanisms by which it has occurred still are subjects of debate.

Strong new evidence of evolution's occurrence comes from *molecular biology,* one of the most exciting areas of current scientific research. This branch of biology deals with the large molecules—in particular DNA (deoxyribonucleic acid) and *proteins*—that determine the nature of all forms of life. DNA contains the *genetic code,* and one of the most profound discoveries of modern SCIENCE is that all living things, from bacteria to MAN, share the same simple code, four "letters" (actually chemical substances) from which three-letter "words" are formed to spell out genetic instructions (see GENETICS). This universal code, prima facie evidence of the unity of life, is explicable only if all living things have descended from one common ancestral form. Molecular biologists have found, moreover, that DNA molecules in closely related *species* resemble each other more closely than do the DNA molecules in distantly related species (Gallant 1984, 399). The DNA in man and chimpanzee, for example, is about 99 percent identical (Gribbin and Cherfas 1982, 117; Mereson 1988)—the chimpanzee is man's closest living relative. The same pattern holds true for proteins, which are composed of *amino acids:* The amino-acid sequences in proteins of closely related species resemble each other more closely than do the amino-acid sequences in proteins of distantly related species. The protein *cytochrome-c,* for example, has the same exact order of 104 amino acids in man and chimpanzee, while the rhesus monkey differs from that order in one amino acid, the horse differs in 11 amino acids, the tuna in 12, and so on (NAS 1984, 22). Such molecular data can be used to construct evolutionary family trees, a practice called *molecular phylogenetics* (Lewin 1988a), and these trees agree remarkably well with evolutionary trees based earlier on anatomical study (Max 1986, 35). In addition, many biologists believe that rates of change in DNA and protein, although apparently not constant, average out well enough over long periods of time that they constitute a fairly accurate "molecular clock" to measure the lengths of time since various life forms diverged from their common ancestors (Ayala 1977, 313; Futuyma 1982, 103). Molecular biologists have also found so-called *pseudogenes,* DNA sequences that have no apparent function and are believed to be the result of copying errors (*mutations*) during transcription of the genetic message. The fact that some pseudogenes are shared by different species is clear evidence that the copying error occurred in a common ancestral species from which the affected species have descended, inheriting the error, that is, the same functionless chemical sequence in a segment of their DNA (Max 1986).

Creationists have no explanation for pseudogenes (see Banach 1988, 18), and their only explanation for the fact that all species share the same genetic code, and that different species have molecular similarities proportional (in the evolutionary view) to their degree of relatedness, is based on the religious DESIGN ARGUMENT. Thus all similarities among species, say the creationists, can be attributed to "the common plan of creation used by the Creator" (Moore 1976, 30). In the creationist textbook *Biology: A Search for Order in Complexity,* John N. Moore and Harold S. Slusher (1970, cited in Newell 1985, 140) argue that similarities in the chemical structure of organisms are "consistent with the concept of an all-wise Creator employing a single effective pattern in his creation." Since creationists seem to consider it only coincidental that the FOSSIL RECORD has an apparently evolutionary order—creationists attribute the fossil order to the Noachian Deluge (see FLOOD, NOAH'S)—they must consider it doubly coincidental that family trees based on molecular biology track so well with those based on the fossil record.

The creationist argument that molecular similarities are evidence of a Creator's common plan is a religious one, and religious concepts are not supposed to enter the thinking of scientists in their search for natural explanations for observed phenomena. And in biology, the natural explanation for the phenomena observed is quite obvious. "For a biologist," says Nobel laureate P. D. Medawar (quoted in Newell 1985, 183), "the alternative to thinking in evolutionary terms is not to think at all."

BIRD

A member of the winged, feathered Aves class of vertebrates (backboned ANIMALS). There are over 8,500 living bird species, ranging in size from the Cuban bee hummingbird (two-and-a-half inches long, weighing one-tenth of an ounce) to the ostrich (as much as eight feet tall and 300 pounds) (Sick 1985, 1).

Birds are descendants of REPTILES, possibly DINOSAURS (Horner and Gorman 1988, 71; McGowan 1984, 110-115; Wilford 1985, 217-231). Birds bear a strong resemblance to reptiles particularly in their skeletal framework; note also the possession of scales and the laying of shelled eggs (McGowan 1984, 110-115). Birds first became abundant during the Jurassic period (180-135 million years ago). In 1986 the discovery was reported (Weisburd 1986) of a fossil bird that is 225 million years old, which would make the fossil specimen (named *Protoavis* by its discoverer) the earliest known form of bird. An excellent TRANSITIONAL FORM in the FOSSIL RECORD is the reptile-bird *ARCHAEOPTERYX*. Creationists, however, cannot allow transitional (hence evolutionary) forms to exist, so they consider *Archaeopteryx*, teeth and all, to be "an undoubted true bird" (Gish 1985, 117).

BOTANY

See PLANT.

CAMBRIAN EXPLOSION

The "sudden" appearance during the Cambrian period (570-500 million years ago) of a wide variety of complex, multicellular marine organisms with shells or hard skeletons. It was once thought that the eon preceding the Cambrian, called appropriately the Precambrian eon (the first 87 percent of EARTH history), contained no fossils, or remains of LIFE, at all. It is now known that Precambrian rocks contain fossilized traces or microfossils of single-celled organisms that are 3.5 billion years old. And there are now late Precambrian fossils of complex, multicellular, soft-bodied marine organisms (called collectively the Ediacaran fauna) from as late as about 670 million years ago (Kutter 1987, 345-355; Strahler 1987, 402, 516).

The proponents of creation "science" interpret the Cambrian explosion as evidence for CREATION. They make much of the fact that the FOSSIL RECORD contains no TRANSITIONAL FORMS between the completely soft-bodied marine ANIMALS of the late Precambrian and the more varied, mostly shelled or skeletal marine animals of the Cambrian. (First in number among Cambrian fossils are the *trilobites* ["three-lobed ones"], extinct marine *arthropods* with external skeletons [Cloud 1988, 334; Fenton and Fenton 1989, 192-212].) In short, we seem to have in the Cambrian period an ABRUPT APPEARANCE of *metazoans* (multicellular animals) with hard parts (Conway Morris 1989, 339). "It at least seems reasonable to suggest," say creationist biologists Wayne Frair and Percival Davis (1983, 56), "that the abrupt change reflects some special activity of God." (Perhaps, but special divine activities do not come under the heading of SCIENCE.) More emphatically, Duane Gish (1986) of the INSTITUTE FOR CREATION RESEARCH states that "complex forms of life appear abruptly" in the Cambrian rocks, and "not a single ancestor for any of these animals can be found anywhere on the face of the earth."

Gish allows that these animals appearing abruptly in the Cambrian include things like shellfish, sponges, and worms. He fails to mention that not a single AMPHIBIAN, BIRD, INSECT, MAMMAL, or REPTILE fossil appears in Cambrian rocks; the first land animals do not appear until the Devonian period, some 100 million years after the Cambrian (see LIFE). Still, Gish (1985, 61, 69) argues that evidence from the Cambrian is "remarkably in accord with predictions based on creation," that in fact "the rocks cry out, 'Creation!' " Yet in the same source (1985, 35), Gish states that during "the creation week" God created "a *finished* creation," all the basic kinds of animals and PLANTS, as described in the biblical book of Genesis. How can Gish have it both ways? How does the Cambrian period—a span of millions of years of varied marine life with no "kinds" of land plants or land animals even in existence—fit into the finished creation of Genesis? Gish doesn't say—he simply has his cake and eats it too!

No evolutionist can say, hundreds of millions of years after the fact, exactly why life "exploded" as it did during the Cambrian. Plausible contributing factors have been suggested, however, that together make it less of a mystery. (It should be noted that the "explosion" was in fact gradual, lasting as much as 15 million years in the early Cambrian, though still a very short time in geologic terms [Eldredge 1982, 46-47].) A major factor must have been adaptive radiation (see ADAPTATION), rapid diversification as organisms moved out into the unoccupied habitats that abounded in the Cambrian world (Futuyma 1979, 81; Cloud 1988, 321; Simpson 1967, 21-22). An increasing amount of free oxygen in the atmosphere due to algal photosynthesis may have been influential in this burst of evolutionary activity (Cloud 1988, 334; Eldredge 1982, 47). The development of hard parts would have been selectively advantageous (see NATURAL SELECTION), and organisms with hard parts were naturally more likely to become fossilized than their soft-bodied forebears (Maynard Smith 1975, 107; Simpson 1967, 20-22). In short, while many details of the Cambrian explosion remain subject to speculation, rapid biological diversification is not surprising in a world that, in Stephen Jay Gould's words, was "virtually free of competition," a world of "unparalleled opportunity" in which "experimentation reigned" (1989, 228).

CATASTROPHISM

The belief that geologic changes during EARTH history have been due to violent catastrophes as opposed to gradual processes (see UNIFORMITARIANISM). Prior to the birth of modern GEOLOGY, most Western naturalists, given their biblically based belief in a very young earth, embraced catastrophism as the only logical explanation for the deformation of rock layers and the past EXTINCTIONS of ANIMALS and PLANTS evident in the FOSSIL RECORD (Newell 1985, 34). As it became clear to geologists that the earth is much older than the BIBLE suggests, uniformitarianism came to the fore. Geologists today recognize that there have been many catastrophes through the ages, but that such events are subject to the same natural laws as govern all other processes and that geologic change on the average has been slow and gradual (Glenister and Witzke 1983, 66-68; Newell 1985, 34-35). Thus plate tectonics, the dynamic theory that has revolutionized geological thought since the 1960s (see CONTINENTAL DRIFT), is uniformitarian with its slow, gradual movement of continental and oceanic plates, yet helps explain the occurrence of catastrophes (e.g., earthquakes at fault lines between plates).

The leaders of the creation "science" movement are Christian fundamentalists who reject the geologic and other scientific evidence that the earth is billions of years old (see ASTRONOMY, RADIOACTIVE DATING, and UNIVERSE). They believe, in keeping with their biblical literalism, that CREATION took place only a few thousand years ago (Aardsma 1988, iv; Morris 1974, 297). To defend this young-earth dogma against the geologic time scale, creationists must "conjure up incredible catastrophes that can do millenia of work in a day" (Boxer 1987, 82). They are therefore catastrophists, though not quite in the tradition of the early naturalists. The creationists propound not a number of separate catastrophes through earth history but rather what Henry Morris, president of the INSTITUTE FOR CREATION RESEARCH (ICR), calls "one great complex of catastrophes in the not-too-distant past" (1985b, 123). He is referring to the worldwide Deluge described in the biblical book of Genesis (1978, 23). Morris (1978, 28) sees the Genesis Flood as "accompanied by great volcanic and tectonic movements," a view intended to account, from a young-earth perspective, for such phenomena as the movement of whole continents—though the Bible, which creationists consider "inerrant" and "infallible" (Morris 1984a, 47; Whitcomb 1984, 31), mentions no such volcanic or tectonic activity in its account of the Flood.

It is an example of what more than one observer calls creationist "gobbledygook" (Davis 1986; Eldredge 1982, 130) that ICR catastrophists pejoratively label modern historical geologists as uniformitarians—prophesied in the Bible, we are told (Gish 1985, 51; Morris i984a, 130), as latter-day "scoffers, walking after their own lusts"—when in fact uniformitarians (virtually all modern scientists with respect to the constancy of natural laws) find in earth history far more catastrophes (floods, earthquakes, volcanoes, cosmic impacts, mass extinctions) than do the creationists with their one-Flood spectacular (see FLOOD, NOAH'S).

CHEMISTRY

The study of the *elements* that constitute matter, including their compounds or interactions. Chemistry has been called "the most central of scientific disciplines" (Brauman 1988), and certainly it has been central to the processes of cosmic and biological EVOLUTION. According to generally accepted theory, the first elements, hydrogen and helium, formed during the hot early UNIVERSE (see BIG BANG), and it was from clouds of these gases that the first STARS condensed. The heavier elements—carbon, oxygen, etc.—were forged in the incredibly hot interiors of the first-generation stars. When some of these stars exploded as supernovas, they scattered the new elements into space, enriching the clouds of gas and dust from which new stars formed (Cohen 1988, 66). Second-generation stars thus incorporated the heavier elements, which would again be dispersed into space with the next supernovas. We are one result of this celestial chemical process of element formation or *nucleosynthesis;* we are literally "children of the stars," every atom in our bodies once inhabiting the interior of a star (Silk 1980, 255). Creationists deny any such notion, of course, as they reject the concept of cosmic evolution.

To become living earthlings, we star children had to undergo another chemical process that creationists consider highly improbable. It is believed that LIFE on EARTH arose naturally as a result of chemical evolution involving the prebiological synthesis of organic compounds, in particular *amino acids* and *nucleotides,* life's basic building blocks (Chang et al. 1983). In a number of laboratory experiments, amino acids and nucleotide bases have formed readily by natural chemistry under simulated primitive-earth conditions (Chang et al. 1983; Miller and Orgel 1974). That is a long way, of course, from producing life. The great unsolved mystery is how *proteins* (made of amino acids) and *nucleic acids* (made of nucleotides) went about self-assembling and came to be associated with each other, allowing self-replication—a living system—to begin (Freske 1981, 13-14; see ABIOGENESIS). It should be noted that organic compounds, evidence of the same type of prebiotic synthesis that seems to have led to life on earth, have been found in interstellar space (Chang et al. 1983, 91; Hartmann

1985, 470). This raises the possibility, at least, of "a cosmic chemistry of life" (Raloff 1986) of which life on earth, whatever its initial mechanism, is but a local reaction.

Compelling evidence that we earthlings have evolved is found in the chemistry of the *genetic code* (see GENETICS). The presence in all living organisms, from bacteria to MAN, of the same simple code, its "letters" consisting of but four chemical bases (adenine, cytosine, guanine, and thymine), cannot be a matter of concidence. The four-letter code's universality is scientifically explainable only as a result of evolutionary descent of all present life forms from a common ancestral form, the original bearer of the code. As further biochemical evidence of evolution, molecular biologists are able to construct evolutionary family trees based on the degrees of similarity in the nucleic acids and proteins in different species, which trees agree remarkably well with those constructed by paleontologists based on fossils (Lewin 1988a; Max 1986, 35; see BIOLOGY). Creationists claim, necessarily, that such biochemical data is evidence not of evolution but of CREATION, the genetic code's universality and the molecular similarities between species being attributable to a common plan or design by the Creator. The creationist DESIGN ARGUMENT seems incompatible, however, with the many imperfections and maladaptations found in nature. (See also THERMODYNAMICS.)

CLASSIFICATION

See TAXONOMY.

CONTINENTAL DRIFT

The theory that the EARTH's land masses separated from one or more ancient supercontinents and continue to move relative to each other. The idea that continents were once joined long suggested itself by the matching coastlines on opposite sides of the Atlantic and by certain similarities and contrasts between both extinct and present forms of

LIFE on separate continents (Spencer 1983, 258-259; Stokes 1982, 196-197). In 1915 German meteorologist Alfred Wegener proposed his theory that the present continents had broken adrift from a single ancient land mass that he called *Pangaea* ("all lands"). Wegener's theory sparked much interest and debate, then fell into disrepute because neither Wegener nor anyone else could identify a mechanism by which continents could drift. The first step in the revitalization of Wegener's theory came in the 1950s with the discovery through seafloor *remanent magnetism* that the earth's magnetic poles have "wandered" over geologic time, and that the continents, when compared to the traced polar wandering paths, have apparently moved relative to each other (Eicher 1976, 90). Then in the 1960s came the discovery of *seafloor spreading*—the mechanism that was missing from Wegener's theory—and with it the birth of *plate tectonics*, a theory of the earth's structure, including drifting continents, that has revolutionized geological thought.

According to plate tectonics, the *lithosphere* (the earth's *crust* and part of its upper *mantle*) is composed of several large slabs or plates that float along on the *athenosphere*, the less rigid underlying mantle. The driving force behind the motion of the plates is not yet fully understood, but major factors appear to be convection currents in the underlying mantle as well as the continuous creation of new seafloor. Oceanic plates move away from each other at *midocean ridges*, leaving rifts where molten rock from the mantle wells up, cools, welds itself to the trailing edges of the plates, and thus creates new seafloor to replace the old floor moving away (Kutter 1987, 459). The moving plates eventually plunge, in a process called *subduction*, beneath the edges of other plates, to descend into the mantle for recycling. Thus seafloor spreading strikes a balance between new lithosphere being created and old lithosphere being subducted.

Lithospheric plates scrape, jostle, and collide with each other as they move, thus causing earthquakes, volcanoes, and mountains (Cloud 1988, 194). The continents themselves do not move independently but are "passive riders" (Stokes 1982, 198) on the more buoyant lithospheric plates that are too light to be subducted. It is believed that the supercontinent that Wegener envisoned in fact existed some 225 million years ago, smaller continental plates having slowly converged, only to break up again, first into the continents *Gondwanaland* and *Laurasia* some 180 million years ago, and eventually into the continents of today (Kutter 1987, 461). Thus continental plates, for all the battering and breaks they endure, live to a ripe old geologic age (the earth's oldest known rocks are nearly 4 billion years old), whereas new seafloor cleaving to its oceanic plate (moving at a rate of a few centimeters per year) can look forward to no more than about 200 million years before subduction.

Creationists have been ambivalent toward continent drift. Some accept it, even claiming that it is referred to in the biblical book of Genesis ("the earth was divided" [10:25]). The Creation-Science Research Center's Kelly L. Segraves (1975, 162) finds it "logical" to conclude that when GOD "scattered the nations" from the area of Babel, "he also divided the continents" (see BABEL, TOWER OF). Some others, though, have tended to agree with creationist geologist Andrew Snelling (quoted in Strahler 1987, 204) that continental drift is "highly speculative and questionable." Snelling's statement (made in 1984) is no longer tenable, however, for continental drift has since become a demonstrable fact: Annual rates of plate motion have been precisely measured using two space-science techniques known as Very Long Baseline Interferometry and Satellite Laser Ranging (Strahler 1987, 212; Weisburd 1985). For creationists who believe (as do the leaders of the INSTITUTE FOR CREATION RESEARCH) that the earth is only a few thousand years old (Aardsma 1988, iv; Morris 1978, 91), the present extent of continental separation, assuming that today's slow rates of motion are not significantly different from the past, poses an obvious problem: millions of years of movement. Creationist young-earthers have no choice but to argue that in the past the continents' displacement, as part of the "residual catastrophism" (Morris 1985b, 128) of the biblical Deluge (see FLOOD, NOAH'S), was so fantastically swift that science writer Robert Schadewald (1983, 28-30) has dubbed it "continental zip." The overall predicament that plate tectonics has created for young-earth creationists has been summarized well by creationists Frair and Davis (1983, 74): "More creationist geologists are urgently needed to address these problems."

COSMOLOGY

See BIG BANG; CREATION; UNIVERSE.

CREATION

The process by which the UNIVERSE came into being. That process is believed by creationists to have been the act(s) of a supernatural Creator (see CREATIONISM). The study of creation (and, more broadly, of the universe's EVOLUTION and structure) is *cosmology*. (A narrower, less used term, dealing solely with the universe's origin, is *cosmogony*.)

Most scientists accept the BIG BANG theory according to which the universe in its present form began with the explosion of a *singularity*, an indescribably dense point of matter/energy, some 10 to 20 billion years ago. The theory is based on evidence that the universe is expanding (see ASTRONOMY), which means that initially all the matter in the universe must have started from one superhot spot. However, scientists as yet have no way mathematically to describe such a singularity, nor does the big bang theory tell us what, if anything, existed before the explosion. "We do not exclude the possibility of a prior phase of existence," says astronomer Joseph Silk (1980, 61), "but we can say essentially nothing about it." One speculation is that the universe oscillates, cyclically expands and contracts, in a perhaps eternal series of big bangs and big crunches (Chaisson 1981, 27-28; Mallove 1987, 34; Weinberg 1977, 150-155). Another speculation, first proposed in 1973 by physicist Edward P. Tryon (1989, 155), is that the universe was "created from nothing as a spontaneous quantum fluctuation" (see Bartusiak 1987; Ferris 1988, 352-362; Thomsen 1985). (Creationists, ironically, misinterpret creation in the BIBLE as *creatio ex nihilo*, "creation out of nothing." The book of Genesis describes GOD as forming the world out of preexistent chaos [Hiers 1989; May and Metzger 1973, 1; Vawter 1977, 37-38]. The only reference to creation out of nothing is in the apocryphal 2 Maccabees 7:28.) As Tryon (1989, 157) admits, among the questions that "creation from nothing" doesn't answer is, What is meant by "a state of nothingness prior to our universe"? Tryon's notion that the universe began as a quantum fluctuation is, of course, highly speculative. Equally so is physicist Alan Guth's suggestion that our universe is one of so many inflating "bubbles" in a "metauniverse" in which new bubbles or "baby universes" are continually being created (Guth 1988b; Begley, Rogers, and Springen, 1988; Lemonick 1989).

The leaders of the so-called creation "science" movement are Christian fundamentalists who believe in the literal truth of the two creation stories in the biblical book of Genesis. Thus Duane Gish (1985, 23), vice president of the INSTITUTE FOR CREATION RESEARCH (ICR), states that the first two chapters of Genesis "present the broad outlines of creation in the form of simple historical facts." The ICR (Morris 1985b, 205-206) has an interesting explanation for the fact that Genesis contains two creation accounts: God wrote the first one (1:1-2:4a), Adam (the first MAN) wrote the second one (2:4b-25), and Moses did the editing. This fails to explain, however, why the EARTH's original state is a watery chaos (1:2) in the first account and a waterless plain (2:4b-6) in the second; why there are six separate days of creation in the first account but no time frame given in the second; and why, among other incongruities, man is the first of all things created (2:7) in the second account and the last thing created—both male and female (1:26-27)—in the first account.

The Genesis creation stories are clearly two separate traditions that the Hebrews wished to preserve despite contradictions. It is generally agreed among biblical scholars that the book of Genesis, like the Old Testament as a whole, is "the work of many hands and the product of many centuries of religious development" (Hooke 1947, 13; see Friedman 1987 and Hiers 1988). It is evident, moreover, that the biblical authors had some familiarity with Mesopotamian mythology and, when it suited their theological purposes, made use of it (see Pritchard 1969). The second biblical creation account is the older one, written by what scholars call the Yahwist or J source (ca. 950 B.C.), and the creation therein of Eve from Adam's rib, combined with other elements from the story of Paradise and the Fall, suggests a relatedness to the Sumerian myth of Enki and Ninhursag (see ADAM AND EVE). The first creation account, from what is called the Priestly or P source (ca. 400 B.C.), seems to be related to the Babylonian creation epic called *Enuma elish* (Speiser 1969, 60-72), in which the Babylonian god Marduk slays the dragon Tiamat who personifies the waters of primordial chaos. In Genesis the Hebrew word for the "deep" (1:2) is *tehom*, a corrupted form of the name of the Babylonian dragon (Anderson 1966, 385; Hooke 1947, 34). This suggests the existence of a Hebrew creation myth in which God, like Marduk, slays a sea dragon in primordial battle. And indeed we find that myth preserved in the Bible, not in Genesis but elsewhere in poetic passages (Job 26:12-13, 41:1-34; Isaiah 27:1, 51:9; Psalms 74:13-14). (Similarly, in Canaanite mythology the god Baal slays his rival Yamm, whose name means "sea" [Ginsberg 1969, 131].) In the Babylonian epic, Marduk splits Tiamat in two and uses half of her to create the sky, "ceiled" so as to hold back the waters of chaos (Speiser 1969, 67). This is paralleled in Genesis (1:6-7) by God's creation of the "firmament," a solid dome (the Hebrew word translated as "firmament" is *raqia*, meaning hammered metal [Rad 1961, 51]) dividing "the waters from the waters." (The biblical Hebrews, like their ancient Near Eastern neighbors, believed in a flat, domed EARTH.) The order of the six-day creation in Genesis also bears a general resemblance to the order of creation in the Babylonian story (Hooke 1947, 35).

There are important theological differences, of course, between the Babylonian and Genesis creation myths, one difference being the elimination in Genesis of the primordial dragon. The authors of Genesis reworked the original polytheistic mythology in favor of monotheism and the Israelite understanding of God and his relationship to man. Thus the biblical story of creation, in the words of Jesuit geologist James Skehan (1986, 29), is "the beginning of salvation history and not a scientific treatment"; it was not intended "to convince the people of Israel, let alone modern man," that this way or that was "how [creation] was actually accomplished." This view reflects the consensus of modern biblical scholars, a consensus well expressed by Judaic studies professor and ordained rabbi Dr. Frederick Greenspahn (1983, 31, 37): "The Bible is not a science text but a religious one. . . . The fundamental purpose of the creation narratives is to interpret the meaning of the universe rather than to make a scientific statement as to its origin or history."

In sum, the Genesis creation accounts are not natural history or SCIENCE as the creationists insist they must be. Rather, the accounts are a prescientific attempt by the authors of the Bible to convey a theological truth—"In the beginning God created"—that science can neither confirm nor deny.

CREATIONISM

The belief in the CREATION of the UNIVERSE, including MAN and all other LIFE forms, by a supernatural Creator. In the Judeo-Christian heritage this has traditionally meant belief in creation as specifically described in the biblical book of Genesis. Creationism in modern America refers specially to an activist movement of Christian fundamentalists who wish to have a "scientific" formulation of biblical creationism taught in the public schools. This movement, which calls itself creation "science" or "scientific" creationism, arose in the 1960s in reaction to a reemphasis on the teaching of EVOLUTION in public school SCIENCE curriculum (Edwords 1980, 4; Moore 1976, 86; Nelkin 1982, 39-87; Overton 1982, 310-311). The movement is thus a renewal of the creation/evolution controversy that has continued sporadically ever since 1859, the year of publication of English naturalist Charles Darwin's *On the Origin of Species*. The modern movement is also part and parcel of the American religious Right's war against the "religion of secular humanism," of which evolution is seen as a basic tenet (see HUMANISM).

The leading creationist organization is the INSTITUTE FOR CREATION RESEARCH (ICR) in Santee, California. Its president is Henry M. Morris, holder of a Ph.D. in hydraulic ENGINEERING and, with some forty books to his credit, the leading voice of the creationist movement. Morris believes (1984a, 109-110) that the theory of evolution was invented by SATAN "to deceive the nations and to turn men away from God." ICR vice president Duane T. Gish, with a Ph.D. in biochemistry, is an accomplished debater who refers (1985, 28) to evolution as the "fish-to-Gish" theory. Like Morris, Gish is a biblical literalist, as is ICR cofounder Tim F. LaHaye, a Baptist minister who believes (1980, 10) there is a humanist conspiracy for "a complete world takeover by the the year 2000." Other major creationist organizations—all of them Christian fundamentalist—are the Bible-Science Association (Minneapolis), which publishes the *Bible-Science Newsletter*; the Creation Research Society (Ann Arbor, Michigan), publisher of the *Creation Research Society Quarterly*; the Creation-Science Research Center (San Diego), led by Kelly L. Segraves; and Students for Origins Research, publisher of *Origins Research*.

Dr. Morris (quoted in Bates 1976, 78) has stated that "evolutionary belief . . . is the root cause of man's present distress and perplexity," and that "Christian scholars," through "a comprehensive system of scientific Biblical creationism," must seek "to turn back the deadly tide of evolutionary humanism in our schools and society." While the ICR creationists acknowledge (Morris 1982a, 9; 1985b) that creation "science" is not really science at all but a belief based ultimately on faith, they argue that the theory of evolution is not science either but a belief of the humanist religion. So to demonstrate "who has more evidence for his faith, the creationist or the evolutionist" (Gish 1985, 25), the ICR has promoted what it calls the *two-model approach* to any classroom study of origins. This approach is supposed to be objective, avoiding, in the guise of creation "science," any overt religious references, with the students themselves deciding in their wisdom, after comparison of evidence, which model makes the most scientific sense. However, the authors of *Scientific Creationism*, the ICR's quasi-official textbook for such study, state their conviction at the outset that "the creation model will always fit the facts as well as or better than the evolution model," that man and his world "are not products of an evolutionary process but, rather, are special creations of God" (Morris 1985b, iii, 10).

The creation model postulates that the Creator "simply called into existence" the universe, including every "kind" of ANIMAL and PLANT, using special processes that are no longer operative and that are therefore inaccessible to scientific inquiry (Morris 1985b, 17; Gish 1985, 11, 35). Nothing about this Creator or the act(s) of creation can be known outside of divine revelation (Morris 1984a, 139). This seems hardly an auspicious start for a scientific discussion of origins. The creationists argue, however, that scientific evidence for creation does exist in presently or historically known processes. And they have accordingly built their principal "scientific" case for creation on something called *flood geology*. This is the concept that all of the EARTH's beds of sedimentary rock, including the extensive FOSSIL RECORD therein, were laid down by the waters of one cataclysmic, worldwide Flood. It is no accident, of course, that this harmonizes nicely with the story of Noah's Flood found in Genesis (see FLOOD, NOAH'S). They also argue that the age of the earth is only a few thousand years, a theory that harmonizes nicely with biblical chronology. This means that the vast majority of the world's geologists are egregiously wrong in their assessment of the earth's age, and that what paleontologists see as an unmistakably evolutionary order in the fossil record is actually the order, based on habitat and mobility, in which the various kinds of animals were caught by the rising waters of the worldwide Deluge (Morris 1978, 28; 1986, 74). Thus the creationists, set in their conviction that the book of Genesis is literally true, argue that "the long geological ages of evolutionary history never really took place at all," and that evolution, which would require all those millions of years to reach its present stages, is therefore "impossible" (Morris 1985b, 251). That leaves creation—using the two-model approach—as the only alternative.

Other creationist arguments against evolution and the *geologic time scale* include the alleged impossiblity of ABIOGENESIS or the development of life from nonlife; the alleged contradiction between evolution and THERMODYNAMICS; the alleged absence of TRANSITIONAL FORMS in the fossil record; and the alleged unreliability of RADIOACTIVE DATING. All of these creationist arguments are flawed as is fully detailed in the respective entries. Some, such as flood geology (for full discussion, see GEOLOGY), may even strike one as "comic relief" (Murphy 1982, 51). The problem is that skillful use of "sciencese" language (Morowitz 1985, 222) can impress a lay audience. To quote Gordon Stein (1987, 407), "most creationist arguments are effective only if they are directed to the scientifically illiterate. Unfortunately, there are far too many of those available to listen." Creationism has aptly been called the best organized movement in the history of American pseudoscience, and thus the most dangerous (Schadewald 1983, 34). The "two-model approach" is more than a pitch for fair play. It represents what the creationists themselves see as a clash of WORLD VIEWS, those of biblical fundamentalism and secular modernity (what Morris calls "evolutionary humanism"), and the two are irreconcilable (Morris 1988a). The theory of evolution is supported by evidence from ASTRONOMY, comparative ANATOMY, EMBRYOLOGY, GENETICS, GEOLOGY, molecular BIOLOGY, PHYSICS—in short, virtually every field of biological and physical science. It is pure nonsense for the ICR to state (1987, iv) that "Evolution is contrary to all the real facts of science." But the creationists do not confine themselves to revising the natural sciences. They would revise the SOCIAL SCIENCES as well, beginning with history, anthropology, and linguistics. Morris considers the entire population of the earth to be descended from the three sons of Noah starting as recently as 4000 B.C., and he traces the origin of human languages to the "miraculous linguistic dispersion of the nations at Babel" (Morris 1978, 47, 53; 1985b, 193; 1974, 273; see BABEL, TOWER OF.)

It is little wonder that members of the scientific community have at times responded intemperately to such "abusing" (Kitcher 1982) of the sciences by creationists. Scientists have called creationists "cranks" (McGowan 1984, 188), "incompetents" (Gallant 1984, 298), "liars" (Eldredge 1982, 112), "charlatans" (Bennetta 1988b, 20), and "an extremist group of religious bigots" who "play fast and loose with the facts" (Cloud 1983, 149). One molecular biologist (Dickerson 1986, 17-18) puts it this way: "The young-earth biblical literalists who reject radioisotope dating, the fossil record, geological history, and evolutionary biology are idiots, and should be ignored, not argued with. . . . These people are fools." The creationists, for their part, consider evolutionists with their "uniformitarian" view of earth history (see UNIFORMITARIANISM) to be "willingly ignorant" as prophesied in 2 Peter 3:3-6 (Gish 1985, 51; Morris 1984a, 130). Evolutionists are also misled by the devil as creationists read 2 Corinthians 4:4 and Revelation 12:9 (Morris 1982a, 10-11; 1982b, 126). Gish (1986) calls the evolutionist opponents of the ICR's two-model approach "book-burning bigots." Some examples of more subtle pejorative labels: Astronomer Carl Sagan is an "evolutionist god-papa" (Keith 1982, 188); origin-of-life researcher A. I. Oparin (whom Morris calls O. A. Oparin) was not just a Russian chemist but a "Russian communist chemist" (Morris 1984a, 232); geneticist Richard B. Goldschmidt was "a rabid evolutionist" (Gish 1983, 186-87); and biologist Richard C. Lewontin is "Stephen Jay Gould's fellow atheist and Marxist at Harvard" (Parker 1987, 7). There is also ICR cofounder LaHaye's (1980, 95) warning that evolution and the other "tenets of humanism" are "not the weird ideas of a few obscure imbeciles." In other words, there are plenty of imbeciles involved.

It is important to note that the views of "scientific" creationism are not shared by the majority of Protestants, Catholics, and Jews in America (Frye 1983a). Two-thirds of the plaintiffs who successfully brought suit to overturn the 1981 Arkansas law requiring "balanced treatment" for creation "science" and evolution in public schools (see *McLEAN v. ARKANSAS*) were ministers or other leaders of religious organizations (*Creation/Evolution* 5:33). The U.S. Supreme Court ruling in 1987 that Louisiana's similar "balanced treatment" law was unconstitutional (see *EDWARDS v. AGUILLARD*) was welcomed by the National Council of Churches (Anderson 1987). Most American religious denominations support strongly the separation of church and state, do not preach biblical literalism (see BIBLE), and have no problem with the idea of evolution as GOD's method of creation.

Fundamentalist attempts to legislate the teaching of creationism in the public schools came to an end with the Supreme Court's decision in the Louisiana case. But that judicial defeat has only spurred the creationists to greater efforts at the local community level, through the type of "education and persuasion" (ICR 1987, iii) of teachers and school boards that historically they have always been good at. They have introduced some alternative names for the creationist cause —*origin science* (Geisler and Anderson 1987) and the "theory" of ABRUPT APPEARANCE in complex form—and founded new organizations with names like the Foundation for Thought and Ethics (Bennetta 1988b, 22). Creationists present themselves as defenders of "academic freedom" (see Fezer 1988). The *Edwards v. Aguillard* decision, says the ICR's George Aardsma (quoted in Boxer 1987, 80), was "against *forcing* teachers to teach creationism in public schools," but "the *opportunity* to teach creation is still there." And teachers, says ICR attorney Wendell Bird (1987, ii), have a right to teach "a variety of scientific theories" about origins and to sue "if punished or prohibited." Eager to support such suits is the Academic Freedom (formerly Creation Science) Legal Defense Fund (AFLDF), headed by former Louisiana state senator Bill Keith (see *EDWARDS v. AGUILLARD*). "Our best and most victorious days are still in the future," says Keith (quoted in Bennetta 1987, 7). Or as Henry Morris (1987e) told ICR supporters following *Edwards v. Aguillard:* "If God be for us, who can be against us" (Romans 8:31)?

CREATOR

See GOD.

CRO-MAGNON MAN

See MAN.

DARWINISM

See NATURAL SELECTION; also EVOLUTION.

DESIGN ARGUMENT

The argument that the apparent order and purpose observed in the world is evidence of design by a divine Creator. All things, says "scientific" creationist Richard Bliss (1988, iv), reflect "the order and purposeful design of the Master Designer." This is essentially a re-statement of the so-called *argument from design,* one of the classical arguments for the existence of GOD. But creationists do not use it to try to prove God's existence; being biblical literalists, they assume God's existence as a given (see BIBLE). Creationists use the design argument principally as an argument against EVOLUTION. Before considering the creationist use, however, we need to look first at the traditional argument from design, for the creationist restatement contains the same weak analogy by which the traditional argument is flawed.

The British theologian William Paley (1802), in his book *Natural Theology*, gave the argument from design perhaps its most familiar expression. If one finds a watch on the ground, says Paley, one must assume it to be a contrivance that was "put together for a purpose," that there was "an artificer or artificers" who understood its construction and designed its use. "Contrivance," says Paley (1802, 10), "must have a contriver; design, a designer." And just as a watch must have a watchmaker, so "the contrivances of nature," surpassing those of MAN, must have had an intelligent author, a "designing Being" (1802, 329). The argument from design had been effectively posed (and then effectively refuted) several years earlier by the British philosopher David Hume. "Look round the world," says the character Cleanthes in Hume's *Dialogues Concerning Natural Religion* (1779, 143). "You will find it to be nothing but one great machine, subdivided into an infinite number of lesser machines." The adapting, throughout nature, of means to ends, says Cleanthes, "resembles exactly, though it much exceeds, the productions of human contrivance," so we are led to infer, "by all the rules of analogy," that "the causes also resemble," that "the Author of nature is somewhat similar to the mind of man," and so we "prove at once the existence of a Deity."

The argument from design was not new with Cleanthes. Indeed, what Hume's character calls the "curious adapting of means to ends" throughout nature was a concept ridiculed twenty years earlier by Voltaire (quoted in Wilford 1985, 46), who in *Candide* has Dr. Pangloss assert, "Everything was made for a purpose. . . . Observe that noses have been made for spectacles; therefore we have spectacles." The horse, someone said, was conveniently designed for man to ride on, and the purpose of tides is to help ships in and out of port (Bowler

1989, 53). Hume was the first, however, to mount sustained objections (through his character Philo) against the analogy upon which the argument from design is based, though he was not the first to note that the analogy is a weak one (Ferre 1973, 675). When we speak of manmade contrivances, says Hume (1779, 149-151), we have experience to fall back on, we know from experience that man has contrived such things in the past. But we have no such experience regarding the UNIVERSE as a whole. As Hume's Philo asks Cleanthes, "Have worlds ever been formed under your eye?" Since we have no experience "of the origin of worlds," how can we say there is any real "similarity between the fabric of a house, and the generation of a universe"? Thus the analogy between the universe and human contrivances like houses is not very close (Smart 1962, 217). It is therefore Philo's contention (Hume 1779, 177) that "we have no data to establish any system of cosmogony," for our limited experience "can afford us no probable conjecture concerning the whole of things."

Natural theology, which sought to find knowledge of God in nature independent of revelation, had been "virtually abandoned" on the Continent by about 1800 but continued to flourish in England (Mayr 1988, 237). Its popularity explains why Paley and others could continue so effectively to promote the argument from design after Hume had just as effectively debunked it. In 1859, however, came the publication of *On the Origin of Species*, in which Charles Darwin convincingly set forth an evolutionary mechanism, NATURAL SELECTION, that made design no longer a necessary explanation for the ADAPTATION of organisms to their environment. The *Origin* was a mortal blow to the argument from design; "historians accept the year 1859," says the distinguished biologist Ernst Mayr (1988, 170), "as the end of creditable natural theology."

Since creationists believe in the literal truth of the biblical record of CREATION, they do not worry about weak analogies or the credibility of natural theology. As creationist leader Henry Morris (1984a, 138) frankly states, "The only way we can possibly know anything about cosmic beginnings is through divine revelation." Creationists find it necessary, however, to use the design argument against the theory of evolution because there is no other argument they can possibly use against some of the most compelling evidence that evolution has occurred. Specifically, creationists contend that the sharing of the same genetic code by all living organisms (see GENETICS) and the basic anatomical similarities among so many diverse species (see ANATOMY) are evidence not of evolutionary descent from a common ancestral form but of the "primeval planning" of a "common Designer" (Morris 1985b, 22, 33). But this raises a crucial question, the whole issue, in fact, of theodicy—the justification of the ways of God to man—that philosophers and theologians have wrestled with down through the ages. The question is simply posed by Hume (1779, 205): "Is the world in general, as it appears to us in this life, different from what a man . . . would *beforehand* expect from a very powerful, wise, and benevolent Deity?" A common enough answer is no, the natural world does not conform to our expectation of what such a Creator would have created. The world does seem to conform, however, to our expectation of what things might look like if produced by evolution (Futuyma 1982, 198; Thwaites 1983, 19). Organisms, notes paleontologist Norman Newell (1985, 156), "are not consistently well engineered"; they have parts that appear to have been improvised or modified from parts that originally served other purposes. This is predicted by evolutionary theory, but is hardly the "optimal design" we would expect of an intelligent designer (Futuyma 1982, 126). Natural selection produces both adaptation and maladaptation in organisms; blind and impersonal, it operates under constraints, able to work only with what is already available and with what genetic variations additionally provide. Thus nature produces "contraptions rather than contrivances" (Ghiselin 1986, 18). The natural world teems with examples of poorly designed, even useless, anatomical structures. Such examples include the clumsy legs (evolved from fins) of AMPHIBIANS (Edwords 1983, 169); the panda's thumb, improvised from a wrist bone (Gould 1980); the musculature, better suited for life on all fours, that supports human viscera (Gould 1987, 68; Halstead 1984, 253); VESTIGIAL ORGANS such as the stubby hind limbs on some sperm whales (Thwaites 1983, 18); and the teeth that develop, and then are absorbed, in whale and anteater embryos (Futyma 1982, 199)—

the list of dubious structures could go on indefinitely. Creationists argue that complex organs could not have come into being by chance but surely must have been been designed. A favorite example is that marvelous organ the eye. But the eye did not appear full blown; it developed like other complex organs in a step-by-step process just as evolutionary theory would predict. Creatures with eyes had ancestors with simpler eyes, who in turn had ancestors with simpler eyes still, until we're all the way back to single light-sensitive cells (Dodson 1985, 988; Mayr 1988, 409). The eyes of humans and other vertebrates, moreover, are not well designed. The retina's photoreceptor cells, instead of pointing toward the light, are in effect wired in backwards, so that some of the incoming light gets screened out by the wiring (Dawkins 1986, 93; Diamond 1985a; Thwaites 1983, 19). "A camera designer who committed such a blunder," notes Jared Diamond (1985a), "would be fired immediately."

And then, of course, there is the problem of pain and suffering. The suffering that animals endure can be seen in part as an inevitable consequence of evolution by natural selection or "survival of the fittest," but is hard to reconcile with the concept of a Master Designer. Darwin (quoted in Greene 1959, 303) cited the example of the ichneumonidae, parasites that feed inside the live bodies of caterpillars, and could not persuade himself that "a beneficent and omnipotent God" would design such creatures, "or that a cat should play with mice." When creationists discuss the wonders of the ANIMAL kingdom, they tend to leave out the likes of ichneumonidae, tapeworms, and bedbugs (Edwords 1982, 2). Why a Master Designer would bless the EARTH with such creatures is as difficult to explain as why the vast majority of all animal species that have ever lived have gone extinct, "just as if no one cared" (Futuyma 1982, 201-202). The world is understandable "as a result of muddle and accident," said the mathematician and philosopher Bertrand Russell (1957, 93), "but if it is the outcome of deliberate purpose, the purpose must have been that of a fiend."

Creationists have an explanation for the suffering and imperfections in the world, but it is not a scientific one. In its "Tenets of Scientific Creationism" (Morris 1984a, 363), the INSTITUTE FOR

CREATION RESEARCH (ICR) is purposefully vague on the subject, stating that "the universe and life have somehow been impaired since the completion of creation," so that there have been "negative" changes in "an originally-perfect created order." In their openly religious moments, however, the ICR creationists leave no doubt at all about the cause of those negative changes. It is "nothing less than the Curse," says ICR president Henry Morris (1978, 74), "pronounced by God on man's entire dominion because of man's sin" (see ADAM AND EVE), a Curse that is reflected in SCIENCE, according to Morris and the ICR, "by the law of increasing entropy" or disorder (see THERMODYNAMICS). "Why else," asks the ICR's George Aardsma (quoted in Boxer 1987, 82), "would the world contain repugnant things?"

DINOSAUR

An extinct REPTILE that flourished during the Mesozoic geologic era (spanning the Triassic, Jurassic, and Cretaceous periods) from 245 to 65 million years ago. The dinosaurs (literally "terrible lizards"), of which there were two orders (Saurischia or "lizard-hipped," and Ornithischia or "bird-hipped"), ranged in size from 6 to 7 pounds (as small as chickens) to as much as 90 tons. Dinosaurs ruled the EARTH for much of the Mesozoic, only to disappear completely, along with many other creatures, during a mass EXTINCTION at the end of the Cretaceous. The causes of the extinction are not known, though a currently favored theory postulates global environmental change due to an asteroid or comet colliding with the earth (Cloud 1988, 405-412; Dixon et al. 1988, 93). The dinosaur's closest living relative is the crocodile, though many experts believe BIRDS to be descendants of the lizard-hipped—not, ironically, of the bird-hipped—dinosaurs (Horner and Gorman 1988, 71; McGowan 1984, 110-115; Wilford 1985, 217-231).

Since young-earth creationists like those at the INSTITUTE FOR CREATION RESEARCH (ICR) believe that all forms of LIFE (or biblical "kinds") were created during the biblical six-day CREATION some 10,000 years ago (Gish 1985, 35; Aardsma 1988, iv), they have little choice but to believe that MAN and the dinosaurs lived contemporaneously. Creationists speculate that the dinosaurs either died during the biblical Flood (see FLOOD, NOAH'S) or, if taken aboard the ark (see ARK, NOAH'S), became extinct due to the Flood's "residual effects" on climate and food supplies (Morris 1978, 32; Moore 1976, 81). Creationists suggest that certain dragonlike creatures depicted in the BIBLE are actually dinosaurs of Old Testament times. Thus the ICR's Duane Gish (1977, 16) states that the description of Behemoth in the Book of Job (40:15-24) is "a pretty good description of a dinosaur." ICR president Henry Morris (1984a, 351-353) tells us that dragons (Hebrew *tannim*) are mentioned "at least twenty-five times in the Old Testament," and that if *tannim* is translated simply as "dinosaurs" the significance of all those references becomes "perfectly clear and appropriate." Actually the Old Testament descriptions of the sea monsters Behemoth, Leviathan (Job 3:8, 41:1-34; Psalms 104:26; Isaiah 27:1), and Rahab (Job 9:13, 26:12; Isaiah 51:9) are poetic passages reflecting an ancient Near Eastern creation myth in which the Creator slays a dragon of chaos (see CREATION).

Man and dinosaur are separated in the FOSSIL RECORD by over 50 million years, and if fossil evidence is ever found that man and dinosaur were contemporaries the world of evolutionary BIOLOGY will certainly be set on its ear. No wonder, then, that creationists have for years been looking for just such evidence along the Paluxy River near Glen Rose, Texas. Many a dinosaur roamed the Texas mud flats of Cretaceous times, so dinosaur tracks are still preserved in the limestone bed of the Paluxy and in the rock at other sites in the Glen Rose area. And ever since a 1950 article by creationist geologist Clifford Burdick, there have been creationist claims of giant human footprints found together with the Texas dinosaur tracks. (The fact that the alleged "man tracks" are giant-sized fits well with the creationists' belief in biblical inerrancy, since Genesis [6:4] states that "there were giants in the earth in those days.") A central figure in the Paluxy man-track claims is the Reverend Carl Baugh, who has regularly led creationist excavation teams in the area and in 1984 opened his Creation Evidences Museum. (For discussion of Baugh's alleged prehistoric "hammer-in-stone," "Moab skeleton" [alleged Cretaceous human bones], and "Glen Rose Man" [a fossil tooth, now determined to be that of a FISH], see Hastings 1985, 1987, and 1989.)

A number of scientists, including paleontologists James Farlow of Purdue University and Stephen Jay Gould of Harvard, have journeyed to the Glen Rose area. None of the man-track claims have held up under their scrutiny. In the early 1980s a team of experts led by anthropologist Laurie R. Godfrey—the team called itself "Raiders of the Lost Tracks"—did extensive fieldwork in the area and concluded that all the alleged man tracks observed were actually dinosaur tracks, invertebrate burrow casts, natural effects of erosion, and (in a minority of cases, as with the casts of footprints that inspired Burdick in 1950) simple forgeries (Cole, Godfrey, and Schafersman 1985; Godfrey 1985; Hastings 1985; see also Kuban 1986). Even the ICR was impressed enough by such findings to back off from its earlier enthusiasm for Paluxy man-track claims. But hope, as Alexander Pope said, springs eternal in the human breast. The ICR continues to provide its followers with Paluxy River updates as Reverend Baugh keeps digging for man tracks.

DNA

See GENETICS.

EARTH

The third planet of the SOLAR SYSTEM in distance from the sun. The study of the earth is GEOLOGY. The biblical Hebrews (see BIBLE) believed that the earth was flat (Isaiah 11:12; Rev. 7:1), beneath it the waters of "the deep" (Genesis 1:2, 7:11), above it the "firmament" (Gen. 1:6-8), a solid dome—the Hebrew *raqia* means hammered metal (Rad 1961, 51)—in which were affixed the sun, moon, and STARS (Gen. 1:14-18). Above this dome were the waters that produce rain, falling through "windows" in the dome (Gen. 7:11). This was the common conception of the UNIVERSE in the ancient Near East and was simply taken for granted by the biblical writers (Anderson 1966, 384-385; Murray and Buffaloe 1983, 465). The leaders of "scientific" creationism contradict themselves by not taking this biblical model literally even though they believe—as they profess when not limiting themselves to purely "scientific" discussion—that the Bible is "absolutely inerrant" (Morris 1984a, 47; see CREATIONISM).

ASTRONOMY has long since swept away the old, cherished notion of the earth as the physical center of the universe. Creationists believe, however, that the earth remains "the center of God's interest" (Morris 1984a, 162). And it is their biblical literalism that forces creationists to argue that the earth is only several thousand years old (see, for example, Ackerman 1986; Aardsma 1988, iv; Morris 1978, 91). This reflects, too, their desire to show that EVOLUTION has not had time to occur. "I want an earth as young as I can get it," says creationist geophysicist Glenn Morton (quoted in Schadewald 1986, 8). But the creationist young-earth argument is simply untenable in light of the overwhelming geological evidence (see GEOLOGY; CONTINENTAL DRIFT; FOSSIL RECORD) that this planet "is a very old place" (Miller 1984, 36). Evidence from astronomy indicates that the earth condensed into a solid body from the *solar nebula* about 4.6 billion years ago (see SOLAR SYSTEM). The evidence also indicates that the universe at that time had already been expanding for billions of years. All evidence, in sum, contradicts the belief of creationist leader Henry Morris (1974, 134) that the earth, "as implied in Genesis 1:1," is "the original material component" of the cosmos. The cosmos, in the words of chemist David E. Fisher (1987, 4), existed long before the earth "was even a mote of dust in its Creator's eye."

Creationists do not argue as did Archbishop James Ussher that the earth was created at 9 A.M. on October 23, 4004 B.C. (Cloud 1988, 9), but their arguments make about as much sense. For example, Morris, their most prolific spokesman, argues in *Scientific Creationism*—the quasi-official textbook of the INSTITUTE FOR CREATION RESEARCH (ICR)—that the fossil record is not what it so obviously appears to be: a record (layered in often miles-deep sedimentary rock that required millions of years to accumulate) of organisms evolving from simpler to more complex forms. Rather it is the record, claims

Morris (1985b, 117-120), of contemporaneous organisms drowning—in what just happens to look like an evolutionary order—in the biblical Flood of Noah (see FLOOD, NOAH'S; for discussion of *flood geology*, see GEOLOGY). Morris (1985b, 157-158) also argues that the earth's *magnetic field* is decaying at such a rate that the earth can't be more than 10,000 years old. It is evident from seafloor *remanent magnetism*, however, that the magnetic field has reversed itself several times over a period of millions of years (Abell 1983, 36-37; see GEOMAGNETISM).

Morris and his fellow young-earthers try especially to discredit RADIOACTIVE DATING, which has yielded ages of 3.96 billion years for the earth's oldest known rocks (Monastersky 1989) and 4.3 billion years for its oldest known mineral fragments (*Science News* 130:136). The creationists argue that radioactive dating is unreliable and therefore proves nothing (Gish 1985, 51; Moore 1976, 39-41; Morris 1984a, 269; Slusher 1981). If that is true, "we need a whole new theory of nuclear and subatomic physics" (Hammond and Margulis 1981, 56). Even allowing for margins of error in the radioactive dating of rocks, it stands to reason that if the earth is only about 10,000 years old, the ages for older rocks as radiometrically measured should be closer to 10,000 years than to billions (Gallant 1984, 298).

It should be noted that while "young-earth" creationism is orthodox creation "science," not all fundamentalists are young-earthers. The so-called *gap theory*, popularized among fundamentalists by the *Scofield Reference Bible*, assumes an indefinite time gap between the first two verses of Genesis (see McIver 1988c). The original earth (Gen. 1:1), after much geological time, somehow met with ruin (became "without form and void" [1:2]), which accounts, so gap theorists claim, for extinct fossil creatures. God then recreated the earth in six days a few thousand years ago. (As to why God would have destroyed the original earth, see SATAN.)

Morris and his fellow young-earthers argue that the gap theory is an unbiblical, unscientific compromise with the evolutionists and their geologic ages (Morris 1978, 87; 1984b, 58-59; 1985b, 231-243). Young-earthers also reject the so-called *day-age theory*, which departs from biblical literalism by assuming that the Genesis "days" of creation refer to ages rather than twenty-four-hour periods (Morris 1985b,

221-230). (The Genesis order of creation, be it days or ages, contradicts both the order of cosmic evolutionary theory, as already noted, and the order of PLANTS and ANIMALS in the fossil record [see LIFE] [Asimov 1981].)

For discussion of the creationist argument that the earth was created with "apparent age," see APPEARANCE OF AGE.

EDWARDS v. AGUILLARD

The case in which the U.S. Supreme Court in 1987 ruled unconstitutional a 1981 Louisiana "Balanced Treatment" law requiring the teaching of creation "science" in public schools whenever EVOLUTION is taught. The statute, said the court, sought "the symbolic and financial support of government to achieve a religious purpose" and thus violated the First Amendment of the U.S. Constitution prohibiting an establishment of religion (Raloff 1987). The ruling brought an end to Christian fundamentalist attempts, begun in the late 1970s, to have the teaching of "scientific" creationism legislated into public school curricula. The ruling did not address the broader question, however, of whether any public school teaching of CREATIONISM is unconstitutional. Thus while *Edwards v. Aguillard* is a landmark decision in creation/evolution litigation (see also *EPPERSON v. ARKANSAS* and *McLEAN v. ARKANSAS*), it is probably not the last one.

The legislative history of the Louisiana law is instructive in terms of the nonscientific motives and methods of the creationists who instigated and supported it. The bill was drafted by Paul Ellwanger, a South Carolina respiratory therapist who headed an organization called Citizens for Fairness in Education. Ellwanger had earlier drafted an Arkansas "Balanced Treatment" law enacted in March 1981 (see *McLEAN v. ARKANSAS*). "I view this whole battle," Ellwanger told a Louisiana legislator, "as one between God and anti-God forces" (Lewin 1987b, 23). The Louisiana bill was introduced by State Senator Bill Keith, whose twelve-year-old son had, in Keith's words (1982, 3), been ridiculed and harassed by a substitute SCIENCE teacher at school for his creationist views. Extensive testimony in favor of the bill was provided by a group called the Pro Family Forum, which presented to the legislature a written Summary of Scientific Evidence for Creation. This evidence included an explanation of GEOLOGY in terms of "a worldwide flood" (see FLOOD, NOAH'S), the "fixity" of original ANIMAL and PLANT "kinds" (see TAXONOMY), and a "relatively recent inception" of the EARTH (Amici Curiae 1986, 9-10). The Pro Family Forum also identified seven books that it considered appropriate to help teachers prepare to teach creation "science." Six of the books were publications of the INSTITUTE FOR CREATION RESEARCH (ICR), which believes, in the words of spokesman Ken Ham (1989a), that the biblical book of Genesis "must be taken literally" and "is foundational to true science, true history, true philosophy, etc." The seventh book was a BIOLOGY text by the ICR's Harold Slusher and ICR Technical Advisory Board member John N. Moore. In 1977 the Indiana Superior Court held that the purpose of Slusher and Moore's book, which had been adopted for public school use by the Indiana Textbook Commission, was "the promotion and inclusion of fundamentalist Christian doctrines in the public schools" (Boles 1983, 181).

Since it was constitutionally essential to avoid any religious or biblical references (direct or indirect) in its language, the Louisiana bill as passed did not contain an actual definition of creation "science." Instead, it contained this tautologous statement: "Creation-science means the scientific evidences for creation and inferences from those scientific evidences" (Zetterberg 1983, 395). It was "a bold trick," says biologist William J. Bennetta (1988b, 22): "a law that promoted the teaching of 'creation-science' but refused to say what 'creation-science' was."

Upon passage, the law was promptly challenged in a suit against Governor David Treen and other officials by a group of educators, religious leaders, and parents (*Aguillard v. Treen*). In 1985 a district court ruled that the statute was unconstitutional, a judgment affirmed that same year by a federal appeals court. The defendants then appealed to the U.S. Supreme Court, where the case was retitled *Edwards v. Aguillard*, appellant Edwin Edwards being then-Louisiana governor and Don Aguillard, the original namesake plaintiff and now an appellee, being a public school teacher (Bennetta 1988c, 16). By this time, creation "science" as promoted by the creationist appellants seemed to bear no resemblance to the young-earth flood geology that the Pro Family Forum had presented to the Louisiana legislature. CREATION was now something called ABRUPT APPEARANCE. The creationists had submitted to district court five affidavits—from a biology professor, a CHEMISTRY professor, and three theologians—stating that creation or creation "science" is not inherently religious but refers, rather, to "abrupt appearance in complex form" (Bennetta 1988b, 25). A friend-of-court brief filed with the Supreme Court by seventy-one Nobel laureates, seventeen state academies of science, and seven other scientific organizations called the creationists' "abrupt-appearance construct" an insufficiently defined "post hoc invention, created for the purpose of defending this unconstitutional Act" [Amici Curiae 1986, 18]. To a degree, the Supreme Court concurred: It viewed the affidavits as irrelevant. The Supreme Court was more interested in the intent of the Louisiana legislature than in a definition of creation from people who had had nothing to do with the legislation (Scott 1987, 6).

Creationist attorney Wendell Bird, in oral arguments before the Supreme Court justices, stated that, yes, some of the law's supporters had religious motives, but the law's primary purpose was to expand students' "academic freedom," to allow them "to hear additional scientific evidence on the subject of origins"; moreover, creation, Bird said, does not necessarily involve a Supreme Being (Lewin 1987b, 22). Opposing attorney Jay Topkis, in his turn before the justices, compared Bird to Tweedledum in *Through the Looking Glass.* "He wants words to mean what he says they mean," said Topkis, but "that didn't fool Alice, and I doubt very much that it will fool this court" (Scott 1987, 6)—at which point Chief Justice William Rehnquist said, "Don't overestimate us" (McKinney 1986, 11). Rehnquist's remark got a good laugh, but Rehnquist, as it turned out, wasn't kidding. When the Supreme Court voted 7 to 2 to declare the Louisiana law unconstitutional, the dissenting votes were those of Rehnquist and Justice Antonin Scalia.

Justice William J. Brennan Jr. wrote the court's majority opinion. He stated that the Louisiana act violated the establishment clause of the First Amendment in that the purpose of the Louisiana legislature "was clearly to advance the religious viewpoint that a supernatural being created humankind." Brennan called the act's stated purpose—the promotion of academic freedom—"a sham." The act "actually diminishes academic freedom," said the court, by forbidding the teaching of evolution when "creation science" is not also taught, a prohibition that "undermines the provision of a comprehensive science education" (Epstein 1987; *Free Inquiry* 7[4]:20; Hastey 1987, 31).

Albert Shanker, president of the American Federation of Teachers, hailed the court's decision as a rescue of the nation's schools "from narrow-minded fanatics trying to impose their beliefs on others" (Epstein 1987). The Reverend James Stovall, executive director of the Louisiana Interchurch Conference, called it "a day of victory and celebration" (Martz and McDaniel 1987, 14). Conversely, television evangelist Pat Robertson—who at the time was running for president—called the decision "an outrage to every American who believes he or she was created by God" (Anderson 1987). ICR president Henry Morris 1987f) warned that America was "in imminent danger of judgment from the Creator we are now brazenly repudiating." Despite this, however, *Edwards v. Aguillard* was not a complete defeat for creationism. The court ruling dealt only with the legislative intent of the Louisiana law; it did not settle the larger question of whether public school teaching of creationism per se is unconstitutional. Such teaching would not necessarily be unconstitutional, says Wendell Bird (1987), if adopted "for a secular purpose." In other words, teachers still have a right, Bird argues, to teach a variety of "scientific" theories about origins and to sue if punished, and schools have a right to encourage or require the teaching of all such "scientific" theories.

The limited scope of the *Edwards v. Aguillard* ruling has virtually guaranteed that the creationists will have another day in court. Soon after the ruling, the ICR (1987b, iii)—while reiterating its long-standing position that creationism is better promoted through "education and persuasion" than through legislation or litigation—was looking forward to "some future test case." And the Creation Science Legal Defense Fund that had helped get the case to the Supreme Court stood ready to help support the next fight. Renamed the Academic Freedom Legal Defense Fund, the fund is headed by none other than Bill Keith, former Louisiana state senator. Says Keith (quoted in Bennetta 1987): "We still are going to blow evolution out of the public schools!"

EMBRYOLOGY

The study of the growth and development of *embryos,* which in humans are the prefetal stage of LIFE in the womb spanning the first two months of pregnancy. There is a striking similarity in the embryos of vertebrate (backboned) ANIMALS—FISHES, REPTILES, BIRDS, and MAMMALS including MAN. Charles Darwin (1859, 439) noted this fact in the *Origin* with a remark about the naturalist Louis Agassiz: "Having forgotten to ticket the embryo of some vertebrate animal, he cannot now tell whether it be that of a mammal, bird, or reptile." And Darwin (1859, 443) drew the obvious conclusion, as do scientists today, from such similarity: Vertebrates evolved from a common ancestor. Human and other mammalian embryos even develop temporary grooves similar to gill slits found in fishes, evidence of the remote ancestors that mammals and fishes share (National Academy of Sciences 1984, 20).

Creationists argue that embryonic similarities are evidence not of common ancestry but of common creative design. (For discussion of this line of thought, see DESIGN ARGUMENT.) They also like to attack the so-called biogenetic law or *recapitulation theory* of German biologist Ernst Haeckel (1834-1919), who believed that embryos during their development go through a repetition, a sort of evolution-in-review, of the adult stages of their ancestors ("ontogeny recapitulates phylogeny"). But the creationists attack a straw man. Scientists today are well aware of the fact that Haeckel overstated the case. Embryos develop from generalized to specialized, developing first the features of their larger taxonomic group, then progressively the defining characteristics of order, of species, of individuals (Gould 1982, 41). While it is true that sometimes in developing embryos there is "an imperfect repetition of ancestral forms" (Newell 1985, 180), this cannot be considered a "law." Creationist leader Henry Morris (1988d) nonetheless argues that "millions" still believe in "recapitulationism" today, and that "abortionists," who "must deny that the fetus is human," use the recapitulation theory as a pseudoscientific justification for "the holocaust of abortionism."

ENERGY

See RELATIVITY; THERMODYNAMICS.

ENGINEERING

The managing of engines, and the application of SCIENCE and the development of technology to the benefit of MAN. Branches include aeronautical, chemical, civil, electrical, and mechanical engineering. It has not escaped notice by evolutionists as well as by creationists that a significant number of the leaders of the "scientific" creationist movement are engineers. Henry M. Morris, cofounder and president of the INSTITUTE FOR CREATION RESEARCH (ICR), holds a Ph.D. in hydraulic engineering from the University of Minnesota—he majored in hydraulics the better to study Noah's Flood (Morris 1984b, 136-137)—and for many years was chairman of the civil engineering department at Virginia Polytechnic Institute (Numbers 1982, 542). Other engineers prominent in the creationist movement have included an engineering dean at Iowa State University and a professor of aerospace, mechanical, and nuclear engineering at the University of Oklahoma. ICR administrative vice president John D. Morris (son of Henry) holds a Ph.D. in geological engineering from Oklahoma, and the late Luther Sunderland, a pioneer of the ABRUPT APPEARANCE "theory" of CREATION, was an engineer with General Electric.

It has been argued by creationists that people in such technical professions as engineering, given the highly structured and ordered nature of their work, naturally tend to think in terms of order and design (Nelkin 1982, 86). A quite different assessment, by professor of engineering (and evolutionist) John W. Patterson (1983, 152), is that engineers "are comparatively ignorant of biological processes, genetics, etc." and "are infatuated with arguments from design." The argument that apparent design in nature implies a Designer certainly had an influence on Henry Morris, who as a professor of civil engineering at Rice Institute used to study the structural design of the butterflies and wasps that flew in through his office window (Numbers 1982, 541). "Teaching structural design," states Morris (1987, 188), "made me intensely conscious of the fact that the marvelous structural design of plants and animals could not be the result of chance." But the concept of design by a divine Creator does not explain, as does the theory of EVOLUTION by NATURAL SELECTION, the many imperfections and maladaptations that are found in the living world. Natural selection "does not work as an engineer works," notes Francois Jacob (1977, 1164), but "like a tinkerer," managing with whatever biological structures and genetic variations are at hand. Consequently, organisms "are not consistently well engineered" (Newell 1985, 156); in fact, they turn the argument from design, in the words of Michael Ghiselin (1986, 18), into "the argument from incompetent design," hence into "an argument for atheism" (see DESIGN ARGUMENT).

Patterson (1983, 150) first entered the creation/evolution controversy because of what he terms the "grossly erroneous if not deceitful arguments" advanced by creationists about THERMODYNAMICS, a subject he had taught to engineering students for many years. Patterson states that biologists, geologists, or paleontologists, unlike engineers, could never publicly endorse a pseudoscience such as "scientific" CREATIONISM and hope to achieve or retain prestigious academic positions or high offices in professional societies. Patterson sees engineering societies as seemingly "uninterested in policing themselves, as regards either ethical irresponsibility or scientific incompetence." That may or may not be a fair assessment of engineering societies, but anyone interested in cases of irresponsibility and incompetence on the part of engineers should be sure to read the creationist book *How Did It All Begin?* (original title: *From Goo to You by Way of the Zoo*) by electrical engineer Harold Hill (1976). Here are three examples (see also LAMARCKISM) of what Hill wants his readers—the book is dedicated to "the young people of today"—to believe: Intelligent radio signals are being received from outer space, shoe leather can be turned into gold, and Hill's friend Dr. Donald Liebman ("a completed Jew") has "a scientific instrument"—Hill calls it "a glory meter"—that can detect whether or not you've been born again. Hill's book has a foreword, incidentally, by the late Wernher von Braun, one of the world's most famous engineers.

ENTROPY

See THERMODYNAMICS.

EPPERSON v. ARKANSAS

The case in which the U.S. Supreme Court ruled in 1968 that a 1929 Arkansas statute prohibiting the teaching of EVOLUTION was unconstitutional. The law had been challenged by Little Rock high-school teacher Susan Epperson, who was subject to prosecution if she used new BIOLOGY books, adopted by her school district, that included the theory of evolution (Dolphin 1983, 20). In its ruling the Court declared that it was "clear that fundamentalist sectarian conviction was and is the law's reason for existence." The law was an attempt, said the Court, "to blot out a particular theory because of its supposed conflict with the Biblical account (of man's origin), literally read" (Edwords 1980, 13). The law thus violated the First Amendment that prohibits any "establishment of religion."

Epperson v. Arkansas helped determine the course of the modern creationist movement. The Arkansas statute was a relic of the fundamentalist antievolution movement of the twenties (see SCOPES TRIAL). Since evolution after *Epperson* could no longer be outlawed, the creationist strategy became one of seeking legislation to require equal time for CREATIONISM whenever evolutionary theory was taught. This strategy led to more court cases and defeats (see *McLEAN v. ARKANSAS* and *EDWARDS v. AGUILLARD*), after which the creationists settled on their current strategy (successful in the past) of local-level influence and pressure.

EVOLUTION

In its organic or biological sense, the process of "descent with modification" (Darwin 1859) of all living organisms from simpler ancestral forms. (For inorganic or cosmic evolution, see UNIVERSE.) While notions suggesting evolution date back to antiquity, the English naturalist Charles Darwin, in his book *On the Origin of Species* (1859), was the first to amass the scientific evidence for biological evolution so comprehensively as to convince most of the world's scientists of the evolutionary descent of all LIFE forms. With the twentieth-century development of the SCIENCE of GENETICS, Darwin's central concept of NATURAL SELECTION was merged with the new understanding of *heredity*, giving rise to the *modern synthesis* or modern synthetic theory of evolution, known also as *Neo-Darwinism*.

The basic principles of evolution can be simply stated. Organisms within a *population* tend to produce more offspring than the *environment* can support. Among a population's individuals, genetic *variation* due to *mutation* and *recombination* will allow some to adapt better than others to changing environmental conditions. Those organisms better adapted—those naturally selected, in effect, by the environment—will live longer and produce more offspring, passing on their favorable characteristics to succeeding generations. When part of a population becomes geographically isolated, a new *species* can emerge as ADAPTATION to new conditions proceeds. Thus *reproduction*, variation, and environment, acting over vast geologic ages, have led to constant evolutionary change.

But how did life arise to begin with? This question involves not Darwinian but chemical evolution (Chang et al. 1983, 53) and is still problematical despite some exciting experimental research (see ABIOGENESIS). Many evolutionists are theists who believe that life was originally created (see GOD and WORLD VIEW). Solving the mystery of life's origin is in any case not vital to evolutionary BIOLOGY. Biological evolution is what happens—and the evidence clearly shows that it has—once life has arisen.

The evidence for biological evolution begins with the FOSSIL RECORD, in which simpler forms of life are followed by more advanced forms, including TRANSITIONAL FORMS between major groups, over a total span of some 3.5 billion years (as measured by RADIOACTIVE DATING). Such a general sequence of life forms from simple to more complex is a major "prediction" of evolutionary theory, that is, it is exactly what we should expect to find if evolution has indeed occurred. Moreover, the ongoing discovery of new fossils means that evolutionary theory, unlike untestable claims, is potentially falsifiable (see SCIENCE). Each fossil tests the theory anew. "Millions of conceivable paleontological discoveries could disprove evolution," says biologist Douglas Futuyma (1982, 170)—the conceivable discovery, for example, of a fossilized MAMMAL in Precambrian rock—"but none has ever come to light."

Another major prediction of evolutionary theory is that all living things, being related by common descent, should "resemble each other in descending degrees" (Darwin 1859, 128). And that is exactly what we find, a "hierarchy of resemblance" (Eldredge 1981, 18) among all of EARTH's organisms. *Homologous* structures (see ANATOMY), such as the similar bone structure in the wing of a bat, the leg of a horse, and the arm of a MAN, are prime evidence from comparative anatomy of the shared evolutionary origin of the organisms involved. The anatomical evidence is complemented by that from *molecular biology:* All living things share the same *genetic code* (see GENETICS), and molecular genetic differences between species can be used to construct family trees that harmonize well with the family trees that paleontologists construct based on fossils (see BIOLOGY). Evolutionary theory is also supported by EMBRYOLOGY, with the close embryonic resemblance between humans and other vertebrates (backboned ANIMALS) clearly suggesting a common ancestor.

The theory of evolution predicts, however, that in addition to similarity among organisms we should find great *diversity.* Such diversity would be a natural consequence of eons of genetic variation and adaptation. And we indeed find diversity that is virtually beyond measure, as many as 10 million living species (the estimates vary), not to mention the untold millions that have suffered EXTINCTION. Evolution is the only scientific theory that brings a unifying order to this otherwise bewildering variety of life forms past and present.

A statement by distinguished geneticist (and Christian believer) Theodosius Dobzhansky (1973) is often quoted by biologists for its simple truth: "Nothing in biology makes sense except in the light of evolution."

The evidence for evolution is also biogeographical. According to the theory, "we should expect closely related species to be found in close proximity," says paleontologist Chris McGowan (1984, 5), "especially those with limited powers of dispersal," such limitations being why, for example, we find kangaroos only in Australia and hummingbirds only in the Americas. The geographical distribution of organisms speaks so strongly of evolution and poses such problems for creationists that the subject has been all but ignored in creationist writings (see BIOGEOGRAPHY).

Creationists are fond of saying that evolutionary theory is not true science because evolution cannot be directly observed. While this is a distortion of the nature of science (can we "observe" gravity or a quark?), it is certainly true that large-scale change or *macroevolution* occurs too slowly to be observed by mere mortals. Macroevolution must be inferred from such evidence as has already been cited. But there are occurrences of *microevolution* or small-scale change within species that *can* be observed in one's lifetime. INSECTS, for example, become immune to pesticides, bacteria become immune to antibiotics. These are cases of changed environments naturally selecting genetic mutations or recombinations that prove resistant and thus spread through the species. Animal and PLANT breeders, through *artificial selection*, operate on evolutionary principles all the time (see NATURAL SELECTION).

Creationist objections to evolutionary theory begin with the fact that the theory conflicts with a literal interpretation of the biblical story of CREATION. Creationist leaders such as Henry Morris and Duane Gish of the INSTITUTE FOR CREATION RESEARCH (ICR) are Christian fundamentalists who will tolerate no such conflict (see BIBLE). They must therefore take scientifically untenable positions in their attempts to refute the theory. Thus the fossil record, according to creationist writings, is not evidence of evolution at all but rather of Noah's Flood, its now fossilized victims left by the sorting action of the waters in an order that today appears evolutionary simply by coincidence (for discussion of this *flood geology*, see GEOLOGY). This is perhaps the most indefensible (both geologically and logically) of all creationist arguments, but one that the biblical book of Genesis, taken literally, forces the creationists to make. When examining an evolutionary theory, says the ICR (Morris 1985b, 215), "the Word of God must take first priority, and secondly, the observed facts of science." Creationists also use flood geology in their argument that the earth is only a few thousand years old, hence evolution has not had time to occur. They must then come up with yet more *pseudoscience* (see SCIENCE) to try to refute the evidence from ASTRONOMY and RADIOACTIVE DATING that the age of the earth is about 4.6 billion years.

Creationists claim that the fossil record contains no transitional forms, forms that we should find in abundance, they say, if evolution is true. But while the fossil record is indeed imperfect—we are fortunate, given the odds against a body being fossilized and recovered, that the record is as good as it is (Futuyma 1979, 78; McGowan 1984, 93)—there are plenty of intermediate forms. Examples of these are ARCHAEOPTERYX, *Seymouria* (see REPTILE), and the *mammal-like reptiles* (see MAMMAL). The fact that evolutionists argue among themselves about why there aren't *more* transitional forms (see PUNCTUATED EQUILIBRIA) is cited by creationists as evidence that the theory of evolution itself is somehow in "troubled waters" (Morris 1982b). But when scientists argue about evolution, they are arguing about *how* evolution has occurred, not *if*. There are still many unresolved questions about evolutionary mechanisms, and paleontologists have their "bones of contention" about this or that fossil (see Lewin 1987), but evolution itself remains "the most fundamental organizational concept in the biological sciences" (National Academy of Sciences 1984, 22).

Creationists never fail to argue that evolution, being a process of increasing order or complexity, is a violation of the second law of THERMODYNAMICS. But while the universe overall is going from order to disorder—the thermodynamic principle of increasing *entropy*—order may temporarily develop (as it obviously does here on earth) in regions far from equilibrium (that is, where there is an ample energy source, in our case the sun), as long as there is an offsetting increase in universal entropy (most solar energy is lost into space). It has been demonstrated that all that is needed to cause new forms of order to arise spontaneously in far-from-equilibrium conditions is an influx of energy (Prigogine 1969; Prigogine and Stengers 1984). His work in this area won thermodynamicist Ilye Prigogine the Nobel Prize for CHEMISTRY in 1977.

Creationists argue that the similarity manifest among organisms is evidence not of common evolutionary origin but rather of common creative design (see DESIGN ARGUMENT). But this argument does not speak well of the Creator's creative ability. While the similar bone structure in the leg of a rat, the wing of a bat, and the fin of a porpoise may suggest common design, an "engineer, starting from scratch," notes Stephen Jay Gould (1984a, 122), "could design better limbs in each case." The design argument invites a virtually unlimited number of questions that can't be logically answered, such as why did God create parasites, put nipples on males, and design wings for flightless birds. It is evolutionary theory, not the concept of conscious design, that predicts the bizarre diversity, imperfections, and often useless genetic by-products that we find in nature. Natural selection is a process that is "blind" (Dawkins 1986) and works only with what is at hand, thus evolution is "very much a string and sealing wax operation" (Ruse 1986, 17). Maladaptation is a common result, with most species in fact having gone the way of extinction.

Which brings us to another religious objection of the creationists. Evolution, says Morris (1978, 73, 88), is "a cruel spectacle," a process of "appalling inefficiency and barbarity" that a gracious God "would not allow, let alone invent." (Evolutionists might reply that a gracious God would not invent this harsh world we live in by placing a curse—as creationists believe that he did (Morris 1985b, 211-214)—on all living things, for all time, for what two people did at the beginning [Mattill 1982, 18; see ADAM AND EVE].) But the theory of evolution neither implies nor denies God's existence (Dolphin 1983a, 26) and has nothing to say about ethics. To quote Futuyma (1979, 9): "Evolution and natural selection *are*, but whether they *ought* to be is a question of value that falls outside the realm of science."

Creationists insist, however, on making evolution a moral issue.

They closely identify evolutionary theory with HUMANISM, which ICR cofounder Tim LaHaye (1980, 57) calls "the world's greatest evil." According to LaHaye (1975, 5), the theory of evolution "has wrought havoc in the home, devastated morals, destroyed man's hope for a better world, and contributed to the political enslavement of a billion or more people." As expressed by a creationist group called CAVE (Citizens for Another Voice in Education), "Animal origins leads to animal ethics" (Saladin 1980, 59). "And how can we explain," asks Morris (1963, 77), "the well-nigh universal insistence that all things have come about by evolution? . . . The answer is Satan!"

Such creationist moralizing fails to appreciate that any concept, no matter how worthy, can be twisted to evil ends. If evolutionary theory has at times been used for social ill—as it was, for example, by the followers of Herbert Spencer (see NATURAL SELECTION)—the same can be said of the Christian religion. Morality requires no theological base; it grows out of the experiences of people (Burke 1986). Generations of evolutionists, "from Darwin to Dobzhansky," have been persons of exemplary character (Futuyma 1982, 181), not the immoral people that creationists think evolutionists must be.

To teach biology without evolutionary theory is, in the words of George Gaylord Simpson (1964, 34), "like teaching physics but leaving out atoms." As for the effect of that theory on students, it has possibly never occurred to a creationist that a student, far from collapsing into moral degeneracy, might agree with Darwin (1859, 489) that when all beings are viewed "not as special creations, but as the lineal descendants" of a few prehistoric life forms, they seem "to become ennobled." Perhaps the most frequently quoted passage from Darwin's writings is the positive vision with which he closes the *Origin*. It seems appropriate to close with it here: "There is grandeur in this view of life, with its several powers, having been originally breathed into a few forms or into one; and that, whilst this planet has gone cycling on according to the fixed law of gravity, from so simple a beginning endless forms most beautiful and most wonderful have been, and are being, evolved." (See also LIFE; MAN; WORLD VIEW.)

EXPANDING UNIVERSE

See BIG BANG; UNIVERSE.

EXTINCTION

The state of an ANIMAL or PLANT species or lineage having ceased to exist. Extinction is a natural consequence of biological EVOLUTION. Those species (or individuals within a species) that through genetic variation become better adapted than others to changing environmental conditions will produce the most offspring and will thus tend, over generations, to displace the others through *differential reproduction* (Dobzhansky 1985, 743; Mayr 1970, 107; Simpson 1967, 257, 268). This is the process that Charles Darwin called NATURAL SELECTION, and while it leads to ADAPTATION it also leads, as Darwin (1859, 128) noted, to "much extinction." In the words of the late paleontologist George Gaylord Simpson (1964, 21), "the statistically usual outcome of evolution" has not been selection but "obliteration." It is estimated that over 99 percent of all species that have ever existed on EARTH have gone extinct (Mayr 1988, 106; Newell 1985, 63). We are living, moreover, at a time of one of the greatest *mass extinctions* in earth history. Several mass extinctions, affecting an array of organisms above the species level, have occurred in past geologic ages, and are events for which natural selection or other biological processes are by themselves not adequate explanations. It has been theorized, for example, that the extinction of the DINOSAURS and many other organisms at the end of the Cretaceous period about 65 million years ago was occasioned by climatic change due to collision with the earth of an asteroid or comet (Cloud 1988, 405-412; Dixon et al. 1988, 93; Eldredge 1987, 209-210). There are as yet no certain explanations for mass extinctions (see Newell 1985)—with the exception, that is, of the one presently occurring. The destruction by MAN of natural habitats, particularly through deforestation, is destroying at least 1,000 species a year, a rate that could rise in the 1990s to 10,000 species a year (one species per hour), until within the next century half of the world's species—the majority, in the tropical rain forests, not even yet named or studied—may be lost, taking with them potential medicinal and other benefits left, in the words of entomologist E. O. Wilson, "forever unmeasured" (Wilson 1985, 122, 138; Roberts 1988).

The INSTITUTE FOR CREATION RESEARCH (ICR), America's leading creationist organization, quotes the BIBLE to the effect that death is GOD's punishment for the sin of ADAM AND EVE (for example, Romans 5:12, 1 Corinthians 15:20-26). In their "scientific" mode, the ICR creationists, who are all Christian fundamentalists, state that extinctions as well as "imperfections in structure, disease, aging," and "other such phenomena" are evidence of "the universal entropy principle" (see THERMODYNAMICS) by which the world is "impaired" (Morris 1984b, 363; 1985b, 58). In their "Biblical" mode, however, they make clear that that impairment is due to "the Curse of God on all man's dominion" (Morris 1985b, 215), that "death and bloodshed of man and animals" entered the world "as a result of Adam's sin" (Ham 1989a). ICR president Henry Morris (1978, 30-32) attributes the extinction of the dinosaurs to Noah's Flood and its "devastating residual effects" (see FLOOD, NOAH'S). He describes the FOSSIL RECORD as "a continuing testimony to God's sovereign destruction" of the original CREATION "in the great Flood." (Such deliberate mass destruction of LIFE, taken as literal history by fundamentalists, would seem to be a rather severe judgment by God against his own creation, but Morris [1970, 131; 1984a, 211; 1987b; 1988b; 1989b] likes to quote Hebrews 12:29: "Our God is a consuming fire.")

Creationists use the fact of extinction to attack the idea that evolution represents "progress." In its Morris-edited textbook *Scientific Creationism* (Morris 1985b, 53), the ICR calls it "strange logic" that the "large array of extinct animals in the fossil record" is considered by evolutionists to be "evidence of evolution." Similarly, creationist John Klotz (1985, 181) wonders how mutation, which is usually harmful or neutral (see GENETICS), "can lead to an improvement in living things as the theory of evolution demands." If evolutionists really believe that natural selection acting on mutation causes evolution, says the ICR (Morris 1985b, 57), they should "favor all measures" to increase mutations and "thus facilitate further evolution." But such a statement is based on the false assumption that evolutionists believe evolution to be progressive or "good." The idea that evolution is somehow *teleological* or purposeful, or that it involves some inner drive toward perfection (a concept called *orthogenesis*), was popular in the late nineteenth century, but is not taken seriously by any competent biologists of the late twentieth (Mayr 1988, 244-247). As Douglas Futuyma (1982, 138, 142) points out, whether a mutation is "good" or "bad" depends on the environment, and we do not go around building "leaky nuclear reactors"—at least not on purpose!—to cook up mutations and facilitate evolution because evolution "isn't either good or bad," it "just happens." Natural selection is an uncaring, impersonal process in which there is no goal or purpose or plan. For a relatively few lucky species, adaptation (but never perfection) has resulted. Historically, however, almost all species have gone the way of extinction. "If that is a foreordained plan," said George Gaylord Simpson (1964, 23), "it is an oddly ineffective one."

EXTRATERRESTRIAL LIFE

See LIFE.

FISH

Aquatic, vertebrate (backboned) ANIMALS with gills and fins. There are over 30,000 species of fishes in three major groups: *jawless fishes*, such as lampreys and hagfishes; *cartilaginous fishes*, such as sharks and rays; and the largest and most familiar group, the *bony fishes*, such as trout, bass, and perch (Greenwood 1985, 289). The earliest known fishes are also the oldest known vertebrates, jawless fishes from the Ordovician geologic period about 450 million years ago (Dobzhansky 1985, 747). Jawed, bony fishes evolved by the time of the Devonian period (about 400 million years ago), with a lobe-finned group called the *crossopterygians* probably giving rise to the AMPHIBIANS, the first vertebrates to adapt to LIFE on the land.

Creationists argue that the EVOLUTION of fishes and other vertebrates from invertebrate ancestors is "purely an assumption" since no TRANSITIONAL FORM between invertebrates and vertebrates has been found in the FOSSIL RECORD (Gish 1985, 65, 88; Morris 1985b, 82). The fossil record is indeed incomplete, since the first *chordates* (the phylum Chordata that includes vertebrates) were not likely fossil candidates, being small, comparatively simple creatures that probably lacked a hard skeleton (Colbert 1980, 5). However, there are primitive chordates alive today that approximate what the form ancestral to vertebrates must have been like. Consider the *Amphioxus*, a lancelet or small fishlike creature that spends much of its time burrowed in sand and feeds by straining food particles from water (McGowan 1984, 75; Romer 1966, 11). It has more features in common with vertebrates than with any other invertebrate, and is generally believed to be a present-day relative of the organisms ancestral to us vertebrates (McGowan 1984, 75-76; Colbert 1980, 5; Romer 1966,11; Stebbins 1982, 275; Strahler 1987, 405). *Sea squirts* in their larval form are very similar to *Amphioxus* and are further evidence of the invertebrate-vertebrate connection (McGowan 1984, 76). A fossil form called *Pikaia* resembles *Amphioxus* and confirms that such creatures existed during the Middle Cambrian period (Fenton and Fenton 1989, 341; Strahler 1987, 405); the first fossils believed to be remains of vertebrates date from the Late Cambrian and Early Ordovician (Fenton and Fenton 1989, 343). Vertebrate paleontologist Chris McGowan (1984, 76) rightly criticizes the creationists for putting so much emphasis on the lack of transitional fossil forms while ignoring living animals.

One living animal that creationists do *not* ignore, however, is the *coelacanth*. This fish was thought to have gone extinct millions of years ago until the one known surviving species (*Latimeria*) was discovered in 1938 (Fricke 1988). What creationists like about the coelacanth is that it is a crossopterygian, the type of lobe-finned fish, as noted above, that is believed by evolutionists to have been ancestral to the amphibians. "It is hard to see," says the INSTITUTE FOR CREATION RESEARCH (ICR), how coelacanths could have "become amphibians" when they are still the same as they were when the transition supposedly began (Morris 1985b, 82-83). The coelacanth is a so-called living fossil, and "the very existence of 'living fossils,' " argues one "scientific" creationist (Moore 1976, 54), "is evidence for fixity of kinds." But while there is uncertainty as to why living fossils such as the coelacanth change so little over time (see ADAPTATION), the fact that they exist in no way negates the evidence for evolutionary change in related lines. And no evolutionists claim that coelacanths "became amphibians." The coelacanth is not even considered to be in the direct line of fish-to-amphibian descent. There were two groups of crossopterygians, and it was the *rhipidistian* group—not the related coelecanths—that is believed to be ancestral to amphibians (Dixon et al. 1988, 44-48). Thus all that evolutionists claim about the coelacanth is what creationists will never admit: It is "our closest living fishy relative" (Wallace, King, and Sanders 1981, 642).

FLOOD, NOAH'S

The worldwide Deluge sent by GOD, according to the biblical book of Genesis (6:5-8:22), "to destroy all flesh" for the sins of MAN. Only a 600-year-old man named Noah, who "found favor in the eyes of the Lord," was spared along with his family and pairs of all "kinds" of ANIMALS, surviving the Flood in an ark built according to God's instructions.

The Genesis Flood narrative is believed by most biblical scholars to be a conflation of two main literary sources, designated (in what is called the *documentary hypothesis*) as J (the Yahwist account) and P (the Priestly account). The two accounts were composed about 500 years apart, and there are contradictions between them. Thus Noah is told by God (Yahweh) in the J document to take into the ark seven pairs of all clean animals and single pairs of all others (7:2), while in the P source all animals enter by twos (7:8-9). In J the Flood lasts 40 days and nights (7:17), in P 150 days (7:24). J and P can generally be distinguished from each other (in the original Hebrew) throughout the Flood story. The prescribed dimensions of the ark (6:14-16), the opening of the firmament and upsurging of the subterranean waters (7:11), the landing of the ark "upon the mountains of Ararat" (8:4), and God's covenant with Noah (9:1-17) are details from the P source. Noah's sending out of the raven and the dove (8:6-12), and his burnt offering for the pleasure of Yahweh ("the Lord smelled the pleasing odor") (8:20-22), are from the J source.

The story of Noah's Flood so strikingly resembles that of Utnapishtim in the ancient Babylonian epic of Gilgamesh that some degree of direct or indirect Hebrew borrowing seems indisputable. In the Babylonian tale (see Speiser 1969, 72-99), Utnapishtim is warned by the god Ea of the coming deluge, builds a ship, takes animals aboard, and weathers the storm. The ship grounds atop a mountain, whereupon Utnapishtim sends out a dove, a swallow, and a raven, and then burns an offering, the gods smelling the odor and crowding around "like flies."

Ancient flood traditions are found among many peoples, with two now fragmentary Mesopotamian myths—one in which the Noah character is the Sumerian king Ziusudra (Kramer 1969, 42-44), the other in which he is named Atrahasis (Speiser 1969, 104-106)—predating the one in the Gilgamesh epic. What distinguishes the Genesis myth from its predecessors is firstly the elimination by the biblical writers of the original polytheistic context, and secondly the presentation of the Flood as divine judgment against sin. (In the Atrahasis myth, by way of contrast, a flood is sent because people have become so numerous and noisy that the supreme god Enlil can't sleep.)

The INSTITUTE FOR CREATION RESEARCH (ICR), headed by America's leading "scientific" creationist Henry Morris, considers Noah's Flood to be literal history. In its quasi-official textbook *Scientific Creationism* (Morris 1985b, 252), the ICR calls the Genesis Flood "the real crux" of the CREATION/EVOLUTION dispute, for the ICR's creationists consider the Flood, not evolution, to be the answer to the order of the FOSSIL RECORD. That order is one of simpler to more complex fossil organisms as we move from older to younger rock strata—exactly the order that we would expect to find if LIFE on EARTH has evolved. But the ICR (Morris 1985b, 117-120) argues that the fossils are of organisms that were "originally created contemporaneously" and were drowned in a "great hydraulic cataclysm" that laid down all the earth's beds of sedimentary rock. Such a flood, the ICR maintains, would leave its drowned victims roughly in the order of their habitat elevations and their ability to flee from the waters. We are apparently supposed to attribute to coincidence the fact that this order of drowning turns out to look the same as an evolutionary order. We must also share the amazement (rhetorical, of course) of philosopher Michael Ruse (1982, 315) that in fleeing the Flood "*not one* human being," or horse or cow or tortoise, was so slow or stupid or crippled as to lag behind and get caught "at the bottom of the hill," thus to become fossilized with simpler organisms in a lower rock layer. (For a discussion of the sequence of fossil life forms, see LIFE.)

We also have to wonder where all the water came from, not to mention where all of it went. It has been estimated (Newell 1985, 38) that over 4.4 billion cubic kilometers of water, to a height of 9 kilometers above present sea level, would be needed to completely cover the earth's surface ("and all the high hills, that were under the whole heavens, were covered" [Gen. 7:19]). In other words, Noah's Flood would have required over three times the amount of water (oceans, lakes, atmospheric moisture, and so on) that is presently in the earth's *hydrologic cycle*. Even a flood only three kilometers above present sea level—enough to cover about one-third of Mount Everest—would require more water than the earth has available (Newell 1985, 38). Morris and his fellow "scientific" creationists must therefore resort to fancy. They hypothesize that before the Flood there existed "a vast thermal blanket of water vapor" in the earth's atmosphere, and that this "vapor canopy" not only provided the pre-Flood world with a "marvelous greenhouse effect" but provided ample atmospheric water for the Flood (Morris 1985b, 124-125). Not only does the creationist "vapor canopy theory" have no basis in either SCIENCE or the Bible, but the atmospheric pressure and composition resulting from such a canopy would have prevented earthly life from existing (see Strahler 1987, 195-197).

The implausible nature of creationist *flood geology* is discussed elsewhere in detail (see GEOLOGY), as are the problems associated with literal belief in the voyage of Noah's ark (see ARK, NOAH'S). The only thing, it seems safe to say, that could conceivably lead someone to accept the historicity of Noah's Flood is a commitment to biblical literalism. This is virtually admitted by the creationists themselves. "If the Bible is the Word of God," says the ICR (Morris 1985b, 251), then the "long geological ages never really took place at all." This "*forces* one to find another explanation" for the earth's sedimentary rocks and fossil record, and therefore the biblical Deluge "*must be accepted* as the basic mechanism" (italics added). In *The Genesis Flood,* a 1961 book that helped to inspire the modern creationist movement, Morris and coauthor John C. Whitcomb make the following statement: "Our conclusions must unavoidably be colored by our biblical presuppositions, and this we plainly acknowledge" (Whitcomb and Morris 1961, xxi). Those are words well worth remembering when evaluating "scientific" creationist arguments, for creationists today, wanting a say in public school science education, are not always so candid about their biblical presuppositions.

FOSSIL RECORD

All of the recorded *fossils*—remains, traces, or impressions—of ANIMALS and PLANTS of past geologic ages. The study of past LIFE forms through fossils is called *paleontology.* Most fossils are found in the stratified or layered *sedimentary rocks*—formed by successive particle deposits solidified over the ages—that cover most of the EARTH's land surface and seafloors. Fossils are found, moreover, in sequence, simpler forms being in the lower or older rock strata and more complex forms being in the upper or younger strata. This is exactly the fossil sequence that we would expect to find if it is true that life has evolved (Eldredge 1982, 41). We would predict, based on the theory of EVOLUTION, that the earth's oldest known fossils would also be the simplest, and they are: traces of microorganisms in rocks that according to RADIOACTIVE DATING are 3.5 billion years old (Kutter 1987, 346-349; Strahler 1987, 516). We would also predict that no fossils of a species will be found in rocks that predate the evolution of that species. For example, we have never found a fossilized MAMMAL in Silurian rock, and we predict that we never will (Futuyma 1982, 207).

It is a favorite argument of "scientific" creationists that there are no TRANSITIONAL FORMS in the fossil record to support evolutionary theory (see, for example, Gish 1985, 249-250; Moore 1976, 51-53; Morris 1977, 29-32). New forms, say the creationists, appear abruptly in the fossil record with no trace of ancestors (see Gish 1985, 250; 1986). It is certainly correct to say that the fossil record is imperfect and contains a great many gaps. However, this in no way discredits evolutionary theory. Given the odds against a dead organism becoming fossilized (and, once fossilized, being found), it is actually remarkable that the record is as good as it is (Futuyma 1979, 78). There are millions of known fossils, including about 250,000 animal and plant species (Whittaker 1979). And to say that among these remains there are no transitional forms is simply not true. Perhaps the clearest example of a transitional form is the fossil reptile-BIRD ARCHAEOPTERYX. The extinct genus *Seymouria* is an AMPHIBIAN-reptile mosaic. As fossil intermediates between REPTILES and MAMMALS, the mammal-like reptiles are dead giveaways. Between extinct ape and early MAN are intermediate fossils called AUSTRALOPITHECINES. Many more transitional forms could be cited. Paleontologists acknowledge, however, that intermediates, particularly at the species level, are rare, and that consequently new forms tend to appear abruptly in the fossil record (see ABRUPT APPEARANCE). However, no competent paleontologist would agree with creationists that this is evidence that the new forms were divinely created. (Creating new forms after old ones would be "progressive creation," which most creationists reject as unbiblical [see Morris 1985b, 220-211], so the creationist argument is muddled.) Rather, many paleontologits now agree with the theory of *geographic* or *allopatric speciation,* according to which new species arise rapidly in small, geographically isolated populations (see PUNCTUATED EQUILIBRIA). When a newly evolved species then extends its range, it appears "suddenly" in the fossil record; the intermediate is unlikely to ever be found (Futuyma 1982, 83).

The fossil record, then, is rather slim pickings with respect to species-level transitions (Godfrey 1983a, 201; McGowan 1984, 96). Overall, however, the fossil sequence includes many transitional forms and is compelling evidence that all forms of life have evolved. The fossil evidence has been strikingly supplemented by advances in molecular BIOLOGY, specifically in the study of proteins and the genetic material DNA (see GENETICS). Molecular biologists are able to use the degrees of similarity in the DNA and proteins among different species to construct evolutionary family ("phylogenetic") trees, which track very well with phylogenetic trees based on fossils (Lewin 1988a; Max 1986, 35; see BIOLOGY). Indeed there are molecular scientists such as Thomas H. Jukes (1988, 5) who believe that the importance of the fossil record in studying evolution is now secondary to that of molecular biology. Fossils cannot tell us, for example, whether MAN is more closely related to rabbits or to mice, but molecular biology can (Edey and Johanson 1989, 358). (The closer relationship is of mice and men.) On the other hand, fossils can tell us things about extinct species, such as morphology or structure, that molecular biology cannot. "That's why," says paleontologist Donald Johanson (Edey and Johanson 1989, 368), "you'll always need people like me to go out and find fossils."

How do creationists explain the fossil sequence of simpler to more complex organisms with its clear implication? It's easy: Creationists contend that the evolutionary nature of this sequence is an illusion. The earth, they argue, is only several thousand years old (Aardsma 1988, iv; Morris 1978, 91)—a biblically based belief that forces them to reject, among other things, the validity of radioactive dating—so that evolution has not had time to occur. They believe that the organisms found in the fossil record all lived contemporaneously, and were drowned by a worldwide Deluge that overtook them in the order of their habitat elevations and degrees of mobility (Whitcomb and Morris 1961, 271-276; Morris 1978, 28; 1985b, 111-120). We are therefore asked to believe: (1) that one great flood could have laid down all the layers of fossil-bearing sedimentary rock that cover most of our planet to a depth of as much as 12 miles; (2) that such a raging deluge would leave an orderly fossil sequence instead of a random mix; and (3) that this orderly fossil sequence has an evolutionary appearance by coincidence. We are also asked to accept as historical fact the biblical Flood of Noah (see FLOOD, NOAH'S), since that, of course, is the worldwide Deluge in question (Whitcomb and Morris 1961; Moore 1976, 45, 57; Morris 1985b, 250-255; 1984a, 312-

364). Creationists consider the Genesis Flood story to be literal history in spite of its clear derivation from Mesopotamian mythology (Lambert 1965; Kramer 1969, 42-44; Speiser 1969, 72-99, 104-106). This all comes under the creationist heading of *flood geology* (see GEOLOGY), and the Flood interpretation of the fossil record has been aptly summed up by Nobel Prize–winning biologist P. D. Medawar (1983, 94): "A man who believes that fossils are the remains of organisms inundated by Noah's flood can believe anything: no effort of credulity would be too much."

FUNDAMENTALISM

See BIBLE.

GAP THEORY

See EARTH; SATAN.

GENESIS

See BIBLE.

GENETICS

The study in BIOLOGY of *heredity* and *variation* in organisms. Heredity in all living things is encoded in DNA (deoxyribonucleic acid), located in what are called *chromosomes* in cell nuclei. DNA consists of four chemical substances called *nucleotides*: adenine (A), cytosine (C), guanine (G), and thymine (T). These four "letters" form three-letter sequences (*codons*), and these triplets (of which there are 64) are the "words" of the *genetic code*. A *gene* is a segment of DNA holding a series of triplets, forming "sentences," part of the instructions or "blueprint" for construction of the organism. More specifically, genes, using RNA (ribonucleic acid) as a "messenger," instruct an organism's cells in the production of *proteins*, compounds essential to the organism's life and development. Proteins are composed of chains of usually hundreds of *amino acids*. (Though there are only twenty different kinds of amino acids, there are some ten trillion amino-acid combinations [Dulbecco 1987, 22].) The function of each protein is determined by its amino-acid sequence, and that sequence is dictated by the genes. Proteins, thus genetically programmed, are "the machines of life" (Frauenfelder 1988, 156), acting "together to construct all living things" (Scott 1986, 29).

Variation occurs through the sexual *recombination* of genes—the reason why each sexually reproduced individual is different from all others (Mayr 1988, 99)—and through *mutation*, which is a change in genetic material due to an error in the code's "translation" or some other random factor such as radiation. Most mutations are genetically harmful or neutral, but environment acting upon favorable mutations, selecting them, so to speak, for survival, is a major feature of the theory of EVOLUTION by NATURAL SELECTION. When Charles Darwin (1859) discussed natural selection in *On the Origin of Species*, the mechanisms of heredity were still a mystery. The pioneering work of Austrian botanist Gregor Mendel (1822-1884) went unnoticed until 1900, when what are now called the Mendelian laws of inheritance were brought to the scientific world's attention (Asimov 1982, 639). This laid the foundation for modern genetics, which, coupled with Darwin's theory of natural selection, gave rise to what is called the *modern synthesis* or Neo-Darwinian theory of evolution. The actual structure of the DNA molecule—the famous *double helix*—was discovered by James Watson (1968) and Francis Crick in 1953. Watson now heads one of the most ambitious scientific projects of all time, a complete mapping of the human *genome*, the complete set of genetic instructions—some 3 billion letters long (Jaroff 1989, 64)—that make a human being. The potential medical benefits of such knowledge in terms of treating genetic defects and diseases through *genetic engineering* (called also *gene-splicing* and *recombinant DNA technology*) appear virtually unlimited. (So do potential ethical problems, considering ability to make "better" human beings [see Suzuki and Knudtson 1989; Elmer-Dewitt 1989].)

Creationists say it is "hard to believe" that genetic mutation, being random and usually harmful, could lead to evolutionary "improvement" in organisms (Klotz 1985, 181). The fact is that mutation doesn't "lead" anywhere; a mutation simply happens, and is random in the sense that it arises irrespective of an organism's adaptive needs. It is the *environment* existing at the time that *leads* or *acts*, for environmental conditions determine whether a mutation is of any adaptive value. It is the environment that naturally selects—or eliminates. (It is interesting that creationist John Klotz [1985, 181-184] devotes four pages of his book *Studies in Creation* to raising questions about favorable mutation, without one mention of the crucial environmental factor.) Also, mutations, if neutral or not harmful, accumulate in a population's gene pool, so that there is a large store of genetic variability available when circumstances arise requiring some adaptive change for survival. Whether or not the "right" mutation is already there in the gene pool is, of course, a matter of chance (Futuyma 1982, 143). (As for the creationist notion that "improvement" in organisms is a requirement of evolutionary theory, see EXTINCTION.)

Creationists argue that "such complex systems as the DNA molecule could never arise by chance" (Morris 1985b, 62). But much depends here on what one means by "chance." Origin-of-life experiments (see ABIOGENESIS) have shown that amino acids and other organic molecules form spontaneously under simulated primitive-earth conditions. This has nothing to do with chance; it is based on chemical laws. It is true that scientists do not yet know the exact process (if they ever will) that led from such prebiological CHEMISTRY to the first "self-replicating nucleic acid-protein aggregate" (Mayr 1988, 67), that is, to the first form of life. Certainly no evolutionist suggests that DNA or the genetic code simply arose full blown. It was a slow, gradual, step-by-step process, and while it is improbable that any *particular* nucleotide sequence would have arisen by chance, the probability that *some* kind of viable sequence would have arisen is high (Futuyma 1982, 62, 184). And that, of course, is exactly what happened. Living things "got stuck," in the words of biologist Douglas

Futuyma (1982, 204), "with the first system that worked."

The fact that the same simple, four-letter genetic code is shared by all living things is strong evidence indeed for the theory of common evolutionary descent. How else could the millions of living species of ANIMALS and PLANTS have all wound up with the same four-letter code? Creationists argue that this universal code is evidence, not of evolution, but of one basic blueprint or design by a divine Creator (see DESIGN ARGUMENT). But that is a religious, not a scientific, argument. There is only one possible *scientific* explanation for the genetic code's universality: All living things have descended from one common ancestral form. (For further discussion of molecular evolution, see BIOLOGY.)

GEOLOGY

The study of the EARTH. *Physical geology* deals with structure and composition, while *historical geology* deals with the earth's past ages and the EVOLUTION of its LIFE forms. Historical geology thus includes *paleontology*, the study of the FOSSIL RECORD contained in the stratified or layered *sedimentary rocks*—solidified accumulations of particles and precipitated material—that cover most of the earth's land surface and virtually all of it seafloors. A major development in geology since the 1960s has been *plate tectonics*, the theory that the *lithosphere* (the earth's *crust* and part of its upper *mantle*) consists of several large plates that move relative to each other, causing such phenomena as earthquakes, volcanoes, and CONTINENTAL DRIFT.

A guiding principle in geology is the so-called *law of superposition*, according to which each layer of sedimentary rock in an undisturbed sequence lies on top of an older layer. This principle is based on simple observation and the commonsensical assumption—basic to all of SCIENCE—that the laws of nature do not change. The geologic processes observable today are the same as those of past ages though their rates and intensity can vary (Newell 1985, 34; Stokes 1982, 45). This assumption is called UNIFORMITARIANISM, often summarized as "the present is the key to the past." (Uniformitarianism, while traditionally contrasted with CATASTROPHISM, does not deny the geologic importance of catastrophes.) Exceptions to the law of superposition are rock strata that at some time in the past have been disturbed. The original order of deposition is reversed, for instance, when a slab of older rock layer has slid or been shoved—due to gravity (when inclined) or compression—over a younger layer, an example of *thrust faults* (Spencer 1983, 217-218). Sedimentary rock layers can be broken, folded, tilted on end, even completely overturned by tectonic activity after their deposition (Stokes 1982, 80).

Another guiding principle is the *law of faunal succession*, according to which particular layers of sedimentary rock are characterized by particular fossil animals (*fauna*), representing past life forms ranging successively from simpler forms in the older rock strata to more complex forms in the younger strata. (The fossil sequence can be disturbed, of course, in cases of thrust faults and other deformities in the rocks.) The study of stratified rock is called *stratigraphy*, and the association of certain fossils with certain rock strata allows geologists to assign relative ages to rock layers wherever similar fossils are found. In addition, so-called absolute ages can be obtained through RADIOACTIVE DATING. Through these dating methods and the stratified sequence of rocks and fossils, geologists have compiled an idealized *geologic column* and *geologic time scale* of earth history. The scale's 4.6-billion-year age for our planet does justice to the sentiment of James Hutton, the founder of modern geology, who wrote in his *Theory of the Earth* (1795) of finding "no vestige of a beginning, no prospect of an end."

The proponents of creation "science," however, will have none of James Hutton or of modern historical geology. In the words of John Morris (quoted in Schadewald 1988, 15) of the INSTITUTE FOR CREATION RESEARCH (ICR), "Like it or not, if you're going to be a Bible-believer, the earth is young." How young is it? According to the ICR's George Aardsma (1988, iv), the earth (indeed the whole UNIVERSE) was created only "about 10,000 years ago." So how can the geologists be so wrong? According to ICR president Henry Morris (father of John), when geologists turn from physical to historical geology they leave "the strict domain" of science: They operate on uniformitarian "assumptions and presuppositions" that are "basically a philosophy, or even a faith," and "attempt to usurp all authority" in the field of earth history (Whitcomb and Morris 1964, xxvi-xxvii). Geologists, say the creationists, subtly employ circular reasoning by constructing a time scale based on "the evolutionary assumption" and then using it to support the theory of evolution (Moore 1976, 46; Morris 1984a, 312; 1986, 69). The elder Morris (1984a, 332) has accused geologists of ignoring fossils that are "anomalous" or out of sequence, and creationists cite what they call *polystrate fossils*—fossil trees standing vertically through more than one sedimentary stratum—as proof of rapid (as in catastrophic, as opposed to uniformitarian) deposition (Ackerman 1986, 84; Moore 1976, 50; Morris 1984a, 324-325). Creationists also say that radioactive dating is unreliable (Gish 1985, 51; Moore 1976, 39-41; Morris 1983, 15-26; Slusher 1981), so that the ages so derived "prove nothing" (Morris 1984a, 269).

But if, as creationists claim, those billions of years on the geologic time scale "never really took place at all" (Morris 1985b, 251), how can we explain the earth's vast accumulation of sedimentary rock layers, as well as the seemingly evolutionary order of the fossils therein? The creationists answer with what they call *flood geology* (Gish 1985, 51; Morris 1978, 26; 1984b, 42; Whitcomb 1973, 11) or "the general cataclysmic model of the fossiliferous strata" (Morris 1985b, 123), the cataclysm in question being "nothing less than the great Flood of the days of Noah" (Morris 1978, 23) (see FLOOD, NOAH'S). According to the prolific Henry Morris (author of some forty books, including the creationist classic *The Genesis Flood*), all of the earth's fossil-bearing rocks were laid down contemporaneously in one "global hydraulic and sedimentary catastrophe" (1978, 28), with all life forms (save those in Noah's ark) destroyed in the order of where they lived and how well they could flee from the rising waters. Morris also believes that victims would tend to be found in the order of their size and shape, "turbulent water" being a "highly effective 'sorting' agent" (1984a, 329), though in one instance he limits this "hydrodynamic sorting action" to individual sedimentry layers (1984a, 329) and in another to marine invertebrates (1985b, 119). In any case, the only real order in the fossil record, according to Morris, does not reflect an evolutionary progression but rather "ecological communities buried roughly in the order of increasing elevation of habitat" (1986, 74) with a dash of "hydrodynamic sorting" thrown in. As for continental movement, mountain-building, and other phenomena related to plate tectonics, Morris allows that there were volcanic and tectonic "after-effects of the Flood," so that overall there was "one great complex of catastrophes," though still with "the primary character of a world-wide flood" (1978, 26-28; 1985b, 123). (For the progress of the ark through all of this, see ARK, NOAH'S.)

Flood geology is perhaps the most indefensible of all "scientific" creationist arguments. (For the debt owed by today's flood "geologists" to Seventh Day Adventist George McCready Price [1870-1963] and his book *The New Geology*, see Gardner 1988, 93-98, and Morris 1984b, 79-82.) Sedimentary rocks cover about 75 percent of the earth's land surface and virtually all of its ocean floors, averaging well over one mile in thickness (Spencer 1983, 89). Sedimentary deposits that formed rapidly and those that formed gradually have different characteristics, and it has been recognized for centuries that most sedimentary rocks bear the characteristics of gradual, particle-by-particle, layer-by-layer accumulation (Glenister and Witzke 1983, 57, 68). The notion that all of this layered rock, in places as much as 12 miles thick, could have been laid down in one brief period of time by one big deluge defies the evidence if not common sense. Equally untenable is the creationist explanation of the sequence of fossils, which go from simpler to more complex forms as we move from older to younger rock layers. "How incredible," says philosopher Jeffrie G. Murphy (1982, 51), that in fleeing the floodwaters "not a single higher animal *tripped*, fell way down, and got drowned (and thus fossilized) at a lower level!" It is interesting, too, that the order of fossilized Flood victims just happens to mimic an evolutionary sequence. In reality (and as Henry Morris, holder of a Ph.D. in hydraulic ENGINEERING, should be well aware), a violent flood does not carefully sort out its ANIMAL and PLANT victims. In a flood as cataclysmic as that envisioned by the creationists, all life forms would be tumbled along and thoroughly mixed irrespective of habitat or biological complexity

(McGowan 1984, 61; Schadewald 1983b, 289).

The creationist claim that the geologic column or time scale is based on an assumption of evolution is simply not true. Naturalists noted that fossils from certain layers differ from fossils from other layers, and began establishing the sequence of geologic periods, long before the theory of evolution became generally accepted (Glenister and Witzke 1983, 73-75). These early geologists made no evolutionary assumptions, though today it may certainly be said, with the benefit of hindsight, that the rocks' fossil sequence makes biological evolution "an observable fact" (Cloud 1988, 61). Early geologists, being creationists, tended to attribute the fossil sequence to successive acts of special creation (see Gillespie 1979, 26-27). Today's "scientific" creationists reject this concept, known as *progressive creation,* as unbiblical. Hence they must make do with flood geology.

The creationist contention that geologists ignore out-of-sequence fossils has been called by paleontologist Niles Eldredge (1982, 98) "a vicious lie." As noted above, fossils can be expected to be found out of sequence where there are crustal deformities such as thrust faults. It is the creationists who ignore evidence when they argue that no large-scale thrust faults have ever occurred, any folds or faults in the earth's sedimentary rock having formed "fairly rapidly" during or soon after the Flood (Whitcomb and Morris 1961, 180-211; see Weber 1980, 21-23). Far from ignoring such anomalies as human footprints and dinosaur tracks supposedly found together (see DINOSAUR), and "human footprints in ancient trilobite beds" (Morris 1985b, 122; see Conrad 1981), scientists have helped expose the invalidity of such claims. (For an excellent discussion of "out-of-order fossils" by a scientist, see Strahler 1987, 459-472).

Polystrate fossil trees are, as creationists claim, evidence of rapid sedimentary deposition, but only as a result of local incidents (usually river flooding), not a worldwide deluge (Eldredge 1982, 105; Weber 1980, 14-15). As for radioactive dating, to doubt its results in principle is equivalent to doubting radioactivity. It is true that there are sources of potential analytical error, but the best evidence for overall accuracy is the concordant dates that are obtained using more than one method (Eicher 1976, 121-122). Other geological evidence that the earth is of ancient age includes *coal* beds, *oil* deposits, *coral reefs* (made of the accumulated skeletons of polyp colonies), and *varves* (layers of sediment in lakes and other still bodies of water), all requiring great lengths of time for formation; *tillites* (sedimentary rocks formed from glacial deposits) indicating several past *ice ages* (creationists, calling such evidence "equivocal," recognize one Ice Age only [Morris 1983, 13]); and the earth's *magnetic field,* which seafloor *remanent magnetism* indicates has reversed itself several times over millions of years (see GEOMAGNETISM).

Henry Morris and his colleagues reject the geological evidence for an ancient, evolving earth because their insistence on literal interpretation of biblical creation accounts and biblical chronology leaves them no choice. Scientific evidence that is contrary to their biblically based beliefs is thus something to be dogmatically fought and never accepted. "No geologic difficulty, real or imagined," says Morris (1970, 33), "can be allowed to take precedence over the clear statements and necessary inferences of Scripture." That's creationist "science" in a nutshell. (For a critical view of "scientific" creationism by a Christian geologist, see Young 1982.)

GEOMAGNETISM

The EARTH's magnetic field and the study thereof. The earth is like a dynamo or generator, in that the geomagnetic field is produced by electric currents that in turn are produced by the convection or movement of molten iron and nickel surrounding the earth's solid inner core (Ozima 1981, 33; Weisburd 1984; 1988a; 1988b). That, at least, is the generally accepted theory; the exact details of the field's origin, including what energy source drives the earth's inner convection and what causes the geomagnetic field periodically to reverse itself, have been called "the earth's best kept secret" (Weisburd 1984). Every half million or so years, magnetic north becomes magnetic south and vice versa (Abell 1983, 36; Van Andel 1985, 99; Weisburd 1985a, 218). In addition to these polarity reversals, the strength of the field fluctuates greatly over time. For the past century and a half the dipole component of the field has decreased about 6 percent (Dalrymple 1984b, 3; Ozima 1981, 33).

The polarity and strength of the field in past ages can be determined by what is called *remanent magnetism* in old lava flows. When molten rock or magma boils up from the earth's interior at midocean ridges, it becomes new seafloor upon cooling, pushing the older seafloor outward from the ridges. (According to the theory of *plate tectonics*, this *seafloor spreading* moves plates that move continents; see CONTINENTAL DRIFT.) In the process of cooling, the molten rock becomes magnetized: It forms with "a frozen-in record of the prevailing magnetic field" (Stokes 1982, 208). This record can be recovered from the magnetic strips in the seafloor using magnetometers towed on the ocean surface, and has been correlated with magnetized land rocks dated by radiometric methods (see RADIOACTIVE DATING) to produce a *paleomagnetic time scale* reliable up to 5 million years (Abell 1983, 36-37; Spencer 1983, 266). Pottery can also be used to measure paleomagnetism over several millenia, since fired pottery, like lava, becomes magnetized when it cools, preserving a record of the field as it exists at the time (Schadewald 1983a, 31).

The INSTITUTE FOR CREATION RESEARCH (ICR), headed by Baptist fundamentalists Henry Morris and Duane Gish, argues in its textbook *Scientific Creationism* that the geomagnetic field is "decaying exponentially" at a rate that makes 10,000 years "an outside limit for the age of the earth" (Morris 1985b, 157-158). This view is based on a book by the late creationist physicist Thomas G. Barnes (1983) who ignored the fact that it is only the dipole-field strength that has been "decaying" for a century and a half. As explained by G. Brent Dalrymple (1984b, 3) of the U.S. Geological Survey, the strength of the nondipole field (about 15 percent of the total field) has increased over the same time span, so that the total field has remained almost constant. Barnes' assumption of a steady decrease in the field's strength throughout history is also irreconcilable, of course, with the paleomagnetic evidence of fluctuations and reversals.

ICR president Henry Morris (1984a, 256-257) has attacked the evidence for polarity reversals by stating that the "supposed 'stripes' " of paleomagnetism in seafloor rock "have never been directly observed."

But surely Morris knows that scientists cannot always work by direct observation (see SCIENCE). No scientist has directly observed gravity or quarks or black holes. In 1989 the ICR published an article by creationist physicist Russell Humphreys accepting the "persuasive" evidence for numerous magnetic field reversals. (Morris [1989d] called the article "important and challenging.") Humphreys argues, however, that the reversals all occurred at a rate of "about one per week" during "the Genesis flood." The intent of this argument—which assumes, to begin with, that the Genesis Flood is historical fact (FLOOD, NOAH'S)—is clearly to preserve the creationist notion, based on biblical chronology, that the field, like the earth itself, is only a few thousand years old. But the creationist insistence on a young earth is irreconcilable with the evidence from ASTRONOMY, GEOLOGY, and PHYSICS that the age of the earth is around 4.6 billion years. In some cases, it appears, the geomagnetic field has taken as much as 10,000 years—the ICR's maximum age of the earth—just to complete a reversal (Newell 1985, 114).

It seems safe to say that in the final analysis nothing of any scientific value regarding magnetic field reversals, pro or con, will ever emanate from the ICR young-earth creationists. The ICR is a self-described "ministry" (ICR 1987a; Morris 1987c) that depends partly on the magnetism of debater Duane Gish, though that, too, has experienced reversals (see INSTITUTE FOR CREATION RESEARCH).

GOD

The generic name in monotheistic religion for the Supreme Being and Creator of the UNIVERSE (see CREATION). In the Judeo-Christian tradition, this universal Creator is the Judge and Redeemer of Israel and (in the Christian faith, through Jesus Christ) of all mankind. In the Old Testament (see BIBLE) his personal name is *Yahweh*, translated in English versions as *the Lord* and (inaccurately) as *Jehovah*. Of uncertain meaning, the name is related to the verb *to be*. Suggested meanings include "he is" (Mettinger 1988, 32) and "he causes to be" (May and Metzger 1973, 71). God's other biblical names include

El (Hebrew, *god*) and, as in the first verse of Genesis, *Elohim* (*gods*), considered both a "plural of majesty" and a vestige of early Hebrew polytheism (Perdue 1985, 686).

The God of the Old Testament has often been contrasted with the God (Greek, *Theos*) of the New Testament, the former being seen as a god of wrath and the latter as a god of love. The God of the Old Testament indeed has a temper, epitomized by his decision "to destroy all flesh" (Gen. 6:17) with a flood (see FLOOD, NOAH'S). It has been said, with oversimplifying humor, that God in the New Testament is "in a considerably better mood" (Sullivan 1988). The perceived contrast has been interpreted by some as the reflection of a progression in Israelite religion from belief in warring tribal deities to ethical monotheism. Others would share the view expressed by Thomas Longstaff (1985, 351) that the biblical concept of God is quite consistent (a god of both judgment and mercy), the main difference between the testaments being their conceptual worlds, the New Testament reflecting a later (Hellenistic and early Roman) stage of intellectual history. And then, of course, there are the fundamentalists, who leave anything less than literal interpretation of both testaments to "pussyfooting preachers" and "liberal" scholars. "I'd rather be a fool on fire," says evangelist Freddie Gage, "than a scholar on ice" (*Florida Baptist Witness* 121[221]:17).

Various thinkers down through the ages have attempted to prove God's existence by logic or reason (see DESIGN ARGUMENT) but with arguments always found wanting. The God of the Bible is by definition revealed through the Word, to the extent that the Bible itself for many believers has become, in the words of B. Davie Napier (1962, 54), "alas, an idol—a deified book." It is a tenet of the Christian fundamentalist-led INSTITUTE FOR CREATION RESEARCH (ICR), America's leading creationist organization, that "the Creator of the universe is a triune God—Father, Son, and Holy Spirit," and that the Bible is "the divinely-inspired revelation of the Creator to man" and is "infallible" (Morris 1984a, 363).

Creationists consider it inconceivable that God would use EVOLUTION as his method of creation (a concept called *theistic evolution*). They argue, to begin with, that evolutionary theory is irreconcilable with a literal interpretation of the Bible (Gish 1985, 23-24). That certainly appears to be true, but is of significance only to biblical literalists. The ICR (Morris 1985b, 219) argues that God would not have wasted billions of years "in aimless evolutionary meandering before getting to the point," namely "the creation and redemption of man." The ICR obviously does not share the more humble sentiment of newspaper columnist Horance G. Davis (1986): "I refuse to fault the Lord for taking His time." ICR president Henry Morris (1978, 73) argues that God would certainly not preside over such a "cruel spectacle" as evolution with its "appalling inefficiency and barbarity" (Morris 1978, 73, 88). Now evolution, though an impersonal, amoral process in itself, is undeniably, to borrow the immortal words of Tennyson, "nature red in tooth and claw." But how can Morris call the process a "cruel spectacle" considering the creationist acceptance as literal history of the aforementioned Flood sent by God to destroy all flesh? Was that not a "cruel spectacle"? ("I would like to know," says geologist Preston Cloud [1977, 291], "how [the creationists] reconcile such events either with the teachings of Christianity or with civilized concepts of morality.") In any case, most Protestants, Catholics, and Jews in America seem to have no particular problem being theistic evolutionists. It is the position of the Roman Catholic church that while souls are created by God, the evidence for physical human evolution is "beyond serious dispute" (Flew 1982, 49; McIver 1988a, 16). Most members of the National Council of Churches, according to spokesman Dean Kelley (quoted in Anderson 1987), do not consider evolution to be inconsistent with creation, since evolutionary theory "merely explains our understanding of the mechanism by which God created the universe and life."

Philosophers, theologians, and the man in the street will continue, of course, to speculate about the nature of God. All who believe in divine creation, whether Christian, Jewish, or other, will conceive of the Creator as they intuit or are taught. But SCIENCE deals only with natural phenomena. It cannot confirm or deny God's existence. In one of his sermons the Reverend Billy Graham spoke for scientists as well as himself when he said, "I can't show you God in a test tube." The existence of God is necessarily a matter of religious faith, of which there is no better definition than that found in the Bible (Hebrews 11:1): "Now faith is the assurance of things hoped for, the conviction of things not seen." When ICR creationists express their belief in "an omnipotent, omniscient, personal, purposive, moral Creator" (Morris 1985b, 200), they are making a religious statement in the finest Judeo-Christian tradition. But they are saying nothing scientific whatsoever.

GRADUALISM (GEOLOGY)

See CATASTROPHISM; UNIFORMITARIANISM.

GRADUALISM, PHYLETIC

See NATURAL SELECTION; PUNCTUATED EQUILIBRIA.

HISTORY

See SOCIAL SCIENCES.

HOMO

See MAN.

HOMOLOGY

See ANATOMY.

HORSE

See MAMMAL.

HUMAN EVOLUTION

See MAN.

HUMANISM

A philosophy and conduct of LIFE that sees MAN and his welfare as of central concern. Historically humanism grew out of the Renaissance with its flowering of the *humanities* (the arts, literature, and philosophy) and the beginnings of SCIENCE. Two classical sayings capture the humanist spirit: "Man is the measure of all things" (Protagoras) and "I am a man, and nothing human is alien to me" (Terence). But while modern humanism may be generally described (by both friend and foe) as "man-centered" (LaHaye 1980, 29; Morris 1984a, 103; Lamont 1957, 1), it is hardly a monolithic or well-organized movement. There are self-styled "ethical" (Ericson 1973), "religious" (Beattie 1985), "scientific" (Wilson 1987, 14), and "secular" (Kurtz 1980) humanists among others—seemingly as many different varieties, says humanist philosopher Paul Kurtz (1973, 6), "as there are grades of wine and cheese"—and they often disagree, particularly on how humanism relates (or does not relate) to religion (see almost any issue of *Free Inquiry*). As far as Christian fundamentalists are concerned, however, "a humanist is a humanist is a humanist" (LaHaye 1980, 45). Humanism (usually prefaced with "secular") is attacked by the fundamentalists as a religion itself, its faith being "in the god of Science and Technology" (Webber 1982, 45). Among its tenets, they say, are the theory of EVOLUTION—a "monstrous lie" of SATAN (Morris 1963, 77)—and the philosophy of "no absolutes," which according to Tim LaHaye (1980, 65) has opened the door to "adultery, fornication, perversion, abomination, and just plain *sin*." Moreover, says the Christian Right, secular humanism "has become the established religion of the U.S. public school system" (Schlafly 1981; see also Gish 1985, 23; Morris 1985b, iii; and Schaeffer 1982, 54, 111), so that today most public school students are being "brainwashed in evolutionary humanism" with "all its tragic implications" (Morris

1987a, 4; 1988f).

In 1987 the Christian Right drew national attention to its position on humanism and the schools through two highly publicized court cases. In Alabama a federal judge, finding for six hundred fundamentalist plaintiffs, banned forty-four textbooks from Alabama's public schools for promoting "the religion of secular humanism." And in Tennessee a federal judge found for seven fundamentalist families seeking to protect their schoolchildren from such "humanistic" reading materials as *The Diary of Anne Frank* and *The Wizard of Oz*. Both decisions were overturned on appeal, but fundamentalist antihumanism had certainly thrown a scare into civil libertarians.

LaHaye (1980, 9, 142), who is president of the Washington-based American Coalition for Traditional Values and a cofounder of the INSTITUTE FOR CREATION RESEARCH, believes that "a small but very influential cadre of committed humanists" has taken control of "our government, the UN, education, TV, and most of the other influential things of life." The humanist goal, says LaHaye (1980, 10), is "a complete world takeover by the year 2000." This notion of a humanist conspiracy—detailed in LaHaye's 1980 book *The Battle for the Mind*—is overstating the case, if for no other reason than the fact that organized humanism is "a pitiably small group" (Bullough 1986). (The American organized humanist movement has perhaps 10,000 members, less than some single church congregations in the South [Kurtz 1986, 4; 1987].) As for the fundamentalist charge of humanists taking over the schools, humanist Gina Allen (1981, 9) replies, "Come on, now! Take a poll of your school board, superintendent, principals, teachers, and authors of textbooks. You'll find Episcopalians, Baptists, Methodists, Catholics, etc., but few, if any, humanists."

It can be argued, on the other hand, that, yes, there are humanistic values being taught in the public schools and that this is not only proper but unavoidable. This is because humanism is in many ways indistinguishable from American culture. There is in humanism, despite its varieties of expression, a consensus on several propositions; these include the ideals of liberty, free inquiry, separation of church and state, education, and moral conduct (Kurtz 1980). The fundamental principles of humanism, says Nicholas Gier (1982, 28), are no different from basic American values: "Humanists believe that human beings have intrinsic value and dignity," free will, and moral responsibility—humanism "is as American as apple pie." Humanists also believe in scientific method and reason in the solving of human problems (Kurtz 1980, 5). This belief relates to the future of America in a vitally important way, for science and critical thinking are two areas of instruction that education leaders recognize need strengthening as part of the reform efforts inspired by the alarming 1983 report "A Nation at Risk" (National Commission on Excellence in Education 1983) on the sad state of American educational performance. Despite reform efforts, the condition of American education since 1983 hasn't shown much improvement. A 1989 report by the National Assessment of Educational Progress stated that "fundamental changes" may be needed to help American schoolchildren "develop both content knowledge and the ability to reason effectively about what they know—skills that are essential if they are to take an intelligent part in the worlds of life and work" (Lawrence 1989). Content knowledge in science, whether the religious Right likes it or not, includes the theory of evolution, "the most fundamental organizational concept in the biological sciences" (National Academy of Sciences 1984, 22). Effective reasoning includes the ability to be skeptical, to ask questions, not to accept anything solely on authority as do "scientific" creationists with their belief in absolute biblical inerrancy on every matter with which the BIBLE deals (see Morris 1984a, 47).

Basically humanism, in the words of philosopher Delos McKown (1986, 5), "is about the same as being educated." Efforts to keep "humanistic" ideas out of our public schools are in effect an attempt "to repeal the modern world" (Kurtz 1981, 11). Fundamentalists have used humanism as a buzzword for everything they perceive as clashing with and threatening their biblically mandated WORLD VIEW. They have sought to make humanism a scapegoat for what the late religious humanist Paul Beattie (1985, 13) called "the anxieties of modernity." But as Beattie aptly observed, "The modern world is here to stay; and, painful as it is, the fundamentalists are going to have to get used to that fact."

INDUSTRIAL MELANISM

See ADAPTATION.

INFLATIONARY UNIVERSE

See BIG BANG; UNIVERSE.

INSECT

A member of the Insecta class of *arthropods* (phylum Arthropoda), invertebrate ANIMALS with segmented bodies and jointed limbs. Insect bodies have three segments (head, thorax, and abdomen), three pairs of legs, and typically one or two pairs of wings. (The other arthropods include spiders, scorpions, ticks, centipedes, crabs, and lobsters, to name a few.) Insects are the most widespread form of animal. There are about 800,000 known species, more than the total number of all other known animal and PLANT species combined (Arnett and Jacques 1981, 16; Oldroyd 1985, 196). The total number of living insect species could be as high as 5 million (Wigglesworth 1985, 585); given the ongoing destruction by MAN of natural habitats, we will probably never know the true number (Arnett and Jacques 1981, 16; see EXTINCTION).

Insects and the other arthropods, given their shared peculiarities, would seem clearly to share some common evolutionary ancestor (Eldredge 1987, 129). Creationists, of course, disagree; they would argue that all arthropods, from crayfish to mites, were simply given similar designs by their Creator. (For the problems such a view involves, see DESIGN ARGUMENT.) Creationist leader Henry Morris (1985b, 86) argues that while many fossil insects were larger—"giant dragonflies, giant cockroaches, giant ants, and so on"—than their modern relatives, "their form is no different in essence from that of modern insects." But some 400 kinds of insects are known from the Pennsylvanian geologic period, and most were unlike modern insects (Strahler 1987,

317). Biologist Gene Kritsky (1987) points out that the wings of those extinct giant dragonflies had a very primitive vein system compared to modern dragonflies, and that some fossil roaches had large ovipositors (special organs for egg-laying) that today's roaches do not possess. As for "giant ants," Kritsky notes that there weren't any.

From what did insects and their arthropod cousins evolve? The FOSSIL RECORD is unfortunately one of gaps with respect to the specifics of insect origins. Most insect fossils are isolated wings, the only parts strong and flexible enough to likely be preserved (Steel 1979). It is thus not surprising that the earliest known insect fossils are from the Devonian period (about 400 million years ago) at which time insects had already evolved wings (Oldroyd 1985, 207; Wigglesworth 1985, 596). But while creationists in attacking EVOLUTION describe the origin of insects as "completely blank" (Morris 1985b, 86) and "shrouded in mystery" (Gish 1985, 61), they ignore the inferences that can be drawn from the study of living species. It is generally believed that all arthropods evolved from an annelid or segmented worm (phylum Annelida), the theoretical TRANSITIONAL FORM between worms and arthropods being similar to a group of caterpillarlike living relatives called *onychophorans* (McGowan 1984, 73-74; Starr and Taggart 1984, 580-581; Strahler 1987, 406). These little creatures, of which there are fossils dating back to the Cambrian (over 500 million years ago), are long and internally segmented like worms but have many legs, a pair of antennae, and, like insects, a tracheal breathing system (McGowan 1984, 73-74). An evolutionist at a drawing-board who wanted to "invent a hypothetical link between worms and arthropods," says paleontologist Chris McGowan (1984, 74), "could not do better than draw an onychophoran." And one need not hypothesize to refute the creationist claim (Gish 1985, 61) that there are no insect transitional forms. The oldest known ant fossil is preserved in amber from the Cretaceous period and in form is actually a wasp-ant intermediate. As described by entomologist E. O. Wilson and colleagues (1967, as cited in Kritsky 1987, 15), the specimen (*Sphecomyrma freyi*) "forms a near-perfect link between nonsocial tiphiid wasps and the most primitive myrmecioid ants."

Insects are a class of animal in which evolutionary change has been directly observed. A classic example is that of the peppered moths of industrial England who genetically changed from light to dark color, to blend with soot-darkened tree trunks and thus be less noticeable to predators (see ADAPTATION). Another example is the resistance that many species of insects developed in a few years' time to DDT and other insecticides. These are examples of a few random mutations or gene combinations proving to be advantageous with respect to the environment and thus spreading through the population's gene pool through differential reproduction (Mayr 1970, 111; McGowan 1984, 37). That is NATURAL SELECTION in action.

INSTITUTE FOR CREATION RESEARCH (ICR)

A self-described "ministry," headquartered in Santee, California, that promotes what it calls "the foundational message of creation" (ICR 1987; Ham 1989c). Its president is Henry M. Morris, a Baptist fundamentalist with a Ph.D. in hydraulic ENGINEERING. Morris (1987d; 1988g, 95) describes the ICR, which he founded in 1970, as a "God-called ministry" whose mission is that of "creation evangelism" through a "threefold program of research, writing, and teaching." This program is carried out by eight full-time "science" staff members, with a support staff in 1988 of nineteen full-time employees (Morris 1989e). Morris (1984b, 235) quite correctly states that the influence of the ICR has been "far out of proportion" to its small size in staff and resources. With its many publications and the heavy travel schedule of its speakers, the ICR has been aptly described as "the unofficial nerve center" of the creation "science" movement (Boxer 1987, 82). Morris himself has been called "the Darwin of the creationist movement" (Numbers 1982, 543), though his creationist colleagues prefer "Mr. Creation" (LaHaye 1980, 50). His 1961 book *The Genesis Flood*, cowritten with John C. Whitcomb, helped inspire the modern creationist revival. Morris has since nurtured the cause with some forty other books. He believes that the BIBLE "must be accepted as absolutely inerrant" (1984a, 47), that the "real facts" of SCIENCE "agree perfectly with the Biblical record" (1987a, 4), and that the theory of EVOLUTION is not only "false and absurd scientifically" (1982b, 184) but is "the anti-God conspiracy of Satan himself" (1970, 71).

Morris acknowledges that the research part of the ICR's program of research, writing, and teaching leaves much to be desired, a weakness he attributes partly to control of science, education, and government by an "evolutionary establishment" that "is not about to supply funds or facilities" for CREATION research (Morris 1984b, 250-251). And besides, says Morris (quoted in Bates 1976, 113), "you can't go back and research methods of creation." ICR research has thus focused on field studies aimed at confirming that the EARTH is young, that Noah's Flood really happened, and that everything in Genesis must therefore be literally true. Such studies include trips to see alleged human footprints contemporaneous with DINOSAUR tracks in Texas (*Acts & Facts* 17[12]:3, 5) and expeditions to Turkey to search for Noah's ark (see ARK, NOAH'S). The ICR also conducts annual tours of the Grand Canyon, a spectacular look back into geologic time that young-earth creationists see instead as "overwhelming evidence for the worldwide Flood" (*Acts & Facts* 18[6]:1).

Beyond such excursions, ICR research consists mainly of analyzing and "reinterpreting" the abundance of experimental data published by evolutionists (Morris 1984b, 251-255). "We interpret what others are doing," says ICR vice president Duane Gish (quoted in Boxer 1987, 82), "to show that evolution is not a reasonable scientific conclusion." The writings of Morris, Gish, and others consist of books published under the imprint Master Books, as well as the *Impact* series of articles inserted in the monthly ICR newsletter *Acts & Facts*. (The latter includes such items as an obituary titled "Sidney Jansma Goes to Heaven" and a debate report titled "Evolutionist Debater Descends to All-Time Low.") The ICR also sells audiovisual materials, conducts "Back to Genesis" seminars around the country, and has a weekly radio show called "Science, Scripture, and Salvation."

ICR books and AV materials include openly religious works designed for use in Christian schools as well as supposedly nonreligious (creation-"science") works intended for public school use. The ICR promotes what it calls the *two-model approach*, a supposedly objective comparison of creation and evolution models of "origins," for public school science classes, even though the ICR's druthers are made perfectly clear in the statement that "true education in every field should be structured around creationism, not evolutionism" (Morris 1985b, iv). The ICR's Richard Bliss travels extensively to conduct two-model workshops for public school teachers (Gallant 1984, 291; Morris 1984b, 259). In answer to the charge that the creation model is biblical religion, not science, the ICR claims to draw "a clear distinction" between "scientific creationism" and "Biblical creationism," though "the two are compatible" (Morris 1984b, 362). The former is in fact only a thinly disguised version of the latter. For example, what is called the "deluge in the days of Noah" in the ICR's "Tenets of Biblical Creationism" becomes "a recent global hydraulic cataclysm" in the "Tenets of Scientific Creationism" (Morris 1984b, 362-364). Would Noah's Flood by any other name not rise as high? In his writings Morris has combined "scientific" and "Biblical" creationism with no apparent qualms, as in "scientific Biblical creationism" (1988e; 1989c) and "Biblical/scientific Christian creationism" (1987d). That any distinction between them is purely artificial is obvious from the ICR position, as stated by associate director Ken Ham (1989c), that the biblical book of Genesis "must be taken literally" and is "foundational to the rest of the Bible, true science, true history, true philosophy, etc."

Since 1981 the ICR's "ministries" have included a graduate school, offering M.S. degrees in various areas of "science" from the creationist perspective (Morris 1988g, 96; *Acts & Facts* 18[3]:3). In 1989, however, a state evaluation team recommended to California superintendent of public instruction Bill Honig that the license of the ICR graduate school be revoked (*Acts & Facts* 18[10]:4). As Honig had already stated, "No one is stopping the ICR from granting degrees in religion or creation, but they are holding their people out to have science degrees, which they don't. The vast bulk of what they learn is not science" (Scott 1988, 5). The ICR intends to fight revocation, but as of this writing the graduate school appears unlikely to survive what ICR administrative vice president John Morris (1989a) calls "the sting of the evolutionary crowd's wrath."

An activity that has gained the ICR much public exposure is

its ongoing series of debates with evolutionists on college campuses. Duane Gish, a debater who "hits the floor running" (Numbers 1982, 543), must by now have some two hundred such debates under his belt, and, if one were to judge by the coverage in *Acts & Facts*, he has won every one of them. Gish, with a Ph.D. in biochemistry and years of professional experience in that field, has the most legitimiate scientific credentials on the ICR staff, though it should be noted that his ICR writings deal principally with paleontology, not with biochemistry (Bates 1976, 160-161). In debates he invariably talks about THERMODYNAMICS, the impossibility of LIFE arising from nonlife (see ABIOGENESIS), and the lack of TRANSITIONAL FORMS in the FOSSIL RECORD. In other words, he attacks the idea of evolution, which his evolutionist opponents must then defend in terms understandable to nonscientific audiences usually packed with creationist supporters (Newell 1985, 13). No positive evidence for creation is presented, since that would necessarily get into religion, and it is the creationists themselves who insist that the subject of religion be kept out of the debates. That so many of these encounters have been "won" by the creationists is attributable to the hundreds of hours of practice they have had, as opposed to the lack of debating experience of the evolutionists—often from specialized fields, with little grasp of the wider issues—who are recruited for the occasions (Newell 1985, 13; Shapiro 1986, 256). Even so, the smooth road Gish once had in debates has become rocky as the "evolutionary crowd" has become familiar with and thus prepared for his tactics. Anthropologist Vincent Sarich has debated Gish about one dozen times (*Acts & Facts* 16[12]:2; 17[1]:2; 17[7]:4) and should know Gish's presentation by heart. Biologist Kenneth S. Saladin (1988) has debated Gish twice and reports that Gish on three occasions has publicly denied that the ICR sponsors expeditions to Mount Ararat to look for Noah's ark. Such denials are difficult to explain when ICR president Morris (1984b, 252-253) unequivocally states that the ICR's "most ambitious" research project, "active since 1972," is its Ararat Project, "sponsoring expeditions to Mount Ararat," which expeditions have been led, and duly reported on to ICR supporters, by Morris's son John (1988b; *Acts & Facts* 16[10]:3, 16[11]:2-3, 17[11]:4).

Is it possible that Gish was driven to such denials—driven, in effect, to distraction—by his determination to keep biblical religion out of the debates? Noah's ark is certainly biblical and irrelevant to any discussion of science. Yet it is idle for Gish and his ICR cohorts to pretend that the purpose of these debates (on the creationist side) is anything other than religious. Henry Morris (1984b, 264) notes that such debates often have a "spiritual impact" and not infrequently lead to "conversion to Christ." The ICR, after all, was "raised up," in the words of Ken Ham (1989a), "to proclaim the message of Christ as Creator and Savior in a pagan world." And woe to those who fail to pay heed. One of the ICR's "Tenets of Biblical Creationism" (see Morris 1984b, 363-365) is that those who reject or "neglect to believe" in Christ "must ultimately be consigned to the everlasting fire prepared for the devil and his angels." Which is one way, perhaps, of telling the "evolutionary crowd" where to go.

KIND

See TAXONOMY.

LAMARCKISM

A theory of biological EVOLUTION proposed in 1809 by the French zoologist Jean-Baptiste Lamarck (1744-1829). Though the idea of evolution was gaining acceptance by the beginning of the nineteenth century, Lamarck's was the first scientific theory about how evolution might occur (Futuyma 1979, 6). The theory proved unsatisfactory to scientists and was destined to be eclipsed by Charles Darwin's (1859) theory of "descent with modification" by NATURAL SELECTION.

One aspect of Lamarck's theory was the *inheritance of acquired characteristics,* a common belief of Lamarck's time and the concept for which Lamarckism is now chiefly remembered. According to this concept, an organism in its lifetime can develop some new capability or trait and pass this acquired characteristic along to its offspring.

There is the old notion, for example, that giraffes had short-necked ancestors, but developed distended necks by browsing off high tree branches, so that their offspring inherited long necks (Eldredge 1982, 57; Romer 1966, 2).

The inheritance of acquired characteristics remained a virtually universal belief until the early 1880s (Mayr 1988, 507). Even Darwin subscribed to the notion, though he always considered its evolutionary role subordinate to that of natural selection (Bowler 1989, 178). The concept of the inheritance of acquired characteristics was finally refuted in the 1880s by the German zoologist August Weismann, though it continued to have diehard advocates long afterward (Dobzhansky 1985, 738). Weismann theorized correctly that the material responsible for transmitting heredity is located in the chromosomes, and that acquired modifications of the body cannot affect that material and therefore cannot be inherited (Bowler 1989, 251). Weismann conducted an experiment to support his theory: He cut the tails off 1,592 laboratory mice over 22 generations (Asimov 1982, 463). As expected, the mice continued to bear young with full-sized tails.

Though the notion of the inheritance of acquired characteristics has been long discredited, creationists still like to discuss it—just as they like to discuss PILTDOWN MAN and NEBRASKA MAN—as an example of "evolutionary misconceptions" (Parker 1987, 94). At least some creationists are apparently not above suggesting that the inheritance of acquired characteristics is a current evolutionary concept. For example, creationist Harold Hill (1976, 5-6): "But acquired characteristics can't be passed on genetically, you argue? Shhhh! Don't let the evolutionists hear you say that." Worse, during a March 2, 1981 ABC News "Nightline" program on the CREATION/evolution issue, a teacher from a private Christian school stated that Jews have been circumcising their babies for thousands of years, yet no Jew has ever been born already circumcised. Since no evolutionist on the program responded to this reference to the inheritance of acquired characteristics, the impression was no doubt left in the minds of many of the program's viewers that such outlandish things as babies born circumcised must indeed be expected to occur if evolution is true.

Evolutionists have often accused creationists of misrepresenting and distorting evolutionist views (see Cole 1981). Hill's shushing and the teacher's statement on "Nightline" are two excellent examples of what the evolutionists are complaining about.

LANGUAGE

See BABEL, TOWER OF.

LIFE

A complex property found in the ANIMAL, PLANT, Fungi, Monera, and Protista kingdoms that is "notoriously hard to define" (Wallace, King, and Sanders 1981, 46) and of which there is no generally agreed definition. BIOLOGY texts prefer defining it in terms of the attributes that are shared by life's myriad forms. These attributes include *metabolism, reproduction, growth,* and *responsiveness.* John Maynard Smith (1975, 96) calls such lists of properties "arbitrary" and "of little use," only to replace them with a list of his own: "the properties of multiplication, heredity, and variation." His list has a genetic theme, however, that does make it more useful in terms of considering life's EVOLUTION, for the fact that all forms of life share the same genetic code (see GENETICS) is prima facie evidence that all biological entities have evolved from one common ancestral form. Two equally valid definitions of life, therefore, are "the expression of (genetically) coded instructions" (Dulbecco 1987, vii) and "the ability to evolve" (Scott 1986, 68).

It is the scientific consensus that the first ancestral life form, most likely a bacteriumlike cell (Cloud 1988, 248), arose from nonliving matter through natural chemical processes some 4 billion years ago. This ABIOGENESIS or *spontaneous generation,* impossible under oxidizing conditions, was able naturally to occur on the primitive EARTH due to an absence of free oxygen in the early atmosphere. (Free oxygen was to arise largely as a by-product of life through green-plant *photosynthesis,* life adapting in turn to its presence.) Life may have arisen more than once but the descendants of only one form survived, thus accounting for basic similarities despite eons of diversification (Cloud 1988, 248; Dobzhansky 1985, 746; Maynard Smith 1986, 19-20). Once life existed, NATURAL SELECTION could begin its work: Different *species* arose, some increasing in complexity and diversity, others suffering EXTINCTION, still others persisting in relative stasis, all the while the FOSSIL RECORD of life's history laying itself down to be read.

The first fossil traces of life are in rocks that are 3.5 billion years old (Kutter 1987, 346-349; Strahler 1987, 516), meaning that life probably began less than 1 billion years after formation of the earth itself (see SOLAR SYSTEM.) For almost 3 billion years life consisted of simple, single-celled marine organisms. Then, with the Ediacaran and Cambrian periods (lasting from some 670 million to some 500 million years ago), complex, multicellular marine organisms made their appearance in abundance (see CAMBRIAN EXPLOSION). The earliest known FISH and land plants appeared in the Ordovician period (roughly 500-425 million years ago), the first AMPHIBIANS and INSECTS in the Devonian (405-345 million years ago), the first REPTILES in the Carboniferous (345-280 million years ago), the first *mammal-like reptiles* in the Permian (280-230 million years ago), the first DINOSAURS and MAMMALS in the Triassic (230-180 million years ago), the first BIRDS in the Jurassic (180-135 million years ago), the first flowering plants in the Cretaceous (135-65 million years ago). MAN on this *geologic time scale* is a late arrival, evolving from apelike ancestors within the last few million years.

Such is the consensus, based on a wealth of scientific evidence, the evidence for biological evolution in general being cumulatively overwhelming. Yet the proponents of CREATIONISM hold that none of this ever happened. They are believers in special creation. The first two chapters of the biblical book of Genesis, says creationist leader Duane Gish (1985, 11, 23), relate the "simple historical facts," which are that "all basic animal and plant types (the created kinds) were brought into existence by acts of a supernatural Creator using special processes which are not operative today." Since this is an explicitly religious view, however, creationists in their creation "science" mode, as in the "scientific" guise they adopted before the U.S. Supreme Court in 1986 (see *EDWARDS v. AGUILLARD*), might avoid the word "creation" altogether and speak rather of "origin through abrupt appearance in complex form" (Amici Curiae 1986, 8). But whether it be called CREATION or ABRUPT APPEARANCE, the fact is that the creationist concept of life's origin is utterly untestable and unfalsifiable and is therefore not SCIENCE. Nor does creationism, including its biblically based concept of created "kinds," provide a satisfactory explanation for the truly mind-boggling diversity of life forms past and present. There are over 1.5 million living species that have so far been named and described, the estimated total number of living species running as high as 10 million, with those millions being only a fraction of the number of species now extinct (Newell 1985, 125, 129). Such diversity gives new meaning to the old Elbert Hubbard adage that "life is just one damned thing after another." There are over 2,500 known species of beetles alone, prompting biologist J. B. S. Haldane to remark (Newell 1985, 127) that any Creator "must be inordinately fond of beetles." And what, for example, is the creative purpose of a particular species of fungus that grows only on wings of a particular species of beetle (*Aphenops cronei*) found only in some French limestone caves (Dobzhansky 1973, 126)? "Tapeworms were not put here to serve a purpose," says biologist Douglas Futuyma (1982, 37); they came into existence "not by design but by the action of impersonal natural laws." There is also the problem for creationists that each life form has imperfections and that most species have in fact gone the way of extinction, suggesting that the Creator was something of a bungler if not worse (see DESIGN ARGUMENT).

Gish (1985, 19) and America's leading creationist Henry Morris (1982a, 9; 1985b), vice president and president, respectively, of the INSTITUTE FOR CREATION RESEARCH (ICR), admit that the concept of creation is ultimately unscientific. But they argue that evolution as a concept is no more scientific than is creation, and to try to prove this creationists spend most of their time not doing "creation research" but attacking evolutionary theory. With respect to life's origin, creationists argue that life could not possibly have arisen by chance from nonliving matter. (For their arguments against evolutionary theory in general, see EVOLUTION.) But the fact is that numerous laboratory experiments (see Chang et al. 1983), beginning with the classic Miller-Urey experiment (Miller 1953), indicate that the gradual emergence of life from prebiological materials in the "reducing" or oxygen-free atmosphere of the primitive earth was hardly by chance: It was a highly probable if not inevitable event. The experiments demonstrate that *amino acids* and *nucleotide bases*—organic compounds that are the building blocks of *proteins* and *nucleic acids*, essential constitutents of life—readily form by natural CHEMISTRY under simulated primitive-earth conditions (see ABIOGENESIS).

This is not to suggest that experimenters are on the verge of creating life from nonlife in the laboratory. The laboratory synthesis of life's building blocks has not told us how to assemble the blocks. How did the first molecules capable of self-replication arise, at which point genetic variation and natural selection could begin? The exact process may never be known. But experimental research into life's origins is relatively new, and as such research continues there is no need to fill in present ignorance with supernatural event—a practice known as "invoking the God-of-the-gaps." The origin of life may at present be "the greatest of all evolutionary problems" (Simpson 1967, 15), but all scientific evidence to date supports the view that life arose as a natural consequence of primitive-earth chemical processes. In fact amino acids and nucleotide bases have also been found in meteorites (Cloud 1988, 230; *Science News* 124:150), and other organic compounds have been identified in interstellar clouds, comets, and the atmospheres of the outer planets, all of which suggests that the synthesis of simple organic compounds such as eventually led to life on earth may occur naturally throughout the cosmos (Chang et al. 1983, 91).

Does life exist, then, beyond earth? There is as yet no evidence that it does. Isaac Asimov (1979) and Carl Sagan (Shklovskii and Sagan 1966) are among scientists who argue that the existence of extraterrestrial intelligence (ETI) is highly probable. Other scientists disagree. "It is logically possible," says astronomer Heinrich K. Eichhorn (1989), "that intelligent life is a freak," and evolutionary biologist Ernst Mayr (1988, 67-74) believes that it *is* one, an "incredible improbability." (Note here the distinction made between *any* form of life and intelligent life. The origin of life was apparently quite probable. But such is evolution that for most species, alas, extinction was probable too. So the rise of intelligence—that is, of man, the only genuinely "intelligent" species out of billions of species over geologic time—stands out as improbable [Mayr 1988, 72].) ETI anywhere in the solar system besides earth is almost certainly absent (Eichhorn 1989), and the STARS are so far away that the question "Is there anybody out there?" may never be answerable. There is evidence that Vega, Beta Pictoris, and other relatively nearby stars have planets or preplanetary material orbiting them (Cohen 1988, 176-177; Eberhart 1987, 1988; Kutter 1987, 248; Peterson 1988), but that does not mean that ETI is, or ever will be, in residence.

The search for ETI (SETI) has been conducted in ASTRONOMY, with the help of government funds, using radio telescopes, seeking to detect intelligent radio signals from space. Mayr (1988, 73) calls this "a deplorable waste of taxpayers' money," an opinion that creationists undoubtedly share. Creationists have a natural aversion to the ETI concept. The discovery of other inhabited worlds could be a devastating blow to the creationists' fundamentalist theology that spotlights earthly man as "the center of God's interest" in the cosmos (Morris 1984a, 162). Thus Morris (1978, 63) says that from all indications in the BIBLE, there are "definitely no men, or manlike intelligences, living on other planets or stars." John C. Whitcomb (1984, 27-30) quotes various biblical passages to the same effect. The only extraterrestrial intelligence that man needs to be deeply concerned about, says Whitcomb, "is the intelligence of God Himself."

LIGHT

See RELATIVITY; STAR.

LIVING FOSSIL

See ADAPTATION.

LOUISIANA CREATIONISM LAW

See *EDWARDS v. AGUILLARD.*

MAGNETIC FIELD

See GEOMAGNETISM.

MAMMAL

A member of the Mammalia class of warm-blooded vertebrate (backboned) ANIMALS distinguished by mammary glands and (usually) hair. Mammals, simply stated, are "hairy animals that give milk" (Wallace, King, and Sanders 1981, 649). There are about 4,000 living species, found in three major groups: primitive, egg-laying *monotremes* (the platypus and spiny anteater), *marsupials* (pouched animals such as the kangaroo), and *placentals* (mammals with organs called placentas that connect mothers and embryos). Monotremes and marsupials are largely confined to Australia. Rodents are the most numerous mammals, though MAN is, of course, the most dominant. Man, apes, monkeys, and prosimians are PRIMATES, the highest order of mammals. Other examples of mammals are dogs, cats, horses, and whales.

The first mammals are believed to have evolved about 200 million years ago from an order of REPTILES (subclass Synapsida) called *therapsids.* The early mammals were small, shrewlike creatures who survived partly by staying out of the way of the DINOSAURS. The dinosaurs' EXTINCTION about 65 million years ago marks the beginning of the so-called Age of Mammals, with mammals undergoing much adaptive radiation and structural change (Cockrum 1985, 205). Some of the early mammals adapted to LIFE in the water, and thus were ancestral to the *cetaceans* (whales, dolphins, and porpoises); others took to the air (the bat is a placental); still others to the trees (most primates are tree-dwellers) (Dixon 1988, 196). According to data from molecular BIOLOGY, the common ancestor of apes and humans lived as late as 5 million years ago (Sarich and Wilson 1967; Lewin 1988, 47-49). By about 4 million years ago, the first known *hominids*—members of man's family Hominidae, of which man is the lone survivor—were living in Africa (see AUSTRALOPITHECINES).

The FOSSIL RECORD of mammals is a good one. Creationists have a particularly hard time trying to deal with the well-documented evolutionary connection between reptiles and mammals. (It is a standard creationist argument that the fossil record contains no TRANSITIONAL FORMS between any groups.) The extinct therapsid reptiles from which mammals are believed to have evolved were so intermediate in their characteristics that they are commonly called the *mammal-like reptiles*. Even creationist leader Duane Gish (1985, 92) admits to the "mosaic" nature of these creatures, though he will never admit that their combination of reptilian and mammalian characteristics has transitional significance. Actually the evolutionary transition from reptile to mammal can be followed quite precisely through certain changes with respect to the jaw joints. What basically happened is that two bones of the reptilian jaw (the articular and quadrate bones) evolved into two bones (the hammer and anvil) of the mammalian ear (McGowan 1984, 139; Moore 1984, 498-499). The mammal-like reptile *Diarthrognathus* ("two-jointed jaws") was smack-dab in between, with both reptilian and mammalian jaw joints. In the words of biologist John A. Moore (1984, 499), "One could not ask for a better intermediate between reptiles and mammals."

Gish (1985, 101) states that the ear's organ of Corti (the actual hearing organ, converting sound vibrations into nerve impulses) must have been "created de novo," since there is no structure that is homologous (similar due to common descent) in reptiles. According to paleontologist Robert E. Sloan (1983, 275), Gish is wrong: "The basilar papilla of lizards and crocodiles is exactly homologous with the organ of Corti." Gish (1985, 102) also states that "reptiles have no diaphragms" nor anything homologous to the diaphragms of mammals. Wrong again, says Sloan (1983, 275): "All of the cynodont reptiles for which we know the skeleton had a diaphragm!"

The *horse* is a mammal that has left a particularly good fossil record with respect to its evolution. The earliest known *equid* (member of the family Equidae that includes the modern horse) is the dog-sized *Hyracotherium*, known also as *Eohippus* ("Dawn Horse"), who lived about 60 million years ago. One way to follow equid evolution is to keep counting toes. *Hyracotherium* had 4 toes in each forefoot and 3 toes in each hindfoot. About 30 million years later, *Mesohippus* had 3 toes in each foot; the modern horse has one toe, which ends in a hoof (McGowan 1984, 143-145). But one must not oversimplify, for the evolution of equids is complex, involving much more than toes. Equid evolution is not a straight line but a "zig-zag" (Dodson 1985), and there is considerable disagreement about the details of the story (Kitcher 1982, 115). Even creationists disagree about horses. John N. Moore (1976, 33) says that "horses are horses," that what evolutionists call horse evolution is "only variation *within* the horse-kind." Gish (1985, 85-86) takes a different view, arguing that *Hyracotherium* was so different from the modern horse that it was not a horse at all. And Gish is right, though of course for the wrong reasons. *Hyracotherium* was not a horse; it was an equid ancestor of horses (and of rhinos and tapirs) (Futuyma 1982, 94). Early equid forms are more different from modern horses than are modern zebras and asses, which no one would call horses (McGowan 1984, 148). But Gish (1985, 86) is wrong to say that the idea of the horse as a classic case for evolution is "without real merit." Though equid history is complex, the evolutionary path that led to *Equus caballus*, the modern horse species, can be fairly well traced. To quote Futuyma (1982, 94), "The history of the horse is not perfectly documented, but it is as good as any 60-million-year history is likely to be."

Gish (1985, 78) states that the whales, dolphins, and other marine mammals "abruptly appear" in the fossil record with no transitional forms to indicate their evolution from land mammals. Naturally he does not agree with those evolutionists who consider *Protocetus*, *Pakicetus*, and other members of an extinct cetacean group called *archaeocetes* to be intermediate between modern cetaceans and land mammals (Edwords 1983; Landau 1983). But there are VESTIGIAL ORGANS in modern whales that clearly indicate that their ancestors were land creatures. There have been numerous cases of whales being found with vestigial hind limbs (Conrad 1983). There are also certain whales that in the embryonic stage have teeth and hair, features that in whales disappear before birth but are basic characteristics of land mammals (Edwords 1983, 5; Newell 1985, 178).

Monotremes (the platypus and spiny anteater), the most primitive of living mammals, lay eggs as do reptiles. This is additional evidence of the evolutionary descent of mammals from reptiles. (BIRDS also lay eggs and are believed to be descended from reptiles.) Gish (1985, 93) argues that the platypus could not be ancestral to the other mammals because the platypus appears too recently on the geologic time scale. But evolutionists do not claim that the platypus is ancestral to other mammals. The point is simply made that the monotreme is a mammal that keeps dropping hints, in egg form, of its reptilian ancestry.

MAMMAL-LIKE REPTILE

See MAMMAL.

MAN

The species *Homo sapiens* (Latin "wise man") of the PRIMATE order of MAMMALS. Man is the last surviving member of the hominid family, believed to be related by common ancestry to the pongid family of apes (chimpanzees, gibbons, gorillas, and orangutans). Evidence that man and ape descended from a common ancestor is derived from comparative ANATOMY, the FOSSIL RECORD, molecular BIOLOGY, and behavioral studies. The anatomical similarities are obvious, recalling Charles Darwin's observation (1874, 613) that "man still bears in his bodily frame the indelible stamp of his lowly origin." Darwin was also aware, however, of the inability or unwillingness of many humans to accept such an origin, as he spoke (1859, 482) of "the load of prejudice by which this subject is overwhelmed." Such prejudice is well exemplified today by the "scientific" creationist movement, led by Christian fundamentalists who attack EVOLUTION as a "lie" (Ham 1987; Morris 1963, 82) and the work of the devil (Morris 1982b, 71-76; 1984a, 109-110; see SATAN).

The descent of man, beginning with some tree-dwelling, four-legged forebear (see PRIMATE), may be seen as an odyssey of millions of years involving a shift from the trees to the ground, a change to upright bipedal posture, the enlargement of the brain, and the emergence of technology (Lewin 1987, 32-33). The dryopithecines ("oak apes") of 10 to 20 million years ago were probably forebears of the common ancestor of man and the apes (Lewin 1988c, 42-43; Stebbins 1982, 315). There is molecular biological evidence that the evolutionary lines leading to man and the apes diverged as recently as 5 million years ago (Sarich and Wilson 1967; Lewin 1988c, 47-49). The earliest known hominids (members of man's family Hominidae) are the AUSTRALOPITHECINES ("southern apes"), several fossil species of manlike apes/apelike men who lived in Africa from over 4 million years to about 1 million years ago. The australopithecines walked upright but had ape-sized brains, about one-third the size of modern man's (Brace 1983, 251). Though experts disagree (see Lewin 1987) as to which of these species, if any, was directly ancestral to man (genus *Homo* of the hominid family), the australopithecines, as mosaic creatures with both apelike and manlike characteristics, are excellent examples of TRANSITIONAL FORMS in the fossil record (Brace 1983, 251; Gould 1987, 68; McGowan 1984, 171-177).

The earliest fossil form of *Homo*, based on brain size and simple stone toolmaking, is *Homo habilis* ("handy man"), who lived in Africa about 2 million years ago. He is followed by the brainier *Homo erectus*, who mastered fire and migrated into Asia and Europe less than 1 million years ago. The fossil remains of *H. erectus* include those popularly known as Java Man and Peking Man. (Some creationists [e.g., Keith 1982, 5] have suggested that Peking Man was a hoax because the bones were lost during World War II. The suggestion ignores the fact that casts of the bones still exist and that many other *H. erectus* specimens have been found around the world, including more from the site near Peking [Eldredge 1982, 125-281].) Early man's brain size continued to grow, reaching by about 500,000 years ago an average size equal to modern man's (Futuyma 1982, 111). Heavily built Neanderthal Man (subspecies *Homo sapiens neanderthalensis*), whose brain size actually exceeded the modern average, flourished within the last 100,000 years. Religion may have begun with Neanderthal Man, the first known hominid to practice ritual burial (Noss 1980, 4-5). By about 35,000 years ago, the first anatomically modern human, Cro-Magnon Man (subspecies *Homo sapiens sapiens*), had completely replaced the Neanderthals either by descent or, more likely, through competition or conquest (Lewin 1988c, 128-133). Man reached America, via a land bridge across the Bering Strait, as early as 32,000 years ago (Bower 1986).

The anatomical and fossil evidence of man's evolution has been strikingly supplemented by the work of molecular biologists in studying genetic differences between species. Specifically, structural differences in protein and DNA (see BIOLOGY) can be used to measure how closely related different species are, and, based on calculated rates of mutation, approximately how long it has been since divergence from a common ancestor. Results show that genetically man and the chimpanzee are almost 99 percent identical (Gribbin and Cherfas 1982, 117; Mereson 1988), and that man and ape, as already noted, shared a common ancestor as recently as 5 million years ago.

Creationists, in spite of the anatomical, fossil, and molecular evidence, have characterized the concept of evolution as "an insult to common sense" (Morris 1985a, 23), the "most overpropagandized delusion to confront man since Satan tricked Eve in the Garden of Eden" (LaHaye 1975, 6), and "the most stupid thought to enter the mind of man" (Homer Duncan, quoted in Kurtz 1985, 42). Shorn of scientific pretensions, the creationist scenario for man's origin is strictly biblical. Duane Gish, vice president of the INSTITUTE FOR CREATION RESEARCH (ICR), sees the book of Genesis as a historically factual account of CREATION that "cannot be reconciled with any possible evolutionary theory concerning the origin of man" (1985, 24-25). Man, says ICR president Henry Morris (1978, 47), is "a unique creation of God, entirely without evolutionary relation to the animals, and Adam was the first man" (see ADAM AND EVE). As for the fossil record, the australopithecines, say creationists, were apes, the early *Homo* species were men, and never the twain shall meet. Arguments about whether or not the australopithecines were transitional forms are termed "silly" (Gish 1986), and Morris (1978,

44) holds that even if anthropologists were ever to find some form intermediate between ape and man, "it still would not prove human evolution." As for anatomical and genetic similarities between man and other creatures, these similarities, say the creationists, are evidence not of common descent but simply of "a common purposive designer" (Morris 1982b, 85).

The argument that Genesis is a factual account of origins may be appropriate for Sunday school but has no place in a public school SCIENCE class. Even when presented as creation "science" with no biblical references, CREATION, implying a Creator, is a religious concept that is neither testable nor falsifiable (see SCIENCE). Nor have creationists yet found an effective way to deal with the fossil record. Each time we look at the fossils, it is a test of evolutionary theory. And we see what we *should* see, exactly what the theory predicts, if man has in fact evolved, for as we trace the fossils backward in time, hominid characteristics become more apelike, and stone tools and other artifacts become simpler, clearly indicating that humans are the product of a gradual physical and mental evolution (Futuyma 1982, 112). Why would God, asks paleontologist Stephen Jay Gould (1987, 68), create five successive species—*Australopithecus afarensis*, *A. africanus*, *Homo habilis*, *H. erectus*, and *H. sapiens*—"to mimic a continuous trend of evolutionary change?" If man did not evolve but was part of an "essentially instantaneous" creation (Gish 1985, 35), it would seem that the Creator has practiced deliberate deception by arranging things exactly as if his method of creation was evolution (Dobzhansky 1973, 127).

The argument that anatomical and genetic similarities are evidence of a common designer is merely an extension of the classical *argument from design* for the existence of a Creator (see DESIGN ARGUMENT). Philosopher David Hume (1779) buried that argument over two hundred years ago, although diehards keep trying to exhume it. The design argument says nothing of scientific value, it simply invites questions it's unable to answer. Why, for example, have some humans been born with tails? Evolutionary biology provides perfectly reasonable explanations for such features as gill slits in human embryos and on occasion a neonatal human tail (see VESTIGIAL ORGAN).

Anatomist William King Gregory, tongue in cheek, coined the

term "pithecophobia," which he defined as "the dread of apes—especially the dread of apes as relatives or ancestors" (Lewin 1987, 59). Pithecophobia may aptly describe the real problem that creationists and so many other people in general have with human evolution. It is surely what afflicted the Anglican bishop's wife who remarked, soon after the publication of Darwin's *Origin*, that if the theory of evolution was true she hoped it would not become widely known (Kitcher 1982, 187). If human beings evolved, then man, according to creationist John N. Moore (1976, 81), is "simply a made-over animal" without dignity, value, or worth. Add to that the Christian fundamentalist view of man as fallen and depraved and one is afflicted with a pretty bleak picture of the human condition. "Man," says Morris (1978, 78), "is not an upward-evolving animal but, rather, a lost sinner under the condemnation of death. . . . 'O wretched man that I am! who shall deliver me from the body of this death?' (Romans 7:21-24)." It seems much more productive, for those unburdened by such sectarian baggage, to agree with George Gaylord Simpson that "man has risen, not fallen" (1967, 311), that he is "responsible to himself and for himself," and that because man knows he evolves, he stands in a position, challenging and unique among creatures, "to influence his own biological destiny" (1964, 25).

MAN TRACKS

See DINOSAUR.

McLEAN *v.* ARKANSAS

The case in which U.S. District Court Judge William R. Overton in 1982 ruled unconstitutional an Arkansas "balanced treatment" law requiring the teaching of "creation science" in public schools whenever "evolution science" is taught. A number of creationist bills similar to the one in Arkansas were introduced in state legislatures in the late 1970s through 1981, and the *McLean v. Arkansas* trial in Little

Rock received a great deal of national attention—some even billing it as "Scopes II" (see SCOPES TRIAL)—because of the impact that the outcome was expected to have, one way or the other, on the direction of the creationist movement that by 1981 was at its height.

The Arkansas "balanced treatment" bill was not exactly a home-grown product. Wendell Bird, an attorney for California's INSTITUTE FOR CREATION RESEARCH (ICR), had written a resolution, based on the ICR's "two-model approach" for teaching "origins" in public schools, for adoption (so the ICR hoped) by boards of education around the country. Enter Paul Ellwanger, a South Carolina respiratory therapist and leader of a group called Citizens for Fairness in Education. Ellwanger used Bird's resolution to draft a model bill for state legislatures. The bill's stated purpose was that of "protecting academic freedom," but Ellwanger's real purpose in pushing such legislation was made clear by a letter he wrote to Tom Bethell about "the idea of killing evolution instead of playing these debating games" (Overton 1982, 314). Ellwanger sent a copy of his model bill to a North Little Rock minister, who passed it on to Arkansas State Senator James L. Holsted (Larson 1985, 150-151).

Ellwanger's bill defined "creation-science" as "the scientific evidences for creation and inferences from those scientific evidences." According to the bill, creation "science" includes the following concepts: sudden creation from nothing; the insufficiency of mutation and NATURAL SELECTION in bringing about development of all living kinds from a single organism; changes only within fixed limits of originally created kinds of PLANTS and ANIMALS; separate ancestry for MAN and apes; GEOLOGY explained in terms of a worldwide flood (see FLOOD, NOAH'S); and a relatively recent inception of the EARTH and living kinds (Zetterberg 1983, 400).

Senator Holsted, a self-described born-again Christian fundamentalist, introduced the bill in the Arkansas Senate without consulting any scientists, science educators, the state attorney general, or the state department of education (Overton 1982, 314). Holsted later testified that although the bill "favored the view of the Biblical literalists, of which I am one," he saw no religious constitutional problem because the bill didn't mention "any particular God" (Gilkey 1985, 153-154).

Act 590, as the Holsted bill came to be known, had no trouble passing both houses of the legislature. Arkansas born-again Governor Frank White signed Act 590 into law, without reading it, on March 19, 1981 (Larson 1985, 153).

The law was promptly challenged by the American Civil Liberties Union (ACLU) as an unconstitutional establishment of religion. The ACLU was to spend more money on *McLean v. Arkansas*—two million dollars—than on any other case in its history (*Miami Herald*, January 6, 1982). Namesake plaintiff Bill McLean was the principal officer of the Presbyterian Church in Arkansas. Other plaintiffs included the bishops of the United Methodist Church of Arkansas, the Episcopal Diocese of Arkansas, and the Catholic Diocese of Little Rock, national Jewish groups, professional teachers' associations, and individual pastors, teachers, and parents (Keith 1982, 113-114). The trial began in Little Rock on December 7, 1981 before the late Judge Overton, who was a Methodist and the son of a BIOLOGY teacher (*Miami Herald*, January 6, 1982).

In opening arguments, ACLU attorney Robert Cearley called Act 590 an attempt by the legislature "to define what science is and to force religion into the schools in the guise of science" (Edwords 1982, 34). State Attorney General Steve Clark argued for the defense that "the primary effect" of Act 590 was to further "academic freedom," in that "a controversial scientific theory [referring to creation "science"] should not be squelched or censored" (Larson 1985, 159). Clark called it "mere coincidence" that the law's description of "creation science" resembled certain religious beliefs (Edwords 1982, 34).

The ACLU presented expert witnesses in both religion and science. Biblical scholar Bruce Vawter (quoted in Gilkey 1985, 86), a Catholic priest, testified that the description of "creation science" in Act 590 "has as its unmentioned reference the first eleven chapters of Genesis. The major ideas of creation science are rephrasings, often with the same words, of central concepts or events" in Genesis. United Methodist Bishop Kenneth W. Hicks (quoted in Keith 1982, 124) testified, "The words 'In the beginning, God created,' I hold very dearly. From that point on, I feel it belittles God and does injustice to both religion and science to try to circumscribe the way he did it." Scientists testifying for the plaintiffs included geneticist Francisco Ayala, who stressed (with regard to the two-model approach embodied in Act 590) the impossibility of ever saying in science that there are only two models or theories; geologist G. Brent Dalrymple, who explained RADIOACTIVE DATING and its contradiction of Act 590's concept of a "recent inception of the earth"; biochemist Harold Morowitz, who differentiated between the question of the origin of LIFE and the theory of evolution, the latter being a theory of BIOLOGY that assumes life's presence; and paleontologist Stephen Jay Gould, who discussed the FOSSIL RECORD and its contradiction of creationist flood geology (Gilkey 1985, 137-151).

Some of the scheduled creationist witnesses failed to show up. They had apparently been warned that the case was doomed, due to what creationists considered to be poor handling by the state attorney general (Nelkin 1982, 143; Edwords 1982, 43; Larson 1985, 163). Dr. Norman Geisler of Dallas Theological Seminary testified that the concept of God is not necessarily religious (Edwords 1982, 35). He also testified that unidentified flying objects (UFOs) are "Satanic manifestations for the purposes of deception" (Gilkey 1985, 77). (When asked how he knew that UFOs exist, Geisler said that he read it in *Reader's Digest*.) British astrophysicist Chandra Wickramasinghe testified that mathematically it was virtually impossible for chance chemical combinations to produce life from nonlife (Larson 1985, 160; see ABIOGENESIS). Wickramasinghe, however, is a Buddhist, not a Christian fundamentalist. He described such creationist concepts as a recent inception of the earth and a separate ancestry for man and apes as "claptrap" (Edwords 1983, 37). He also told the court that INSECTS may be more intelligent than humans but "they're not letting on" (Nelkin 1982, 143). Creationist witness Wayne Frair, a biologist, congratulated Arkansas for being "on the very cutting edge of an educational movement" that would teach students how to think (Keith 1982, 135). "If Darwin were alive today," said Frair (quoted in Edwords 1983, 36), "he would be a creationist." Creationist physicist Robert Gentry told the court about the mystery of POLONIUM HALOS (see also Wakefield 1987). CHEMISTRY professor Donald Chittick (now affiliated with the ICR) testified that traditional methods of determining the age of the earth are unreliable (Keith 1982, 136). When asked under cross-examination if he could ever accept any scientific data that conflicted with his belief in the literal truth of the BIBLE, Chittick replied after some thought, "I cannot give an answer" (Edwords 1983, 36).

Judge Overton issued his decision on January 5, 1982. He judged Act 590 on the basis of a test of constitutionality articulated in case law (*Lemon v. Kurtzman, Stone v. Graham*) with respect to the First Amendment establishment clause. According to the three-pronged test, a statute must have a secular purpose, its primary effect must neither advance nor inhibit religion, and it must not foster excessive government entanglement with religion (Edwords 1983, 33-34). Act 590, said the judge, failed the first prong of the test, that of secular legislative purpose. The state had produced no evidence that anyone in the process of passing the bill had considered the question of its legitimate educational value. "It was simply and purely an effort to introduce the Biblical version of creation into the public school curricula." Act 590 also failed the second and third prongs, by advancing biblical religion and excessively entangling the government therewith. It would be an "impossible task," said Overton, for the state department of education "to constantly monitor materials to avoid religious references," particulary when the ultimate source for much of the information that would be needed to teach creation "science" was the book of Genesis.

In finding for the plaintiffs, Overton, drawing heavily from the experts', courtroom testimony, gave no quarter to the creationist defense. "Evolution is the cornerstone of modern biology," he wrote, and any student deprived of instruction "as to the prevailing scientific thought" on such topics as the age of the earth, geology, and relationships among living things "will be deprived of a significant part of science education." Science, Overton said, is defined as that which is "accepted by the scientific community"; science is "what scientists do," and "creation science" as defined in Act 590 "is simply not science." Sudden creation is "an inherently religious concept," and the definition of "creation science" in Act 590 is based on the first eleven chapters of Genesis. The creationists' two-model approach is "a contrived dualism which has no scientific factual basis or legitimate educational purpose." Biologists know that the processes of mutation and natural selection do not account for all significant evolutionary change. The "separate ancestry of man and apes" is "a bald assertion" that "explains nothing and refers to no scientific fact or theory." A sizeable majority of Americans no doubt believe in the concept of a Creator, said Overton, but "the application and content of First Amendment principles are not determined by public opinion polls or by a majority vote." Overton closed his opinion with the eloquent words of Justice Felix Frankfurter: "Complete separation between the state and religion is best for the state and best for religion," and "If nowhere else, in the relation between Church and State, 'good fences make good neighbors.'"

The state of Arkansas did not appeal Overton's decision. Attorney General Clark, who was roundly criticized by creationists for his handling of the case, said that the 1981 Louisiana balanced treatment law, which had also been challenged (see *EDWARDS v. AGUILLARD*) would have a better chance in the courts if there were no appeal in Arkansas confusing the issue (Edwords 1983, 43). "We've lost the battle," said creationist leader Duane Gish, "but we haven't lost the war" (*Miami Herald*, January 6, 1982). Creationist activists would simply redirect their energies, away from seeking legislation to the ongoing practice of pressuring school boards, teachers, and textbook committees. Following the *McLean v. Arkansas* decision, the number of creationist bills introduced in state legislatures dropped and no more have been passed (Larson 1985, 162). The issue of requiring the teaching of CREATIONISM by law would not be finally settled, however, until the U.S. Supreme Court's *Edwards v. Aguillard* decision in 1987.

METEORITIC DUST

See SOLAR SYSTEM.

MOLECULAR BIOLOGY

See BIOLOGY.

MONKEY

See PRIMATE.

MOON

See SOLAR SYSTEM.

MORPHOLOGY

See ANATOMY.

MOTH, PEPPERED

See ADAPTATION.

MUTATION

See GENETICS.

NATURAL SELECTION

The central concept of *Darwinism*, the theory of biological EVOLUTION set forth by English naturalist Charles Darwin (1809-1882) in his book *On the Origin of Species by Means of Natural Selection* (1859). The essence of Darwinism is that as more individuals of a species are produced than can possibly survive, any individuals who vary, however slightly, in an advantageous way "will have a better chance of surviving" and thus be "naturally selected" in the "struggle for existence" (Darwin 1859, 5). Those naturally selected will leave more offspring than others, which offspring, through inheritance of favorable variations, will also be more likely to be selected and leave the most offspring (1859, 61). Darwin (1859, 81) thus defined natural selection in its simplest terms as "the preservation of favorable variations and the rejection of injurious variations" (1859, 61, 81). Such a process will lead over time to "divergence of character," ADAPTATION to environment through "preservation of each profitable deviation of structure and instinct," and EXTINCTION of "less-improved forms" (1859, 223, 459). In this way "the innumerable species, genera, and families of organic beings," wrote Darwin (1859, 458), "have all descended . . . from common parents, and have all been modified in the course of descent."

Darwin chose the term *natural selection* for his theory because of the analogy between this naturally occurring evolutionary mechanism and the *artificial selection* practiced for ages by MAN in the breeding of ANIMALS and PLANTS. The two main differences between artificial and natural selection, according to Darwin (1859, 82-83), are, first, that man can act "only on external and visible characters," whereas "nature cares nothing for appearances" but only for advantageous variation; and, second, that Nature has "an incomparably longer time at her disposal." It must also be appreciated that unlike man, natural selection is not an intelligence or planner but rather what zoologist Richard Dawkins (1986, 5) calls a "blind, unconscious, automatic process" with "no purpose in mind." Natural selection leads to a biological entity's adaptation solely on the basis of that entity's present structure and whatever favorable genetic variation may occur or be already present in the entity's genes when environmental conditions change, a critical juncture in the struggle for existence. Natural selection, as Francois Jacob (1977) has aptly described it, works "like a tinkerer," always making do with odds and ends and never knowing what the outcome will be. Indeed, how often the outcome of nature's tinkering is not adaptive is readily apparent in the fact that more than 99 percent of all species that have ever existed have gone extinct (Mayr 1988, 106; see EXTINCTION).

Darwin was not the world's first evolutionist, but his theory of "descent with modification through natural selection" (1859, 459) was revolutionary because here, finally, was a theory that offered a convincing mechanism—natural selection—by which evolution might occur. Upon reading the *Origin*, British naturalist Thomas Huxley (quoted in Mayr 1964, xv) remarked, "How extremely stupid not to have thought of that." The book was controversial, of course, not only because of the perceived conflict between divine creation and any theory of evolution but because Darwin's theory seemed to do away with *teleology* or the concept of a purpose in nature. The theory replaces design by a Creator (see DESIGN ARGUMENT) with the impersonal process of natural selection as an explanation for adaptation. Darwin presented so strong a case, however, that most of the world's scientists came to accept biological evolution as a result of the *Origin*, even though the genetic causes (*mutation* and *recombination*) of the variations on which natural selection works remained a mystery—"the laws governing inheritance," admitted Darwin (1859, 13), "are quite unknown." The key to solving that mystery was the long-ignored experimental work in heredity by Gregor Mendel (1822-1884), an Austrian botanist and monk who crossbred peas in his monastery garden. Mendel's work came to light in 1900 and led to the modern SCIENCE of GENETICS. It was the integration of genetics and Darwin's theory of natural selection that became known in the 1940s as the *modern synthesis* or Neo-Darwinian theory of evolution. Natural selection is now generally defined as *differential reproduction* (Mayr 1970, 107; Simpson 1964, 24; 1967, 268), which means—in the words of paleontologist George Gaylord Simpson (one of the founding fathers, with biologist Ernst Mayr and geneticist Theodosius Dobzhansky, of the modern synthesis [Moore 1984, 511])—"the consistent production of more offspring, on an average, by individuals with certain genetic characteristics than by those without those particular characteristics" (Simpson 1964, 20). This differs from Darwin's concept only in emphasis, Darwin emphasizing survival and extinction more than reproduction (Simpson 1964, 20) but certainly recognizing the crucial importance of "success in leaving progeny" (Darwin 1859, 62). As for the religious controversy over Darwinism, mainline Christian denominations eventually became willing to live with the notion that evolution is GOD's method of CREATION (a concept called *theistic evolution*; see GOD and WORLD VIEW), though the idea is condemned to this day by fundamentalists.

Many examples can be cited of small-scale evolutionary change or *microevolution* due to natural selection, observable over relatively short periods of time. (Large-scale evolutionary change, or *macroevolution*, occurs too slowly, of course, to be observed in a human lifetime, and must therefore be inferred from microevolution and other areas of evidence such as the FOSSIL RECORD, comparative ANATOMY, and molecular BIOLOGY.) Bacteria evolve resistance to antibiotics within our own bodies, based on simple Darwinian evolution: As bacteria mutate, the few mutations that happen to be immune to the antibiotics will be naturally selected to survive and multiply. This makes development of new antibiotics necessary, so that medical researchers are continually "in a race to stay ahead of bacterial evolution" (Futuyma 1982, 118). Similarly, about half of the more than 500 species of INSECTS that do significant damage to crops have in a few decades developed resistance to insecticides (Newell 1985, 184). A major problem in trying to develop a vaccine against AIDS is the fact that the disease-causing virus mutates so frequently: After infection, thousands of different strains of the virus may soon exist in a single AIDS patient (Marx 1988; Patlak 1989). In this "viral Darwinism," most of the mutations probably soon die out (most mutations in any type of organism are harmful or neutral), but those that prove advantageous to the virus in reproducing and in attacking the body's cells are naturally selected (Patlak 1989). (Not surprisingly, creationist leader Henry Morris [1989], a Baptist fundamentalist, believes that AIDS is one of God's "various judgments" against sin.) Perhaps the most frequently cited example of directly observed natural selection is the adaptive change from light to dark color—for protection from predators on pollution-darkened trees—of peppered moths in England during the Industrial Revolution (see ADAPTATION). Selection can also be observed at work in controlled laboratory experiments, a favorite subject of such experiments being the fruit fly *Drosophila*. Because of its small size and short life cycle, the fruit fly can be raised in great numbers over many generations for genetic study (Rubin 1988).

Proponents of the creation "science" movement do not deny that natural selection occurs (the evidence is simply too strong for denial), but they claim that it operates only on genetic variations built into the originally created "kinds," variations that allow each kind to adapt to differing environments (Gish 1985, 35; Morris 1970, 33; 1985b, 51). This argument is based, of course, on the biblical concept of kinds, categories of which creationists have no established definitions but which are much broader than the scientific concept of species (see TAXONOMY). Creationists argue that natural selection working on a "chance" process such as mutation could not produce any major evolutionary change or any favorable change at all. As Henry Morris (1978, 7) puts it, "a *random* process could never produce an ordered structure for selection to 'select.'"

There are at least three flaws in this creationist contention. First, "random" mutations are not mutations that appear from thin air. Mutations, caused by genetic copying errors (see GENETICS) and various types of radiation, are "random" only in the sense that they arise irrespective of any adaptive need. Mutations within a given species are nevertheless highly constrained genetically; they can arise only within a very restricted range (Mayr 1988, 98), and should therefore not be confused with pure chance. Secondly, mutations can be neutral, neither favorable nor unfavorable, and thus remain in a population's gene pool unexpressed until some environmental change tips the balance. To quote Michael Ruse (1986, 19), a population can have "masses of variation to draw upon" when an adaptive need arises, so that at least some variations in the stockpile "will probably do the job." Thirdly, evolutionists today do not claim that natural selection working on genetic variation is alone sufficient to produce macroevolution or new species. There is much debate among modern evolutionists about what factors in addition to natural selection contribute to major evolutionary change. It is now generally believed, for example, that geographic isolation plays an important role in the origin of new species. The proponents of PUNCTUATED EQUILIBRIA feel that Darwin placed too much emphasis on *phyletic gradualism*, the gradual transformation of one species into another (Eldredge and Gould 1972). The punctuationalists emphasize instead a relatively rapid splitting of a geographically isolated species into two or more new species. They do not deny, however, the role of natural selection in the process (Eldredge and Gould 1972, 206, 223). Creationists like to claim that debates among evolutionists are evidence that evolutionary theory is in disarray, that it is, in Duane Gish's words (1987, i), a "rotting theory," when in fact debates are a sign of intellectual health and vigor (Gould 1984a, 119-120). Debate is essential to scientific progress and is evidence that SCIENCE is at work.

To creationists evolutionary theory is a moral issue (see EVOLUTION and WORLD VIEW), and they often attack what Morris (1984a, 112) calls Darwin's "awful legacy" by attacking not Darwin's theory of natural selection but rather the excesses of a popular sociopolitical philosophy with which Darwin had no involvement. This philosophy, which came to be known as *Social Darwinism*, developed from the writings of Herbert Spencer (1820-1903), a Lamarckian evolutionist (see LAMARCKISM) who believed that social progress is based on "survival of the fittest" (a term coined by Spencer). Social Darwinism was seen as a justification for laissez-faire capitalism, imperialism, the concept of "inferior" races or ethnic groups, and opposition to all forms of welfare (Futuyma 1979, 10).

Spencer's philosophy, popular in Victorian England and early twentieth-century America, led to social injustices, but it was Spencer's philosophy, not Darwin's. Darwin adopted the term "survival of the fittest" in later editions of the *Origin*, but he used it in reference to natural selection as originally conceived and not as applied by Spencer and others to society. If Darwin is nevertheless to be held responsible by Christian fundamentalists for all the social injustices perpetrated in the name of "survival of the fittest," then it would be equally valid to hold Christianity responsible for all the social injustices—such as religious wars, the burning of religious dissenters, and all manner of ecclestiastical fraud and corruption—committed in its name down through the ages. When ICR cofounder Tim F. LaHaye (1975, 5) claims that the theory of evolution has "devastated morals, destroyed man's hope for a better world, and contributed to the political enslavement of a billion or more people," he is clearly attacking Spencerian social thought, not Darwin's theory of biological evolution.

NEANDERTHAL MAN

See MAN.

NEBRASKA MAN

The popular name of a fossilized tooth discovered in Nebraska in 1917 and mistakenly identified by paleontologist Henry Fairfield Osborn as that of a manlike ape. The tooth was actually that of an extinct peccary, a MAMMAL related to pigs. The error was acknowledged in 1927, but creationists won't let evolutionists forget it. "A scientist made a monkey out of a pig," says creationist Duane Gish (1985, 188), "and the pig made a monkey out of the scientist!"

John Wolf and James S. Mellett (1985) provide an excellent account of what happened. The tooth's discoverer, geologist Harold Cook, submitted his find to the eminent paleontologist Osborn in 1922. Osborn stated that it looked "100 percent anthropoid." He announced to the world the discovery of *Hesperopithecus* ("western ape") *haroldcookii*, "irrefutable evidence," in Osborn's words, "that the man-apes wandered over from Asia into North America." Many experts were skeptical, but British anatomist Grafton Elliot Smith went so far as to assist the *Illustrated London News* with a full artistic reconstruction of Nebraska Man. In 1925 other fossil finds at the Nebraska site cast doubt on Osborn's identification, which was retracted two years later. Osborn, as Wolf and Mellett explain, had been misled by associated fossil material originally found at the site and by what Cook himself, years before the discovery, prophetically described as "the startling resemblance" of peccary premolars to anthropoid teeth. Osborn's judgment may also have been clouded, Wolf and Mellett believe, by a desire to embarrass William Jennings Bryan, a Nebraskan and three-time presidential candidate who in the early 1920s was leading a fundamentalist movement to have the teaching of EVOLUTION banned from America's public schools (see SCOPES TRIAL). Osborn mockingly referred to Bryan as "the most distinguished Primate which the State of Nebraska has thus far produced."

A French paleontologist rightly called Nebraska Man "a lesson for paleontologists with too vivid an imagination" (Wolf and Mellett 1985, 34). Creationists love to retell the story as another way to disparage evolutionists (see also PILTDOWN MAN). What creationists fail to mention is that SCIENCE is a self-correcting process, that error and correction are one of the ways by which science advances (Futuyma 1982, 64; Moore 1984, 472; Newell 1985, 58; Wolf and Mellett 1985, 41). Creationists also disserve their audiences by presenting mythology about Nebraska Man as fact. They habitually state that testimony about the tooth and even the tooth itself—creationist accounts vary—were presented as evidence in the famous 1925 Scopes trial (see McIver 1987 and 1988b). According to televangelist D. James Kennedy, defense attorney Clarence Darrow not only confronted William Jennings Bryan on the witness stand with the Nebraska Man evidence, but brought in Henry Fairfield Osborn to testify (McIver 1987, 14). The fact is that according to the court record, not one mention of Nebraska Man was made by anyone during the course of the Dayton, Tennessee, trial (McIver 1988b, 2; Wolf and Mellett 1985, 39). Several scientists were in Dayton to testify in defense of evolution (though the judge did not allow them to do so), but Osborn was not among them. Osborn had already received the first specimens from the renewed Nebraska field work that would discredit his identification of the tooth. Little wonder that during the Scopes trial he stayed "out of reach in New York" (Wolf and Mellett 1985, 39).

So a tooth, says creationist Thomas Heinze (1973, 51), was "all that was needed by some 'experts' to construct (a) whole man." It is relevant to note that in 1987, creationist Carl Baugh of Glen Rose, Texas, announced the discovery of "Glen Rose Man" or "Little David" (or, to use Baugh's "scientific definition," *Humanus-Davidii-Glen Rosii*), a fossil specimen from Cretaceous rock about 100 million years old (Hastings 1987). The INSTITUTE FOR CREATION RESEARCH (*Acts &*

Facts 17[12]:3, 5) reported that the fossil, if it indeed proved to be human, would bolster the case for the Glen Rose "man tracks" (alleged human footprints contemporaneous with dinosaur tracks; see DINOSAUR). And what exactly was the fossil in question? A tooth—now found to be that of a Cretaceous FISH (Hastings 1989). Perhaps the creationists need to be reminded of their own pointed advice (Morris 1985b, 201): "The mistakes of the past by expert anthropologists should not be forgotten."

NOAH'S ARK

See ARK, NOAH'S.

NOAH'S FLOOD

See FLOOD, NOAH'S.

PALEONTOLOGY

See FOSSIL RECORD; GEOLOGY.

PALUXY RIVER

See DINOSAUR.

PEKING MAN

See MAN.

PHYLETIC GRADUALISM

See NATURAL SELECTION; PUNCTUATED EQUILIBRIA.

PHYSICS

The SCIENCE that deals with the forces, properties, and interrelations of *matter* and *energy*. Physics covers various areas relevant to the CREATION/EVOLUTION controversy; these are treated in detail in separate entries and will be mentioned only briefly here. Creationists reject the BIG BANG theory of the UNIVERSE expanding from a primeval explosion or *singularity*, even though expansion is indicated by strong astronomical evidence (see ASTRONOMY) and is predicted by RELATIVITY (Einstein 1952, 133-134). They equate the basic forces of nature with the workings of "the power of God." The leaders of the creationist movement are Christian fundamentalists (see CREATIONISM) who believe that some 10,000 years ago an originally static universe was created by GOD as described in the biblical book of Genesis, which they consider to be literal history (Gish 1985, 23-24; Ham 1989a; Morris 1984a, 47; see BIBLE). Thus creationist leader Henry Morris (1972, 232) states that there is "no better scientific explanation" for the nuclear and electromagnetic forces than Hebrews 1:3: "(Jesus) is upholding all things by the word of his power." Morris (1984a, 69) also sees the universe as a "witness to the Lord Jesus Christ" through *quantum mechanics*, in that the dual (wave-particle) nature of light is analogous to the "hypostatic union" of God and MAN in Christ. Morris sees Christ's divine-human nature exemplified also in the equivalence of mass and energy (see RELATIVITY).

Creationists love to talk about THERMODYNAMICS, a branch of physics dealing with heat. Though there is apparently not one thermodynamicist in the creation "science" movement, the creationists argue (fallaciously) that the thermodynamic principle of *entropy* makes evolution impossible. The creationists equate entropy or increasing disorder with "God's Curse" upon the world as a result of man's fall (see ADAM AND EVE). The creationists would revise *geophysics*, the physics of the EARTH, with their argument that the earth's *magnetic field* is decaying exponentially and cannot be more than 10,000 years old (see GEOMAGNETISM). They touch on *astrophysics*, the physics of STARS and other heavenly bodies, with Morris's (1978, 66-67) suggestion that "apparent disturbances in the stars and planets" are caused by warfare between good and bad angels. And they get into *nuclear physics* by questioning the validity of the rock-dating process, based on radioactive decay rates, called RADIOACTIVE DATING. In other words, creationists question the competency of the world's nuclear physicists. Why? Because rocks, according to biblical chronology, simply *can't* be billions of years old. "We are forced to the conclusion, as Bible-believing Christians," says Morris (1978, 89), "that the earth is really quite young" and that all those radioactive measurements "have somehow been misinterpreted."

PILTDOWN MAN

A fraudulent fossil hominid *species* found in a Piltdown, England gravel pit in the early 1900s. It consisted of a skull with a human cranium (ultimately determined to be that of a medieval woman) and an apelike jaw (in fact that of a 500-year-old orangutan). Thought by many scientists of the time to be ancestral to MAN, the species was named *Eoanthropus* ("Dawn Man") *dawsoni*. It was not exposed as a hoax until the 1950s, following years of scholarly study and dispute, gaining Piltdown Man the reputation of being "the greatest hoax in the history of science" (Blinderman 1986, 4). The identity of the hoaxer remains a mystery, though prime suspects include the discoverer Charles Dawson and the Jesuit paleontologist Pierre Teilhard de Chardin.

Creationists Duane Gish (1985, 188) and Gary E. Parker (1987, 154) point to the long success of this hoax as evidence that scientists can be biased and believe what they wish to be true. The same point has been made by paleontologist Stephen Jay Gould (1980, 108-124), whom Gish quotes at length. (Creationists love to quote, mainly to misquote, Gould, perhaps their favorite whipping boy next to SATAN and Charles Darwin. Creationist leader Henry Morris [quoted in Banach

1988, 18] has described Gould as "an Evolutionist-Atheist-Marxist, whatever you want to call him.") It is important to remember, however, that the Piltdown hoax was exposed by scientists themselves, not by creationists. SCIENCE is a questioning, "self-correcting" process (Futuyma 1982, 164; Moore 1984, 472; Newell 1985, 58), and in the case of *Eoanthropus dawsoni* the process worked well in the end. The great lesson of Piltdown, said anthropologist Earnest Wooton (quoted in Blinderman 1986, 241), is that "it's wrong to fix on scientific discoveries as irrevocable." To quote the ever quotable Gould (1984a, 120) on the subject of certainty: "There ain't no such animal" (a fitting epitaph for *Eoanthropus*).

PLANT

Any member of the *Plantae* kingdom of multicellular organisms. Plants manufacture their own food through *photosynthesis,* the conversion of sunlight into usable energy, and produce oxygen in the process. They are the form of LIFE that supports all other life forms, for ANIMALS must have oxygen to breathe and must eat either plants or other animals for the energy they need. *Botany* is the study of plants.

Plant fossils are often fragmentary and hard to identify, plants having no skeleton and thus being prone to total decay (Calder 1983, 266). Thus, while there are many good fossil remains, there are also many questions about plants' evolutionary history left unresolved by the FOSSIL RECORD. Plants are believed to have evolved from green algae. There is fossil evidence of simple land plants as early as the mid-Ordovician period, some 450 million years ago (Cloud 1988, 335, 401). Land plants underwent rapid diversification during the Devonian, Carboniferous, and early Permian periods, with flowering plants or *angiosperms,* possibly evolving from seed ferns, making their first appearance during the Cretaceous period about 150 million years ago (Franks 1979; Bisacre et al. 1984, 52; Margulis and Schwartz 1988, 260). Since their relatively late arrival, flowering plants have virtually "inherited the earth" (Wallace et al. 1988, 491). They comprise over 90 percent of the 275,000 known plant species (Goldberg 1988, 1461).

Creationists, concerned as they are with keeping animals out of MAN's pedigree, have had little to say about plants, though man of course is kin to plants too. (Based on molecular data, the common ancestor of animals and plants would have lived about 1.2 billion years ago [Jukes 1983, 130; for discussion of molecular EVOLUTION, see BIOLOGY].) Creationist biologist Gary E. Parker (1987, 133) of the INSTITUTE FOR CREATION RESEARCH (ICR) quotes his "professor of paleobotany" (no name or date is provided) to the effect that all we find in the fossil record are different varieties of plant types that we still have today, "plus extinctions in many cases." Parker basically argues that there is nothing about fossil plants that is "hard to understand" as compared with plants today. And indeed there shouldn't be, since "a striking feature of higher plants," in the words of biologist Robert B. Goldberg (1988, 1462), "is their apparent morphological simplicity"—masking "a very complex genetic program" that cannot be seen in fossils.

ICR president Henry Morris (1978, 37-38; 1984a, 236, 370-371; 1985b, 211) argues that plants are not even living things "in the Biblical sense." He bases this view on the fact that plants have no consciousness, breath, or blood. (Plants transpire but do not breathe as do animals. They are bloodless but have tissue that conducts water and food.) This is an important concept to Morris and other ICR creationists because they are biblical literalists who believe that death did not enter the world until after the sin of ADAM AND EVE (Ham 1989b; Morris 1985b, 211; Stambaugh 1989). Since plants, according to the BIBLE, were the food of man and animals before man sinned, plants must therefore not be alive, the creationists reason, else eating them would certainly have killed them. Now it is true that breath and blood in biblical times were both looked upon, in the words of biblical scholar Bruce Vawter (1977, 46, 133), as "the sign and source of life," and that "bloodless, unbreathing" vegetation was seen as "simply a part of the earth itself." It is certainly true as well that plants have no consciousness as do animals. In the early 1970s a book entitled *The Secret Life of Plants* became a bestseller, claiming that plants can perceive and respond to human emotions, appreciate music, and even predict natural disasters. This is nonsense, of course, since plants have no nervous system to allow any such perceptions or feelings (Galston and Slayman 1979). It is quite arbitrary, however, for Morris to exclude plants from the living because plants are "not conscious life" (1985b, 211) or because they lack breath or blood (1984a, 370-371). While biologists have no generally agreed definition of life, they do not consider consciousness, breath, or blood to be required attributes (see LIFE). Morris and his colleagues wish to exclude plants from life on biblical, not on scientific, grounds. Plants and animals share the same genetic code (see GENETICS), a fact unknown to the biblical writers and the strongest evidence there could be for the unity of life. Plants have molecular genetic processes, says Goldberg (1988, 1461), "that are equivalent in complexity to those found in animals." Yet Morris (1978, 38) defines plants as "merely complex replicating systems of organic chemistry." It is a good thing that plants have no feelings, for they would certainly be hurt by creationists.

PLATE TECTONICS

See CONTINENTAL DRIFT.

POLONIUM HALOS

Tiny rings in certain rocks from the Precambrian eon caused by the radioactive decay of polonium isotopes. (The Precambrian covers all of prehistory down to about 600 million years ago. The age of the rocks in question is about 1 billion years [Wakefield 1987, 20]. For discussion of radioactive decay, see RADIOACTIVE DATING.) For several years polonium halos have been promoted by creationist physicist Robert V. Gentry (1986) as evidence of divine CREATION. The halos have become known as "Gentry's tiny mystery," geologist G. Brent Dalrymple having described them in testimony during the Arkansas CREATIONISM trial (see *McLEAN v. ARKANSAS*) as "a tiny mystery" that SCIENCE has yet to solve (Schadewald 1987).

The mystery of the polonium halos lies in the fact that polonium is a product of uranium decay, yet there are no inner uranium halos to indicate that any significant amount of uranium was present in the rocks. Creationist Paul Ackerman (1986, 110) likens this mystery to "a ship in a bottle": If there was no parent uranium, how did the daughter polonium isotopes get into the rocks? Creationists believe that GOD may have put the polonium there, the halos to be "a permanent silent witness" to the fiat creation of the rocks enclosing them (Morris 1985b, 170). In Gentry's (1986, 32) words, the polonium halos may be "God's fingerprint in Earth's primordial rocks."

This is an excellent example of "invoking the God-of-the-gaps," the ill-advised practice of using the divine as an explanation for what science cannot yet explain. The God-of-the-gaps has been an important element in the historical conflict between science and religion, for such a deity must be "in perpetual retreat with each advance of science" (Huchingson 1982). It seems likely that Gentry's tiny mystery will someday be solved. Indeed, various natural explanations for the phenomenon have already been suggested (see Brush 1983, 71; Wakefield 1987, 31). In the meantime Gentry's case is fatally flawed anyway. Gentry wants to associate the halos with creation, but he is wrong in claiming that the rocks in which the halos are found are among the earth's earliest Precambrian rocks. J. Richard Wakefield (1987) has explained in detail how the rocks containing the polonium halos do not represent the oldest rocks in the region (Ontario, Canada) from which the samples came, but are younger igneous material intruding into older rock units. In short, Gentry's tiny mystery has nothing to do with the origin of the earth's first rocks, unless one is willing to believe that the entire geologically complex area from which the rocks with the halos came was created all at once with an APPEARANCE OF AGE, rather than formed over geologic time (Wakefield 1987).

POLYSTRATE FOSSIL

See GEOLOGY.

POPULATION GROWTH

See SOCIAL SCIENCES.

PRIMATE

A member of the highest order of MAMMALS. The order Primates includes *prosimians* (lemurs, lorises, and tarsiers), *monkeys* (New World and Old World), and *hominoids* (superfamily Hominoidea: apes and MAN). Most primates are arboreal (tree-dwelling), their grasping hands and feet and stereoscopic vision (forward-facing eyes) being early ADAPTATIONS to climbing and moving through trees (Lewin 1988c, 34; Stebbins 1982, 308). Most also have tails, the exceptions being apes and humans, though a few human beings have been known to be born with tails (see VESTIGIAL ORGAN). There are over 150 species of primates, found mostly in the tropical rain forests (Lewin 1988c, 32, 34).

The first primates evolved from primitive placental mammals about 70 million years ago and looked more like tree shrews or rodents than monkeys (Godfrey 1983a, 200). The primate FOSSIL RECORD is relatively poor—primates being quick and not as susceptible as some other, less wary ANIMALS to unexpected disasters and burial (Stebbins 1982, 310)—yet the record is good enough to contradict consistently the creationist claim (Gish 1985) that there are no TRANSITIONAL FORMS. The early primate *Cantius trigonodus*, with a strong grasping toe and forward-facing eyes but with primitive teeth not adapted to a diet of tree fruits, bridges the gap nicely between ground-dwelling placental mammal and prosimian ("premonkey") primate (Strahler 1987, 476). The mosaic characteristics of *Aegyptopithecus* ("Egyptian ape") *xeuxis* of the Oligocene epoch (about 35 million years ago) represent the primate form ancestral to monkeys and hominoids (Brace 1983, 249; Stebbins 1982, 314). Apes called the dryopithecines, including *Proconsul*, lived 10 to 20 million years ago and are considered the stock from which the common ancestor of modern apes and humans derived (Lewin 1988c, 42-44; Stebbins 1982, 315). (A dryopithecine descendant, *Ramapithecus*, of which related forms were *Sivapithecus* and *Gigantopithecus*, was once considered a member of man's family Hominidae, but has since been demoted [Lewin 1988c, 44-47; Strahler 1987, 478].) The first hominids, the AUSTRALOPITHECINES of about 4 million to 1 million years ago, may truly be called "apemen." The early man *Homo erectus* represents the transition—whether as a direct australopithecine-modern man link or as an evolutionary cousin—from the australopithecine form to *Homo sapiens* (Brace 1983).

There is evidence from molecular BIOLOGY that man and the apes (chimpanzees, gorillas, orangutans, and gibbons) diverged from a common ancestor as recently as 5 million years ago (Sarich and Wilson 1967), and that man and the chimpanzee remain almost 99 percent genetically identical (Gribbin and Cherfas 1982; Mereson 1988). Some taxonomists now include the chimpanzee, gorilla, and orangutan in the hominid family of man (Brooks 1988, 15-16; Lewin 1988b), and even Linnaeus, the eighteenth-century creationist whose classification scheme made him the father of TAXONOMY, had trouble generically distinguishing man from ape and admitted that perhaps, were it not for the certainty of ecclesiastical wrath, he should have "called man an ape, or vice versa" (quoted in Futuyma 1982, 99).

Creationists argue that anatomical and genetic similarities such as exist between man and the other primates are evidence, not of common descent, but of common creative design. But the DESIGN ARGUMENT offers no answer to an interesting question posed by philosopher Michael Ruse (1982, 5): "Why should God have made such grotesque parodies of humankind as orang-utans and gorillas?" The most logical answer is that man and the apes were not designed at all, but are simply divergent products of EVOLUTION by NATURAL SELECTION, with man having benefited immensely by the shift of Miocene forebears from the trees to open savannas. But logical explanations often make little difference; there will always be those who refuse to believe, on emotional or religious grounds, that man and the ape are related. As British prime minister Benjamin Disraeli (quoted in Seldes 1967, 630) expressed it: "The question is this: Is man an ape or an angel? I am on the side of the angels."

PROGRESS, EVOLUTIONARY

See EXTINCTION.

PSEUDOGENE

See BIOLOGY.

PSEUDOSCIENCE

See SCIENCE.

PSYCHOLOGY

See SOCIAL SCIENCES.

PUNCTUATED EQUILIBRIA

The theory, proposed in 1972 by paleontologists Niles Eldredge and Stephen Jay Gould, that most evolutionary change occurs in relatively rapid, isolated events of *speciation* (the splitting of one species into two) punctuating long periods of *stasis* or nonchange.

Punctuated equilibria is essentially a variant form of the widely accepted theory of *geographic* or *allopatric* ("in another place") *speciation.* According to the allopatric model, a new species arises when a population becomes geographically isolated from its parent species. The standard view was of a species separating into two halves because of a newly arisen geographical barrier, with the two isolated halves then evolving their separate ways (Mayr 1988, 442-443). In 1954 biologist Ernst Mayr (1954) gave allopatric speciation a new twist. Mayr (1988, 444, 461-462) believes that small bands of immigrants become "peripherally isolated" by settling beyond the normal geographic range of their species. In such an environment they are subject to strong selective pressures (see ADAPTATION and NATURAL SELECTION) that can produce "genetic revolutions," the rapid evolving of new species. Mayr thus refers to these immigrant groups as *founder populations*, and he calls his theory "peripatric" speciation to emphasize the peripheral isolation involved.

Eldredge and Gould's theory incorporates Mayr's. They restate Mayr's view that new species arise when small local populations become peripherally isolated beyond the geographic range of the parent species (Eldredge and Gould 1972, 203). What was new, then—besides the name, coined by Gould (Eldredge 1985, 49)—about punctuated equilibria? For one thing, there was the emphasis on stasis, long periods of nonchange between rare speciation events (Eldredge and Gould 1972, 218, 223; Mayr 1988, 462). For another, there was the application of geographic speciation to "thinking about fossils" (Eldredge 1985, 97). Eldredge and Gould used Mayr's theory as an explanation for the rarity of TRANSITIONAL FORMS in the FOSSIL RECORD. "Most fossils," Gould (1984b, 24) explains, "are the records of large, established central populations." If a new species arises from a peripheral isolate beyond the range of the parent species, we will likely not meet the new species until it invades the ancestral range. Thus we find the ABRUPT APPEARANCE of new forms in the fossil record. This scenario, Eldredge and Gould (1972, 197, 217) believe, better explains the rarity of transitional fossil forms than does *phyletic·gradualism*, the idea, emphasized by Darwin in his *Origin of Species*, that new species evolve by the gradual transformation of one species into another. The punctuational theory does not deny that EVOLUTION by gradual change occurs (Eldredge 1985, 145), it simply holds that "most evolutionary change is concentrated in events of speciation" (Gould 1984b, 24).

Eldredge and Gould's theory inspired debate among evolutionists and continues to do so. One reason for this reaction was the "newness" of Mayr's theory (proposed almost 20 years earlier) of peripherally isolated immigrants—the theory had been "completely ignored by paleontologists," as Mayr (1988, 461) himself says, "until brought to light by Eldredge and Gould." Other areas of debate are the emphasis on stasis and de-emphasis on Darwinian gradualism. This delights creationists, of course: They see debates among evolutionists as signs of "a house divided" (Morris 1989a), which, as we all know, is a "house that cannot stand" (Mark 3:25). Creationist leader Duane Gish (1985, 250) calls punctuationalism "just another indication of the bankruptcy of evolutionary theory." Gish (1985, 247-248) claims that the punctuationalists have in effect announced the death of phyletic gradualism, leaving the theory of evolution with no evolutionary mechanism. (Gish's argument is garbled, since phyletic gradualism is gradual evolutionary change, not its mechanism.) Gish (quoted in Sonleitner 1987, 25) also associates punctuated equilibria, with its rapid speciation events, with "Goldschmidt's 'hopeful monster' mechanism"—referring to the late geneticist Richard Goldschmidt's concept of genetic "macromutations" causing abrupt major changes, evolutionary jumps or "saltations," in morphology or structure (Godfrey 1983a, 209-211). Evolutionists, says the INSTITUTE FOR CREATION RESEARCH (ICR), are "still completely in the dark about the supposed mechanism of evolution," as the "so-called punctuationalists" are now "saying the same thing" that creationists have been saying for years, namely that there are "no true transitional forms in the fossil record" (Morris and Parker 1987, 303; Morris 1985b, viii).

None of these creationist claims are true. As noted above, punctuationalism does not deny that gradual change occurs as Darwin described it. "Gradualism," says Gould (1980, 184), "sometimes works well." The point is that gradualism alone is not sufficient to account for new species. If there were no speciation (splitting of species) but only "the transformation of an entire population from one state to another," there could be no increase in the number of species and "life would cease as lineages became extinct" (Eldredge and Gould 1972, 197). Punctuationalism therefore says that evolutionary change may occur "in either of two modes," phyletic evolution (gradualism) or speciation, and that most change occurs, as the fossil record indicates, through rapid speciation (Gould 1984b, 24)—"rapid" in terms of geologic time meaning "hundreds of thousands of years for the origin of most species" (Gould 1980, 213).

Punctuationalism does not dispense with natural selection, the evolutionary mechanism in Darwin's theory of evolution. As Eldredge and Gould (1972, 223) state, it is the small size of peripherally isolated populations and the alien environment that they encounter beyond the species border that bring to bear "selective pressures" strong enough to produce the "genetic revolution" that speciation requires. Speciation assumes adaptation by natural selection. "It is obvious," says paleontologist Norman Newell (1985, 194), "that a new species must be viable." At the same time, Gould (1984b, 22) points out, "there is nothing in the theory of natural selection that precludes a notion of rapid change during very short periods." Again, by "rapid" or "very short periods" is meant hundreds of thousands of years—not overnight saltations or leaps a la Goldschmidt's "hopeful monster."

Punctuationalists do not say, as creationists claim, that there are "no true transitional forms in the fossil record" (Morris 1985b, viii). Eldredge and Gould speak of "the rarity of transitional forms" (1972, 197), of the fact that there is "precious little in the way of intermediate forms" in the fossil record (Gould 1980, 189). But they are referring here to the rarity (not absence) of fine-scale transitions between species, not to any overall failure of the fossil record to document transitional forms (Godfrey 1984, 177). "Transitional forms are generally lacking at the species level," Gould (1981, 37) says, "but are abundant between larger groups." Eldredge, too, states that "intermediate forms abound" (1982, 120), and cites his own work with trilobites (small, extinct marine arthropods), "connected by a compelling array of intermediates" (1981, 19).

Gould (quoted in Godfrey 1984, 179) has made clear his feeling about the creationist treatment of punctuated equilibria: "It's so utterly infuriating to find oneself quoted, consciously incorrectly, by creationists. None of this controversy within evolutionary theory should give any comfort, not the slightest iota, to any creationist." Debate has been called "the life blood of science" (Cazeau 1982, 34), and for creationists to accuse evolutionary biologists of arguing among themselves, says Eldredge (1982, 52), is to accuse them "of doing science."

QUANTUM MECHANICS

See PHYSICS; UNIVERSE.

RADIOACTIVE DATING

Determining the age of a rock or (in some cases) of a fossil based on the *radioactivity* of a chemical *element* contained in the sample. Some elements are unstable, that is, their atomic *nuclei* will spontaneously decay by emitting particles (*radiation*), so that the *atoms* of the element change from one form (called *parent* atoms) into another form (called *daughter* atoms). This process is called *radioactive decay,* and varying atomic forms of the same element are called *isotopes.* While individual isotopic atoms decay randomly, they decay at a constant rate, a different constant rate for each kind of isotope. Each isotope, then, has its own *half-life,* that is, the time it takes for half the parent atoms of that isotope to decay into daughter atoms. Assuming no daughter atoms were present when a particular rock containing the unstable element first crystallized, it is thus possible, the isotopic half-life being known, to determine the rock's *radiometric age* by measuring the ratio of parent and daughter atoms (Eicher 1976, 121).

There are four methods of radioactive dating that are most commonly used. The *potassium-argon* method measures the ratio of the isotope potassium-40 (half-life 1.3 billion years) and its daughter isotope argon-40. The *rubidium-strontium* method measures the ratio of parent-daughter isotopes rubidium-87 (half-life 47 billion years) and strontium-87. The *uranium-lead* method measures the decay of isotopes uranium-238 and uranium-235 (both occurring in all natural uranium) to lead-206 and lead-207 respectively, thus having a built-in cross-check of the radiometric age (Eicher 1976, 129). The fourth method, *carbon-14,* applies to organic material or fossils (see FOSSIL RECORD). Since fossils occur in sedimentary rocks, they can rarely be dated directly by the other methods, which work best on igneous or once-molten rocks (Valentine 1977, 315-316). The carbon-14 method measures the amount of the isotope carbon-14 still left in once-living matter. The half-life is only 5,730 years, but the carbon-14 method is quite accurate for ages up to 40,000 years. (This method made news in 1988 with the determination that the linen of the Shroud of Turin is of medieval origin, thus the long-venerated shroud cannot be the burial cloth of Christ [Waldrop 1988].)

Creationists who believe (as do the leaders of the creation "science" movement) that the EARTH (indeed the entire UNIVERSE) is only about 10,000 years old (Aardsma 1988, iv) are naturally forced to question the validity of radioactive dating. The radiometric age of the earth's oldest rocks is 3.96 billion years (Monastersky 1989). Based on the radiometric age consistently determined for meteorites (relics of the early SOLAR SYSTEM) and corroborated by radioactive dating of material from the moon (Eicher 1976, 129, 139; French 1981, 76-77; Strahler 1987, 128), the earth is around 4.6 billion years old. When creationists claim that radioactive dating is billions of years in error, they are questioning, in effect, the validity of nuclear PHYSICS, on which radioactive dating—not to mention nuclear energy—is based. Yet that is exactly what they claim, for "the earth," says Henry Morris (1978, 91) of the INSTITUTE FOR CREATION RESEARCH (ICR), "is really only several thousand years old, as the Bible teaches."

Morris (1985b, 137-139), in the ICR textbook *Scientific Creationism*, claims that radioactive dating is based on three invalid assumptions—a closed system, no initial daughter component, and a constant decay rate—and is therefore unreliable. There is no such thing in nature, Morris says, as a closed system, so daughter atoms in rocks can be added or lost. Moreover, there is no way to know that no daughter component was initially present. Third, no process in nature operates at an unchangeable rate, so decay rates can't be always the same.

All scientists acknowledge that there is some uncertainty in radioactive dating as in everything else. Our knowledge of half-lives or decay constants is not precise, but is accurate within one or two percent (Eicher 1976, 121; Valentine 1977, 318). There can indeed be daughter components initially present, but there are ways to estimate and allow for the amount (Gallant 1984, 297-298; Strahler 1987,

131). The greatest source of radiometric inaccuracy is loss of daughter atoms through "the failure of rocks and minerals to remain closed systems" (Eicher 1978, 121). Scientists therefore cross-check radiometric results by using independent laboratories and different samples and whenever possible by using more than one method (Newell 1982, 111). When different methods agree, that is, when they yield *concordant* ages, the ages are considered reliable, there being "very low probability that different isotopic systems with different constants would produce the same results by chance" (National Academy of Sciences 1984, 14). Morris (1985b, 133) claims that radiometric dates are so unreliable that most are discarded, notably when discordant with "the previously agreed-on dates." But the U.S. Geological Survey's Dr. G. Brent Dalrymple (1984, 95, as cited in Strahler 1987, 134) points out that "many tens of thousands" of radiometric measurements by as many as 100 laboratories worldwide have been documented in the scientific literature. Certainly, then, there are enough concordant dates to show that this is a successful method of dating rocks (Raup 1983, 156), that we are not dealing with "a few crackpot samples with wildly varying results, as creationists would prefer to believe" (Eldredge 1982, 103). And even allowing for some degree of error in radioactive dating, "it is inconceivable," says geologist David Raup (1983, 156), "that the error could be anything approaching the difference between billions of years and thousands of years."

The assumption that radioactive atoms have always decayed at the same rate is based on our knowledge of the atom and on the principle of uniformity of natural laws (see UNIFORMITARIANISM) that makes SCIENCE possible at all. An atomic nucleus is shielded from the effects of outside conditions, such as temperature and pressure, by the electrical repulsion of the atom's electrons (Brush 1983, 60; Strahler 1987, 131). There have been attempts to alter decay rates despite this shield by using extreme laboratory conditions not likely to occur in nature. Some small rate variations, ranging from 0.1 to 3.5 percent, have been induced in this way, but not in any isotopes used in radioactive dating (Newell 1982, 108; Strahler 1987, 137, citing Dalrymple 1984, 91). Since scientists have yet to find anything that can alter the decay rates of isotopes used radiometrically, there is no reason to believe that those rates have ever been different (Futuyma 1982, 72). Morris (1985b, 142) suggests that cosmic rays, a reversal of the earth's magnetic field, or a process called free neutron capture could influence decay rates. He fails to mention that the idea of cosmic-ray influence was experimentally tested more than 60 years ago, with no change in decay rate observed beyond the experiment's 1 percent margin of error (Brush 1983, 66). This result also takes the wind out of the magnetic-field reversal argument, by which a reversal would allow more cosmic-ray influx (Strahler 1987, 136). (Morris supposedly doesn't accept the idea of magnetic-field reversals anyway; see GEOMAGNETISM.) As for free neutron capture, this would not change a nucleus's decay rate, it would change the decaying nucleus itself, into a new isotopic form with a decay rate all its own (Kitcher 1984, 162; Strahler 1987, 137, citing Dalrymple 1984, 88-89).

Ultimately, however, Morris and his fellow young-earth creationists simply can't be argued with. Scientists can refute claim after creationist claim, but creationists can always fall back on the APPEARANCE OF AGE, a concept that scientists can't refute because it is utterly untestable. Nothing is as old as it may seem, says this argument, because GOD created everything fully functioning from the start, thus everything has an "appearance of age" (Moore 1976, 61; Morris 1985b, 209-210; Whitcomb and Morris 1961, 238). Radioactive minerals, therefore, could have daughter atoms already present at CREATION, the processes of which cannot now be scientifically examined (Morris 1978, 94). So we should not be impressed, says Morris (1978, 95), with the "apparent age" of rock formations, for God has told us the "true age" of the earth—principally through biblical genealogies (1967, 63-64)—and "there is no other way of determining it."

RECAPITULATION

See EMBRYOLOGY.

RELATIVITY

A physical theory proposed in two forms by the physicist Albert Einstein (1879-1955). According to the *special theory of relativity*, all the laws of nature, including the constancy of the speed of light in a vacuum, are the same for all observers in relative uniform motion (Einstein 1952). The theory may thus be said to deal with what is absolute or invariant; indeed Einstein considered calling it "invariance theory," but it was the "relativity" of motion that gave the theory its name (Calder 1979, 2; Ferris 1988, 193). The special theory also postulates the equivalence of mass and energy, as given in Einstein's famous equation $E = mc^2$ (energy equals mass times the speed of light squared).

Einstein's *general theory of relativity* deals with gravity, conceives of the universe as a curved, "four-dimensional space-time continuum," and extends the special theory by holding that the laws of nature are the same for all observers regardless of their state of motion (Einstein 1952; 1956, 57-58). The general theory also predicts an expanding UNIVERSE. Interestingly, Einstein first published his theory in 1915, before there was astronomical evidence for expansion. Assuming the universe to be static, Einstein had to insert a "hypothetical term" into his equations to keep the universe from expanding. When astronomer Edwin Hubble discovered the expansion in the 1920s (see ASTRONOMY), Einstein (1952, 133-134) removed the hypothetical term.

The creationist approach to relativity has been rather confused and inconsistent. Young-EARTH creationists, such as Henry Morris and his cohorts at the INSTITUTE FOR CREATION RESEARCH (ICR), have a particular problem with the constancy of the speed of light. They can't explain how a STAR can appear to be billions of light-years away—meaning that the light from that star has traveled billions of years just to reach us—when the universe, by creationist reckoning, is only a few thousand years old. For a time Morris and other "scientific" creationists thought the answer might lie in the calculations of an Australian amateur astronomer named Barry Setterfield. Setterfield claims that light has been slowing down since it was first created, so that it could have had an almost infinite velocity when it first started out just a few thousand years ago (Morris 1984a, 174). However, ICR physicist George Aardsma (1988) has written a devastating critique of Setterfield's "selection of data" and concludes that creationist support for the "decay of the speed of light hypothesis is not warranted." So the best that creationists can do to cut down on the travel time of starlight is to suggest that GOD created the light en route (see APPEARANCE OF AGE).

Creationists see both good and bad in relativity. For example, they construe the "relativity" in relativity as an argument for the existence of God. Since Einstein emphasized that "all frames of reference" in the world "are relative, not absolute," says the ICR, the universe can therefore "have no independent or absolute existence" and must owe its existence to a Creator (Morris 1985b, 20-21). Creationist John N. Moore (1976, 84), on the other hand, sees relativity as morally corrupting because it can be interpreted to mean that "all things are relative." Henry Morris (1972, 230; 1984a, 59-60) likes the equivalence of mass and energy—it exemplifies, he believes, the hypostatic union or "divine-human nature of Christ" (1984a, 69)—and the concept of the space-time continuum, which he uses to link "Space, Time and Matter-Energy" to the Christian Trinity. Yet Morris (1984a, 173) turns around and draws a distinction between "relativistic mathematics" and "the *real world* of human experience" (emphasis added). Morris doubts, for example, the existence in space of *black holes* (incompatible with the creationist concept of a static universe) because their existence "is deduced solely from relativistic mathématics" (1984a, 167). Morris clearly wants to have his cake and eat it too, choosing only what he likes about relativity though it is all based on the "relativistic mathematics" he disparages.

RELIGION

See BIBLE; CREATIONISM; GOD; SCIENCE; WORLD VIEW.

REPTILE

A member of the class Reptilia of cold-blooded vertebrate (backboned) ANIMALS. The class includes *snakes, lizards, turtles, crocodiles,* and *alligators.* (The word Reptilia comes from a Latin word that means "creeping.") Reptiles were the first vertebrates to become fully land-dwellers, evolving from AMPHIBIAN stock about 300 million years ago, thanks largely to a reptilian innovation (to be passed on to BIRDS and some MAMMALS) called the *amniotic egg* (Dixon 1988, 58; Dowling 1985, 422). The mosaic fossil creature *Seymouria* is representative of the amphibian-reptile evolutionary transition (Wallace, King, and Sanders 1981, 644). The early or *stem-reptiles* gave rise to a variety of lineages, including the DINOSAURS and the flying reptiles called *pterosaurs* (Keeton 1980, 1055). Reptiles so dominated the EARTH during the Mesozoic era (280 million to 65 million years ago) that it is known as the Age of Reptiles. A transitional group called the *mammal-like reptiles* gave rise to mammals, who inherited the earth following the EXTINCTION of the dinosaurs and many other creatures at the close of the Mesozoic. The more than 5,000 living species of reptile are only a shadow of the Mesozoic reptilian heyday (Dowling 1985, 422).

In the "scientific" creationist view, there was no Age of Reptiles. The earth, according to the INSTITUTE FOR CREATION RESEARCH (ICR), is only about 10,000 years old (Aardsma 1988, iv). Dinosaurs didn't rule the earth, they were contemporaries of MAN—the "younger ones" may even have been aboard Noah's ark (J. Morris 1989b; see ARK, NOAH'S). For the sake of argument, however, ICR creationists often discuss the FOSSIL RECORD as if the earth really were a few billion years old. And they argue that the fossil record contains no evidence for either an amphibian-reptile evolutionary transition or a reptile-mammal transition (Gish 1985, 76-78; Morris 1985b, 83-84). The ICR's Duane Gish (1985, 77) argues that *Seymouria,* being a creature of the early Permian, could not be ancestral to reptiles since it post-dates the reptiles by at least 20 million years.

Gish's argument, to an unsuspecting lay audience, would seem to make perfectly good sense. But it is based on a distortion of the meaning of TRANSITIONAL FORM. A form is transitional if it represents a mixture of characters of two groups of organisms, thus clearly indicating that one group evolved from the other. This does not mean that a particular transitional form was necessarily in the direct line of descent. *Seymouria* was obviously not the direct ancestor of reptiles. Rather, *Seymouria* and the reptiles likely shared a common ancestor (Kitcher 1982, 113), with *Seymouria* undergoing less change, and thus more closely resembling the ancestral form, than its reptilian cousins. (For the creationist argument against the transitional nature of the mammal-like reptiles, see MAMMAL.)

SATAN

The Judeo-Christian-Islamic devil or personification of evil. Satan (Hebrew *adversary*) first appears in the BIBLE as a divine messenger, sent by GOD to inflict woes upon an innocent MAN in order to test him (Job 1:6-12). During the intertestamental period, the Hebrew concept of a cosmic devil grew rapidly, possibly under the influence of Persian Zoroastrianism (Cavendish 1983, 627; Hiers, 1974, 40-41; Russell 1977, 217-218), and Satan emerged full blown in the New Testament as the proverbial Prince of Darkness. The tradition that Satan was originally an archangel named Lucifer ("light bearer") who rebelled against God is based on interpretations of Isaiah 14:12 (dealing with a tyrant's downfall), Luke 10:18 ("I saw Satan fall like lightning from heaven"), and Revelation 12:7-12 (referring to a war in heaven and the fall of Satan and his angels).

Satan is still viewed as an actual being by Protestant fundamentalists. "He is indeed a powerful and subtle being," says creationist Homer Duncan (quoted in Kurtz 1985, 42). "I know this because I have had dealings with the old boy for over fifty years." In recent years more Catholics have had to deal with him too, Pope John Paul II having announced that "the demon is still alive and functioning in the world" (*Gainesville [Fla.] Sun*, May 25, 1987). Creationist leader Norman Geisler (quoted in Gilkey 1985, 76) claims to have personally known "at least twelve persons who were clearly possessed by the devil." Kelly L. Segraves (1975, 103), head of the Creation-Science Research Center in San Diego, stated in a 1975 book (not long after the trend-setting horror film *The Exorcist* had made exorcism—the expulsion of evil spirits—a household word) that there are so many cases of demonic possession "one merely needs to read the daily newspapers to verify their existence."

Creationist leader Henry Morris believes (1963, 77; 1970, 71; 1984a, 109-110) that Satan originated the concept of EVOLUTION to deceive mankind. Morris hypothesizes (1982b, 71-76) that Satan first revealed this "grand delusion" to Nimrod and his priests in a sort of "long-range strategy" session at the tower of Babel (see BABEL, TOWER OF). Morris also believes (1978, 66-67) that there is an ongoing cosmic war between the archangel Michael and his angels and Satan and his angels (Revelation 12:7), and he sees in this heavenly warfare "a potential explanation" for such things as "the fractures and scars on the moon and Mars" (see SOLAR SYSTEM).

Creationists also consider Satan to be responsible for unidentified flying objects (UFOs). Materials on the demonic nature of UFOs have been distributed by Master Books, the publishing arm of Morris's INSTITUTE FOR CREATION RESEARCH (see Bennetta 1988a). Segraves (1975) tells us in his book *Sons of God Return* that UFO pilots are "fallen angels and followers of Satan," appearing to contactees as visitors from elsewhere in the galaxy in order to deceive earth's inhabitants and "prepare the way for the antichrist." Geisler (quoted in Gilkey 1985, 77), testifying for the creationist defense in the 1981 Arkansas CREATIONISM trial (see *McLEAN v. ARKANSAS*), stated that UFOs are "satanic manifestations for the purposes of deception." And how did Geisler know that UFOs exist? He read it, he said, in *Reader's Digest*. (For a discussion of the UFO phenomena by scientists, see Page and Sagan 1972.)

Many fundamentalists believe that Satan reigned in a "pre-Adamic" world before his fall. This notion combines the so-called gap theory of CREATION with the Lucifer tradition. The gap theory assumes two creations, the one described in the first verse of Genesis ("In the beginning God created the heavens and the earth") and the familiar six-day creation that followed. The "gap" refers to an indeterminate span of time (accounting for the geologic ages) between the first creation and some cataclysm that left the original earth "without form and void" (Gen. 1:2). According to gap-theory creationists such as televangelists Jimmy Swaggart and the late Herbert W. Armstrong, Satan ruled the original earth until it became corrupted with sin by his rebellion and fall and was destroyed by God (McIver 1988c). Morris and the ICR represent the better-known "young-earth" school of CREATIONISM and reject the gap theory. Satan's sin and fall, say the young-earthers, occurred in heaven, not on earth, and there is "no scriptural reason" to connect Satan with some pre-Adamic earthly cataclysm (Morris 1985b, 231-243).

Since Morris considers evolutionary theory to be a satanic conspiracy, it would seem logical to assume that he sees evolutionists as flat out doing the work of the devil. Morris (1982a, 10-11) allows, however, that this is not the case: Creationists do not consider evolutionists to be "agents of the devil, as some have complained, but only as unknowing victims of the one who has 'deceived the whole world' (Revelation 12:9)."

While the existence in the world of evil—one historian (Russell 1977, 17) aptly defines it as "abuse of a sentient being"—requires no proof, there is no rational basis for its cosmic personification. Belief in Satan or any other supernatural entity is inherently religious and without any scientific foundation. There are neuropathological explanations for alleged cases of demonic possession (see Beyerstein 1988), which was thought in ancient and medieval times—even by Jesus in the New Testament (see Hiers 1974) and obviously (witness Geisler and Segraves) by creationists today—to be a cause of mental illness (Coleman, Butcher, and Carson 1980, 25-36). Morris (1963, 83) indulges in Orwellian newspeak, moreover, when he includes satanism on his list of the evil fruits of evolutionism. It is biblical religion, certainly not evolutionary theory, that established the concept of Satan and continues (in its fundamentalist forms) to promote belief in the old boy's existence.

SCIENCE

The endeavor to understand the UNIVERSE by repeated observations of natural phenomena, and the body of knowledge (Latin *scientia*) tentatively established by such observations. The *scientific method* generally involves forming a *hypothesis* based on the data or *facts* of observation, which hypothesis is then tested through experiments; a hypothesis that passes all tests becomes a generally accepted *theory*, which in turn may pass such rigorous further tests as to be considered scientific *law*. It is important to note that in science we are thus dealing with "different levels of probability" (Cloud 1983, 139), never with certainty. Nothing is ever proved to be true, things are "at best highly probable" (Cuffey 1984, 269). "There is no 'right' theory," says astronomer Martin Cohen (1988, 2), "there are only wrong ones, that fail to explain, predict, or at least accommodate known facts."

What Cohen has essentially described is the concept of *falsifiability* (see Popper 1968). For a theory to be meaningful, it must make testable *predictions* and be potentially falsifiable. Consider the theory of EVOLUTION: Any number of conceivable fossil discoveries—a fossilized MAN, for example, in Silurian rock—would show evolutionary theory to be false. For the theory predicts that fossils, in undisturbed rock layers, will be found in sequence from simpler to more complex forms (see FOSSIL RECORD and GEOLOGY). Evolutionary theory is put to the test (among other ways) each time a new fossil is found, and so far it has passed every test. Theories that pass tests in this way become ever stronger, for the tests are evidence that the theories in question are reliable, that they say something valid about reality.

CREATION by a supernatural being is not a falsifiable hypothesis. There is no conceivable test that could show that the universe was not divinely created. Being untestable, creation is therefore not a scientifically meaningful concept. It is a religious belief. Scientists do not interject religious or supernatural concepts into their speculations because science is a way of seeking natural explanations for observed phenomena. This does not necessarily mean that "most scientists are unbelievers" as stated by creationist leader Duane Gish (1985, 21). (The distinguished geneticist Francisco Ayala, a former Catholic priest, testified in the Arkansas CREATIONISM trial [see *McLEAN v. ARKANSAS*] that many working scientists who subscribe to the theory of evolution are devoutly religious [Overton 1982, 330].) It simply means that there is no place for supernaturalism or miracles in scientific method. The assumption that there are natural laws, and that there is a constancy to those laws, is what makes science practicable (Gould 1984b, 11). Those who mix supernaturalism with science and try to sell it as science, as do the "scientific" creationists, are selling an unnatural mess. They are selling *pseudoscience.* The primary objective of any pseudoscience—astrology (see Culver and Ianna 1988) and parapsychology (see Alcock 1984; Gardner 1981; Hansel 1984) are enduring examples—is not an impartial search for truth but rather the validation of a claim, a fixed idea (our fate in the STARS, extrasensory perception, and so on), supportable only by misuse or distortion of any relevant data (Newell 1985, 24). The fixed idea of creation "science" is that the universe was supernaturally created and is nonevolutionary, when in fact scientists do not know how the universe first came into being (see CREATION) but have accumulated a multidisciplinary body of evidence for cosmic and (in our corner of space) biological evolution that is compelling.

Creationists have admitted that creation "science" is not really science (Morris 1982a, 9; 1985b, 4-10). They do not, of course, call it pseudoscience; rather they acknowledge that creationism is ultimately based on faith. But they argue that the theory of evolution is also based on faith (it is a tenet, they say, of the "religion" of HUMANISM), and that the concept of creation is therefore no less scientific than that of evolution. So both concepts, they say, should be considered in public school science courses as competing scientific "models" of origins—the so-called *two-model approach* promoted by the INSTITUTE FOR CREATION RESEARCH (ICR). But as Frederick Edwords (1981, 20) has rightly observed, such an equal-time approach in a science class amounts to "the betrayal of a public trust," for it implies that informed scientific opinion is equally divided on the creation/evolution issue, which is certainly not the case. The theory of evolution, in the words of the National Academy of Sciences (1984, 22) is "the most fundamental organizational concept in the biological sciences." The obvious purpose of the two-model approach is to let creationism in through the back door. The creationists who promote the approach (and, in the case of the ICR, stand ready to sell schools the teaching materials) are on record as believing that evolution is scientifically "absurd" (Morris 1982b, 184) and "totally irrational" (Moore 1976, 93), and that Genesis, in the words of the ICR's Ken Ham (1989b), is "foundational to the rest of the Bible, true science, true history, true philosophy, etc." So why aren't these people demanding, instead of equal time, a total expunging from the public schools of such an "absurd" and "irrational" theory? Because creationists have already tried and failed (after temporary success) to make the teaching of evolution illegal (see SCOPES TRIAL and *EPPERSON v. ARKANSAS*). The two-model approach is a case of "if you can't beat 'em, join 'em," but it is hardly the way to teach science.

Creationists argue that evolution is not science because it cannot be directly observed. Science, says creationist leader Henry Morris (1963, 58), "is supposed to be based on observation, what one actually *sees* in the real world." It is not true that evolution cannot be directly observed (see EVOLUTION and NATURAL SELECTION), but even if it were true it would not disqualify evolution as a valid scientific theory. While direct observation is a scientific ideal, in practical terms science must often depend on indirect observation or inference. We cannot "see" an electron, yet it is basic to atomic theory. We cannot "see" gravity, we see only its effects as predicted by the theory of gravity. These theories are so well established that no one disputes them. Similarly, the theory of evolution is so well supported by evidence that to most scientists it is beyond reasonable doubt. But evolution, because of what it says about genealogy, upsets many laymen who are quite down-to-earth about gravity. They call evolution "only a theory." But that's a use of the word *theory* in its vernacular sense of mere speculation that is different from its scientific use. As already noted, a theory in science is a well-tested hypothesis, and that describes evolution.

The condition of science education in America has become a national shame and, in the long run, a threat to national security (see National Commission 1983; Byrne 1989; Lawrence 1989; Meisler 1989). In a

1989 report by the Educational Testing Service on the math and science achievement of schoolchildren from several countries, the American children ranked near the bottom (Byrne 1989). According to a survey funded by the National Science Foundation (Culliton 1989), only about 6 percent of Americans can be called scientifically literate. About 50 percent reject the idea of human evolution. Less than 50 percent know that the earth revolves around the sun in one year. Eighty-eight percent believe that astrology has scientific significance. One bright if ironic finding: A whopping 97 percent of Americans know that hot air rises.

It remains to be seen how effective the current educational reform movement in America will be. Yet even as that movement is struggling to get off the ground, creationists are as determined as ever to have creationism taught as science in the public schools. Their legislative efforts have failed (see *EDWARDS v. AGUILLARD*), but creationists, able always to find grassroots support, have been effective in the past in pressuring teachers, school boards, and textbook selection committees to make concessions to the cause. Such local-level action is once again the main focus of creationist strategy.

Some scientists suggest that creationism might well be usefully included in public school science courses—"as an example of bad science" (Wilson 1983, xxii). But such classroom use should properly be the decision of science educators, not fundamentalist pressure groups who think evolutionary theory is the work of the devil (see SATAN). America needs to reverse what in effect has been a policy of "unilateral educational disarmament" (National Commission 1983, 23) as it heads toward the twenty-first century in an increasingly competitive world. To quote paleontologist Niles Eldredge (1982, 149), "Scientific illiteracy will send the United States on a surer and straighter path to hell than ever will that idea we call evolution."

SCOPES TRIAL

The famous 1925 "monkey trial" in Dayton, Tennessee, in which high school teacher John T. Scopes was convicted of teaching the theory of EVOLUTION in violation of Tennessee's Butler Act. The new Tennessee statute was one result of a nationwide Christian fundamentalist movement in the 1920s to promote state laws against the teaching of evolution in public schools. This movement should not be construed as an early version of the "scientific" creationist movement. The fundamentalist movement of the twenties was not an attempt to put biblical CREATIONISM on a "scientific" basis but was aimed purely at banning Darwinism from the schools. "The beast jungle theory of evolution," said fundamentalist Amzi Dixon (quoted in Bates 1976, 20), "robs a man of his dignity, marriage of its sanctity, government of its authority, and the church of her power and Christ of his glory." The movement gained a nationally prominent spokesman in 1922 in the personage of former secretary of state William Jennings Bryan, a three-time presidential candidate now reduced to being what H. L. Mencken called "a tinpot pope in the Coca-Cola belt" (Gould 1983, 277). "All the ills from which America suffers," said Bryan, "can be traced to the teaching of evolution. It would be better to destroy every other book ever written, and save just the first three verses of Genesis" (Cole 1983, 14; Marsden 1984, 96).

The Butler Act of 1925 prohibited any Tennessee public schoolteacher from teaching "any theory that denies the story of the Divine Creation of man as taught in the Bible," and from teaching that "man has descended from a lower order of animals" (Zetterberg 1983, 386). As soon as the act became law, the American Civil Liberties Union (ACLU) offered to pay the expenses of anyone in Tennessee willing to test the law's constitutionality in court. Some civic-minded folks in Dayton thought it would be good to make their little town the scene of the crime. John Scopes, a young Dayton athletic coach and PHYSICS teacher who had briefly substituted for the high school's regular BIOLOGY instructor, agreed to take the rap, though he couldn't remember if evolution had even been discussed in class (Cole 1983, 14; Gould 1983, 265). The whole plot, Scopes later recalled, "was just a drugstore discussion that got past control" (Gould 1983, 270). What began in Robinson's Drug Store, however, soon promised to be a spectacle: The ACLU sent famed trial lawyer Clarence Darrow to Dayton to defend Scopes, and famed orator Bryan volunteered to assist in the prosecution. "Scopes isn't on trial," Darrow announced. "Civilization is on trial." Darrow warned of a "reign of bigotry," saying "No man's belief will be safe if (the fundamentalists) win." Bryan, not to be outdone, declared, "If evolution wins Christianity goes" (Newell 1985, 10). The Dayton trial drew worldwide attention, and newspaper columnist Mencken, there to cover the story, described the Dayton scene, with "tinpot pope" Bryan followed everywhere by "gaping primates," as "better than the circus" (1925a, 161; 1925b, 163).

The trial itself was a bit anticlimactic. Several scientists were on hand to testify for the defense, but were not allowed by Judge Raulston to do so. The whole issue, said the judge, was whether Scopes had taught evolution, and Scopes had admitted as much (Cole 1983, 15). Modern creationists persistently claim that NEBRASKA MAN was discussed during the trial, but the court record indicates no such thing (McIver 1988b; Wolf and Mellett 1985). (Nebraska Man consisted of a fossil tooth, believed by some scientists in the twenties to be that of a manlike ape until it was determined, to the unending delight of creationists, to be that of an extinct form of pig.) Creationists also misquote Darrow for the purpose of making him sound, absurdly, like an advocate of the creationists' so-called two-model approach to teaching "origins" (see McIver 1988b). What remains most memorable about the trial is Bryan himself taking the stand as an expert on the BIBLE, with Darrow then proceeding to run "circles of skepticism around (Bryan's) simple literal interpretation" (Cole 1983, 15). Mencken (1925b, 165) wrote vividly of how Bryan "writhed and tossed" on "Darrow's cruel hook," Darrow even luring "poor Bryan" into denying that humans are MAMMALS. Bryan was publicly humiliated (and died a week later), and even though Scopes was convicted (and fined $100), Bryan and his fundamentalist cause were ridiculed internationally, misleading many into thinking that evolution was the actual victor.

Evolution didn't win. To begin with, Scopes's conviction was thrown out on a technicality: Judge Raulston had fined Scopes $50 too much. The ACLU's plan all along had been a quick conviction followed by an appeal, to get the Butler Act ruled unconstitutional.

Suddenly there was nothing to appeal. As Stephen Jay Gould (1983, 273) says, "All that effort down the tubes of a judge's $50 error." Secondly, the fundamentalist crusade continued. By the end of the decade, over twenty state legislatures had debated antievolution measures, and at least five of them—Arkansas, Florida, Mississippi, Oklahoma, and Tennessee—passed restrictive laws (Numbers 1982, 538). Thirdly and most profoundly, biology textbook publishers were left intimidated by the attention that the Scopes trial had received and by the passions it had aroused. There followed a period of almost 40 years in America during which the subject of evolution received drastically reduced treatment in high school biology texts and frequently no treatment at all. This situation did not change until the Russian launching of the satellite Sputnik in 1957 shocked America into a reevaluation of its public school SCIENCE curriculum. The vigorous reform that followed included a reemphasis on evolution in high school biology courses (Edwords 1980, 4; Overton 1982, 310-311). As H. J. Muller (quoted in Simpson 1964, 36) said angrily in 1959 (the centennial of Darwin's book *On the Origin of Species*), "One hundred years without Darwin is enough!" Fundamentalists, of course, disagreed, and the 1960s brought the beginning of the "scientific" creationist movement (see CREATIONISM).

SECOND LAW OF THERMODYNAMICS

See THERMODYNAMICS.

SECULAR HUMANISM

See HUMANISM.

SOCIAL DARWINISM

See NATURAL SELECTION.

SOCIAL SCIENCES

The group of studies that deal with MAN and society. These include anthropology, economics, history, political science, psychology, and sociology. The leaders of the "scientific" creationist movement believe that there are "two basic opposing world views," CREATION and EVOLUTION (Morris and Parker 1987, xii), and that the evolutionary view is "sociologically harmful" (Morris 1982b, 184, 186). Henry Morris, president of the INSTITUTE FOR CREATION RESEARCH (ICR), specifically identifies the following as examples of evolutionary theory's "evil fruit": fascism, Nazism, collectivism, socialism, communism, anarchism, racism, imperialism, laissez-faire capitalism, secular HUMANISM, naturalism, atheism, pantheism, occultism, determinism, existentialism, behaviorism, Freudianism, Taoism, Buddhism, Confucianism, Hinduism, Kinseyism, Social Darwinism, modernism, satanism, materialism, and homosexual activism (1963, 24, 83; 1982b, 182, 186; 1986, 40-41). Lest anything be left out, Morris adds to these ism's "abortion, the drug culture, animalistic morality, and so on" (1986, 40-41).

Much of the work of social scientists is treated by the proponents of "scientific" CREATIONISM with what can only be described as contempt. The theory of evolution, a guiding principle of physical anthropologists, is called by creationists a "delusion" (LaHaye 1982, 5) and "lie" (Ham 1987) that is "absurd scientifically" (Morris 1982b, 184). If the "scientific" creationists are correct that GOD created the entire UNIVERSE only "about 10,000 years ago" (Aardsma 1988, iv), then Morris (1984a, 451) puts it kindly when he says that dating methods used by archaeologists to report man-made structures as much as 32,000 years old (Bower 1986) are "extremely erratic and unreliable." And if historical linguists would only read the biblical book of Genesis, interpreted literally by creationists (see BIBLE), they would therein be informed that mankind's language differences stem from the confusion of tongues at the tower of Babel (see BABEL, TOWER OF), a miraculous event that Morris (1984a, 431) considers "the only meaningful explanation for the phenomena of human languages."

All schools of psychology postulate some degree of determinism—

the doctrine that all events have causes—in terms of genetic and environmental sources of human behavior (Chaplin 1985, 125; Reber 1985, 193; Skinner 1981). This would seem to suggest that ADAM AND EVE (whom creationists believe to be historical characters) and all of their still unborn descendants received cruel and unusual punishment—"God's curse" on mankind, bringing "death and separation from God" (Morris 1984b, 364)—for yielding to temptation by SATAN. The ICR holds, however, that "man was endowed with freedom . . . to obey or not obey," and all the suffering and death in the world since Eden "is proof enough that (man) chose wrongly" (Morris 1985b, 212). A "real science of human behavior," says Morris (1984a, 369), must be built on "the great Biblical truths of the Fall, redemption, and reconciliation," and "the Bible is our only reliable 'textbook' " on the subject.

Presumably, then, the Bible should be a required text in any psychology course—indeed in any social science course. That includes, of course, history. Ancient history as it is taught by historians gets the heave-ho by Morris in less than one paragraph of his book (one of some forty he has written) titled *The Remarkable Birth of Planet Earth* (1978, 47): "Man is a unique creation of God, entirely without evolutionary relation to the animals"; Adam was the first man; and "the present-day nations, tribes, cultures and languages of men have all been derived from the three sons of Noah, after the great flood" (see FLOOD, NOAH'S). Morris (1978, 50) goes on to explain that man owes his "spiritual heritage" to Noah's oldest son Shem, his "scientific and philosophical heritage" to second son Japheth, and "most of his material comforts" to third son Ham.

Mention should also be made of the creationist argument for a young EARTH based on population statistics. If the world population began, says the ICR (Morris 1985b, 167-169), with two people, the population would reach its present size, based on an average annual growth rate of 0.5 percent, in just 4,000 years (Morris 1985b, 167-169). Since the present annual growth rate is about 2 percent, using only one-fourth of that, or 0.5 per cent, leaves plenty of room, it is argued, for long periods of time when the annual growth rate was far below average due to war or pestilence. (Elsewhere Morris

[1982b, 153-154] uses an annual rate of .44 percent, assuming the world population to have started around 4,350 years ago with eight people [Noah, his wife, their three sons, and their wives], Noah's Flood having wiped out everyone else.) If man, we are told (Morris 1985b, 169), has been on earth for a million years as evolutionists claim, the world population, based on an annual growth rate of only 0.5 per cent, would by now have reached a number so astronomical it would exceed the number of electrons in the universe!

This creationist argument sounds impressive—and totally ignores what is known about the history of populations. Population growth has been linked historically to scientific and technological progress, and prior to the agricultural revolution about 10,000 years ago, the world's small populations of humans should have numbered only a few million people in all (Bogue 1985, 404; Hollingsworth 1983, 250). By the beginning of the Christian era, the world population was 200 to 300 million. It took 1,600 years for the population to double, as death rates remained high, and not until the mid-eighteenth century did the annual population growth rate accelerate, due to improvements in hygienic conditions, medical treatment, and food supply (Bogue 1985, 404-405; Hollingsworth 1983, 250-251). The present annual growth rate of about 2 percent is a phenomenon of recent times—the population explosion—and for most of human history the annual growth rate has been nowhere near the 0.5 percent used by the creationists to produce more people than electrons.

The emphasis in the creation/evolution dispute has been on natural SCIENCE, but the ICR (Morris 1985b, 178) clearly states its belief that the most important differences between the creationist and evolutionist WORLD VIEWS lie in the realm of the social sciences, for it is here that world views "impinge most directly on man's personal commitments and daily activities." It is the ICR's position that "true education in every field should be structured around creationism, not evolutionism" (Morris 1985b, iv), and that literal interpretation of the biblical book of Genesis is "foundational" to "true science, true history, true philosophy, etc." (Ham 1989c). Biologist Wayne Moyer (1986, 50) would certainly seem not to exaggerate when he says that "if ever given the force of law, creationism would eventually dominate the curriculum of every subject to which it could lay claim."

SOLAR SYSTEM

The *sun* and all the *planets*, *moons*, *asteroids*, *comets*, and other celestial objects that revolve around it. The four planets (including the EARTH) that are closest to the sun have rocky surfaces and are known as the *terrestrial* (earthlike) planets, while the four large outer planets, with liquid or even gaseous surfaces, are called the *giant* or *Jovian* planets. (The ninth, outermost planet Pluto is an ungiantlike misfit, being perhaps an escaped moon from Neptune [Fisher 1987, 102].) The sun is one of 100 to 200 billion STARS in the Milky Way Galaxy, and there is a growing body of evidence that Vega, Beta Pictoris, and other nearby stars have planets or preplanetary disks orbiting them (Cohen 1988, 176-177; Eberhart 1987, 1988; Kutter 1987, 248; Peterson 1988). This suggests the possibility—we have no way of knowing—that the solar system is not an unusual galactic phenomenon.

The solar system is believed to have condensed beginning some 5 billion years ago from a *nebula* or interstellar cloud of gas and dust. The exact nature of the condensation process is not yet known and is a favorite subject of speculation among astronomers (Eichhorn 1989). One scenario is that the rotating cloud began to contract due to gravity, the process perhaps triggered by the shock wave from a nearby exploding star or *supernova* (Cohen 1988, 168-169). The central region of the contracting cloud condensed—spinning ever faster as a consequence of the *conservation of angular momentum*—until the temperature inside this center became so high that nuclear reactions began. The center thus became the sun with its radiant energy. Centrifugal effects of the early sun's spin caused the rest of the rotating cloud to flatten into a disk (Fisher 1987, 151-157; Hartmann 1985, 228). Dust particles orbiting in the inner part of the disk would collide and aggregate, gravity compacting them into larger bodies that would themselves bump into each other and compact through gravity, there finally emerging from these the four terrestrial planets (Hartmann 1985, 231-233;

Kutter 1987, 243-244). Some of the larger rocky bodies or *planetesimals* that did not become planets may have been captured by the planets as moons; others bombarded the young planets and moons, leaving craters still visible today on the more geologically inactive bodies as well as on earth. Many collisions among planetesimals were violent, causing the objects to break up. Among leftover debris from the early solar system are asteroids, hundreds of thousands of rocky objects now orbiting in a zone between Mars and Jupiter (Eichhorn 1989; Kutter 1987, 241); comets, far-ranging objects made mostly of ice that the sun's heat turns to luminescent gas when they enter the inner solar system (Sagan and Druyan 1985); and *meteoroids*, asteroidal/cometary fragments that vaporize as "shooting stars" or *meteors* when they happen into the earth's atmosphere or that actually land on earth as rocks called *meteorites* when large enough to escape complete vaporization (Strahler 1987, 127). The early solar system's remaining dust and gas were swept away into interstellar space by the *solar wind*, charged atomic particles that began streaming from the solar surface as the sun reached the early *T Tauri* stage of stellar evolution (Kutter 1987, 249; Strahler 1987, 126).

Such is a likely scenario of the solar system's birth and evolution. The generally accepted *condensation* (called also the *accretion* or *nebular*) theory not only explains much of what we observe in the solar system today but is consistent with present theory about the origin of stars in general (see STAR).

Creationists reject, of course, any such evolutionary view of the solar system's origin. According to Henry Morris (1987b, 265-266), an evolutionary hypothesis faces "insuperable difficulties," the most significant being the solar system's "tremendous variety of structures." Such variegated structures, he believes, could not have a common evolutionary origin, though he fails to explain why he believes this. In fact there are perfectly good evolutionary explanations for such variety. The planets vary in chemical composition, for example, because of the varying temperatures that existed in the solar nebula. In the inner nebula, the planetesimals that were to grow into the terrestrial planets were chemically affected by a range of temperatures, how high the temperature for each planet depending on its distance from the sun, while temperatures in the outer nebula, far from the sun's heat, were so low as to give the giant planets chemical compositions drastically different from those of the terrestrials (Kutter 1987, 242-243; Strahler 1987, 122). Planetary moons show variety in that some likely accreted in assocation with their planets while others, such as the two moons of Mars, may well be gravitationally captured asteroids (Kutter 1987, 185; Strahler 1987, 127). The fact that the axial rotations of Venus and Uranus are opposite to those of the other planets is considered by the INSTITUTE FOR CREATION RESEARCH (ICR) to be "incapable of reasonable explanation" in terms of common planetary origins (Morris 1985b, 32). It is in fact possible that something happened *after* the two planets' origin to account for their retrograde rotation. Among the possibilities are collisions with other celestial bodies that passed through the solar system (Eichhorn 1989; Fisher 1987, 101). Such nonevolutionary explanations for some observations do not in any way contradict the theory that the solar system evolved.

The ICR considers it beyond reasonable evolutionary explanation that 99.8 percent of the solar system's mass is concentrated in the sun while 98 percent of the system's angular momentum is concentrated in the planets (Morris 1985b, 31). This was a legitimate concern about half a century ago, before scientists—as the ICR should know—worked out a reasonable explanation. In fact, the explanation revived the nebular theory that had been favored once before and had fallen into disrepute because of the solar mass/angular momentum problem. The solution involves magnetic lines of force: Generated in the early spinning sun, these lines would extend into the surrounding nebula and have a braking effect on the sun's rotation, transferring angular momentum from the sun to the planets (Fisher 1987, 128-136; Hartmann 1985, 233; Strahler 1987, 123). One has to wonder why the ICR cites the solar mass/angular momentum problem without mentioning the fact that it has been theoretically solved.

The solar system's estimated age of about 5 billion years is based on the RADIOACTIVE DATING of meteorites, which are relics of the early solar system. Meteorites have consistently yielded a radiometric age of 4.6 billion years (Eicher 1976, 139). That is also the radiometrically determined age of some of the lunar material from the Apollo missions (Eicher 1976, 129-130; French 1981, 76; Strahler 1987, 128) and is considered to be the age of the earth. (The oldest known rocks on earth are 3.96 billion years old, all rocks earlier than that having been destroyed by the young earth's intense geologic activity.) ICR creationists believe, however, that the entire universe is only about 10,000 years old (Aardsma 1988, iv). To support this biblically based belief, they have no choice but to argue that radioactive dating is unreliable, thus the dates so determined "prove nothing" (Morris 1984a, 269). The creationists might just as well doubt the validity of atomic theory, upon which such dating methods are based (see RADIOACTIVE DATING). Creationists also say that the sun appears to be shrinking, in which case the sun cannot be billions of years old (Ackerman 1986, 55-64; Morris 1984a, 164). Actually measurements have suggested a solar oscillation, with no apparent long-term gain or loss in the sun's diameter (Strahler 1987, 141-142). Such measurements are extremely difficult, however, and the results are uncertain (Eichhorn 1989). In short, that the sun is shrinking is an unwarranted assumption. (In terms of stellar evolution, the sun is going to get larger, not smaller; see STAR.) The ICR (Morris 1985b, 151-152) also claims that at the present rate of influx of *meteoritic dust* from space, the earth and moon after 5 billion years should each be covered with a meteoritic dust layer more than 180 feet thick. This calculation is based on a long outdated, speculative estimate by Hans Pettersson (1960). The ICR seems unaware of data since derived from space technology that reveals a much lower rate of dust influx—a rate that causes the creationist argument to collapse (see Awbrey 1983; Miller 1984, 42-45; Wheeler 1987).

As in any area of scientific inquiry, there remain many unanswered questions about the solar system's origin. Ironically one of the most frustrating questions involves our nearest celestial neighbor, the moon. Compared to other planetary satellites, our moon is so huge that the earth is in effect a binary or double planet, yet there are differences between earth and moon (such as the moon's lack of iron) suggesting that the two bodies did not evolve in the same physical environment (Hartmann and Davis 1975; Strahler 1987, 128). Thus there are problems with both the *capture theory* of lunar origin, by which the earth managed to capture such a large body gravitationally after the latter formed elsewhere in the solar nebula, and the *accretion theory*, by which earth and moon formed as original neighbors. One speculation that may prove to be true is what astronomer William Hartmann (1985, 101) has called the *impact-trigger theory*, first proposed by Hartmann and Donald Davis in 1975. According to this theory, a large body collided with the earth, ejecting iron-poor crust and upper mantle material in the form of a cloud of hot dust that condensed to form the moon. This could explain why the earth and moon seem to have evolved differently, for the theory is in fact "not purely evolutionary"; it depends, rather, on the same type of "chance encounter" as does the hypothesis that a collision caused Uranus's retrograde spin (Hartmann and Davis 1975). We may never know whether the impact-trigger theory is right or wrong. The point is that differences between earth and moon, while still a challenge to astronomers, is hardly what the ICR (Morris 1985b, 32) calls "the final blow" to any evolutionary theory of the solar system.

How do creationists explain the moon's craters, clear evidence of bombardment by debris from the solar system's evolution? ICR president Morris (1978, 66-67) suggests that such features on solar system bodies are evidence, not of cosmic evolution, but rather of continuing cosmic warfare between the angels of SATAN and those of the archangel Michael. Meteorites, then, may be ammo or debris from divine star wars going on in the heavens.

SPECIES

See TAXONOMY; also PUNCTUATED EQUILIBRIA.

SPONTANEOUS GENERATION

See ABIOGENESIS.

STAR

A giant, self-luminous ball of gas, stabilized by a balance (*hydrostatic equilibrium*) between gravity pulling the gas inward and pressure from within pushing outward. A star's light and outward pressure are produced by nuclear reactions, converting matter into energy, in the unimaginably intense heat of the stellar core. The spherical shape, like that of planets and moons, is an effect of gravity (Chaisson 1981, 77; Kutter 1987, 118). Most stars are not "solitary wanderers in space" but are *multiple star systems* (two or more stars orbiting each other) (Hartmann 1985, 351-363). There are countless stars—one estimate is 10 billion trillion (Sagan 1980, 7)—in the UNIVERSE, in billions of great star groups called *galaxies*. Yet the distances between stars and between galaxies are so tremendous that the universe is mostly empty space. The nearest star to our sun (itself an ordinary star) is 40 trillion kilometers away.

Stars evolve. The following is the generally accepted picture of stellar evolution, though that picture is very incomplete, with many details still tentative (Eichhorn 1989). Stars are born in groups in huge interstellar clouds of gas and dust. The gas is mostly hydrogen, the predominant element in the universe. A *protostar* forms when a fragment of the cloud undergoes gravitational contraction, heating up the gas thereby compressed. Contraction and compression continue until temperatures at the center become so high that nuclear fusion begins, hydrogen being converted into helium. Some hydrogen mass in the process gets converted to energy, which is gradually transported to the star's surface and released, producing light—the star "turns on" (Eichhorn 1989; Russell 1983, 50). Thus stabilized, a star spends most of its life (counted in millions of years) burning hydrogen into helium in its core. This is the star's *main-sequence* stage. (Our sun, a middle-aged main-sequence star, converts hydrogen into helium at a rate of 4 million tons per second [Cohen 1988, 35].) When its hydrogen supply nears exhaustion, a star begins showing its age: Its core contracts, its outer layers expand and become reddish, and it becomes what astronomers call a *red giant*. (In a few billion years our sun will be a red giant large enough to practically fill the EARTH's orbit [Russell 1983, 52], burning the old homestead to a cinder.) The contracted core, however, causes the star's central temperature to rise high enough for a different nuclear fusion, namely the burning of helium into the heavier element carbon (Hartmann 1985, 308-310). Thus the giant lumbers on (for millions of years) till its helium is depleted. Then the star begins to contract under its own gravity, the temperature at its core now insufficient to produce further nuclear reactions using carbon. Now a star's mass becomes crucial to its fate. If the star is a smaller one, the gravitational contraction will not be enough to raise the core temperature to a carbon-burning level; instead the star will continue to contract until becoming a densely compressed *white dwarf*, eventually dimming into a "blackened corpse" after radiating the last of its heat (Jastrow 1979, 58-59). A more massive star, however, can generate high enough core temperatures through contraction to induce further nuclear reactions in a series of arrested contractions, each time producing (along with released energy) a heavier element, all the way up to iron. After iron, though, a star is simply out of its element. Iron nuclei will not yield any mass by fusion and therefore are useless as nuclear fuel; the star consequently begins its final contraction (Eichhorn 1989; Jastrow 1979, 59). The most massive stars, however, do not collapse to the white-dwarf state. Some create such enormous inner pressures in collapsing that they explode as *supernovas*, leaving behind small remnants of their cores known as *neutron stars* or *pulsars*. (A pulsar is a neutron star that spins, emitting light and radio energy in sweeping beams "like a cosmic lighthouse" [Waldrop 1989c].) Other stars are so massive that they collapse right past the white-dwarf state: Gravity pulls them literally out of sight. They become *black holes*, points in space so gravity-bound that not even light can escape.

Such is the general picture. It is important to note that it is stellar evolution, in this view, that brought the heavier elements into being. (The process is called *nucleosynthesis*.) The first stars of the early universe had to be made entirely of hydrogen and a little helium. Carbon, oxygen, and other heavier elements were products of "thermonuclear cookery" in the first stars' interiors (Cohen 1988, 66). These new elements were then dispersed into space by the first supernovas, elements heavier than iron being forged and added to the mix by the extraordinary temperatures of the supernova explosions (Jastrow 1979, 60). Thus the interstellar clouds of gas and dust from which new generations of stars would evolve were enriched with these star-made heavy elements. New stars absorbed them, the process to be continually repeated. It may truly be said, then, that all the atoms in our bodies are products of celestial furnaces; made of stellar debris, we are literally "children of the stars" (Silk 1980, 255). (A less romantic interpretation, voiced by chemist David E. Fisher [1987, 127], is that "we are truly the dregs of creation.")

Creationist leader Henry Morris (1978, 57-62) has argued that stars do not change. He has stated that no astronomer has ever seen one kind of star evolve into another kind. But thanks to the 1987 supernova, astronomers have done exactly that: They had observed and named the star Sanduleak before it exploded, they observed the star exploding, and they predicted, based on stellar evolutionary theory, that behind the clouds of gas and debris from the explosion they would find a neutron star or pulsar (Woosley and Phillips 1988). In early 1989, an international team of astronomers announced that a pulsar was found (Peterson 1989; Waldrop 1989c).

It is certainly true that astronomers cannot watch any one star's entire evolution, since one stage of its life may cover millions of years. But they can observe different stars in different stages of evolution, from newborn stars in the Orion Nebula, for example, through main-sequence stars like the sun, to supernovas and pulsars. Through the science of *spectroscopy*—the study of the *spectrum* of light from stars—astronomers are able not only to identify elements in stars but to learn something about temperature, pressure, and other stellar properties (Hartmann 1985, 259-262, 270). And when certain quantities that characterize observed stars are plotted on what is called a *Hertzsprung-Russell diagram*, the evolutionary pattern can be recognized, with most stars found, as expected, along the diagram's main-sequence region (Eichhorn 1989; Ferris 1988, 260; Hartmann 1985, 277-281).

Morris (1978, 59) believes that the stars were made, along with the sun and moon, on the fourth day of the six days of CREATION as related in the BIBLE. His biblical literalism thus obliges Morris to believe that the sun, moon, and stars were made, as Genesis states, three days *after* the creation of light. There is no way, says Morris, of now determining the source of this initial light, though he suggests that the source was GOD's presence. (According to the BIG BANG theory, there was radiation or light in the universe before stars existed [Eichhorn 1989; Weinberg 1977], but the big bang is a theory that creationists reject.) Morris (1978, 61-62) also believes, based on scripture, that the stars are "only several thousand years old." He recognizes that such a young age is impossible if some stars are billions of light-years from earth (meaning their light has required billions of years to reach us). But Morris gets around this by suggesting that God created starlight en route, before the stars even existed, so that stars only appear to be old (see APPEARANCE OF AGE). As for supernovas, Morris (1978, 66-67) suggests that such "apparent disturbances" in the heavens are attributable not to stellar evolution but to the "continuing cosmic warfare between 'Michael and his angels' and 'the dragon and his angels' (Revelation 12:7)" (see SATAN). These are just a few of the ideas of the leader of the "scientific" creationists who want to help shape SCIENCE education in America's public schools.

SUN

See SOLAR SYSTEM; STAR.

SURVIVAL OF THE FITTEST

See NATURAL SELECTION.

TAXONOMY

The classification of PLANTS and ANIMALS (a *taxon* is a category or group). The classification used today is a modified version of the system of Carolus Linnaeus (1707-1778), the Swedish naturalist who is known as the "father of taxonomy." Linnaeus was a creationist, believing that all types of organisms were specially created. Each was seen as a link in the "Great Chain of Being," and Linnaeus undertook his classification, first published in 1735, "for the greater glory of God" (Futuyma 1979, 4-5; Bowler 1989, 59-65). Yet what Linnaeus unwittingly uncovered with his hierarchical arrangement of organisms was a pattern of inherited relationships (Newell 1985, 135), what Darwin (1859) would later call "descent with modification"—in a word, EVOLUTION. (Which, theistic evolutionists might say, is also "for the greater glory of God"; see WORLD VIEW.)

The basic unit of evolution (Mayr 1988, 253) is the *species* (Latin *kind*). Species are generally defined as interbreeding groups or populations that do not interbreed with other such groups (Mayr 1988, 318). It appears that new species may arise either by *phyletic gradualism* (one species transformed into another through gradual change) or by *speciation* (one species splitting into two or more, following the geographic isolation of populations from the parent species) (Eldredge and Gould 1972). Darwin in his *Origin of Species* emphasized gradualism, while punctuationalists such as Niles Eldredge (1972), Stephen Jay Gould (1984), and Steven Stanley (1981) emphasize rapid speciation (see PUNCTUATED EQUILIBRIA). Neither process rules out the other. Darwin's theory of NATURAL SELECTION still reigns supreme with respect to evolutionary change in general, while punctuational theory is still controversial (Maynard Smith 1988, 123-161; Mayr 1988, 144-145, 180, 192-193).

Species are grouped into *genera,* the genus being the next taxonomic category above species. Linnaeus established the practice of referring to an organism by the Latin names for its genus and species (*binomial nomenclature*). MAN, for example, is *Homo sapiens* ("wise man"), his species *sapiens* being a member (the only surviving one) of the genus *Homo*. Genera are grouped into *families* (man's family is Hominidae), families into *orders* (man is a PRIMATE), orders into *classes* (man is a MAMMAL), classes into *phyla* (man's phylum is Chordata), and phyla into *kingdoms* (man is an ANIMAL). (There are also subcategories: Man's family Hominidae, for example, belongs to the superfamily Hominoidea, and man's subphylum is Vertebrata.) Putting it all together, human beings according to taxonomy are sapient hominids, descended from tree-dwellers, who suckle their young, have spinal cords, and, unlike plants, must eat plants or other animals to subsist.

The classification system is not perfect, being somewhat subjective beyond the level of species and failing to recognize TRANSITIONAL FORMS (McGowan 1984, 97; Newell 1985, 136). The fossil intermediate *ARCHAEOPTERYX*, for example, is classified as a BIRD because it had feathers, even though it was essentially a flying REPTILE. There are also different schools of methodology, with cladistics (based on genealogy) and numerical phenetics (based on numerically encoded resemblances) competing with the traditional school (emphasizing genealogy) (Mayr 1988, 268-284; Valentine 1977, 237-238). Still, it is a major prediction of evolutionary theory that all organisms, having descended from a common ancestral form, will share various characteristics in a hierarchical arrangement, a branching family tree (Futuyma 1982, 205). Not only do we find such a branching arrangement in nature, but it is that arrangement that makes classification possible (McGowan 1984, 97). It is how an eighteenth-century creationist, working from nature, came to devise a system that evolutionists feel right at home with.

Creationists view the Linnaean system as arbitrary and use the biblical term *kind* instead of species. According to Genesis 1:21, GOD created all living creatures "after their kind" (Hebrew *min*). However, there is no established creationist definition of what a kind is. Creationist John N. Moore (1976, 28) states that kind is "difficult to define, . . . but can be used generally for any easily recognized living form of animal or plant." Moore does not say why a kind is so easily recognized but so hard to define. Henry Morris (1977, 29), president of the INSTITUTE FOR CREATION RESEARCH (ICR), says that kind denotes an "originally created entity." Morris does not say what "entity" denotes, though he allows that the Linnaean "family" category may be "a good approximation." ICR vice president Duane Gish (1985, 31) defines a "basic type" as including all "variants" derived from "a single stock." Each type or kind has "remained fixed since creation," says Gish (1983, 202), with genetic variation occurring only "within narrow limits." But then Gish (1985, 31) must hedge, saying we can't always be sure "what constitutes a separate kind." But not to worry. There may be "uncertainty," Morris (1985b, 217) says, as to what the BIBLE means by *kind*, but it is "obvious" that "the word does have a definite and fixed meaning." In other words, the biblical writers knew what they were talking about even if we don't.

Why the creationist vagueness about kinds? It really boils down to numbers: ICR-style creationists believe in the literal truth of the story of Noah's Flood (see FLOOD, NOAH'S), and that means they must keep all the ANIMALS that were aboard Noah's ark down to a reasonable figure (see ARK, NOAH'S). And that means forgetting about species, which number in the millions, and using some broader, more ill-defined concept, like kinds. That's how John C. Whitcomb and Henry Morris (1961, 69), in their creationist classic *The Genesis Flood*, whittle down the total number of land-dwelling vertebrate animals aboard Noah's ark—marine creatures, Whitcomb and Morris assume, were left to fend for themselves—to about 35,000 individuals. There was even room on board for the DINOSAURS.

THEISTIC EVOLUTION

See GOD; WORLD VIEW.

THEORY

See SCIENCE.

THERMODYNAMICS

A branch of PHYSICS dealing with heat, engines, and transformations of energy. A favorite argument of "scientific" creationists is that the theory of EVOLUTION contradicts the *second law of thermodynamics.* Creationists have less to say about the *first law of thermodynamics,* since CREATION seems to contradict that law. (A scientific "law," it should be noted, is not something chiseled in stone—there is no absolute certainty in SCIENCE. A law is simply a statement of something that has been observed to occur invariably under certain conditions.)

The first law is equivalent to the principle of the *conservation of energy.* The law states that energy can be neither created nor destroyed. Creationists, however, arbitrarily limit this law. Energy, they say, cannot *now* be created or destroyed. The INSTITUTE FOR CREATION RESEARCH (ICR) argues that energy could not have created itself, so it must have been created, prior to its present conservation, "by a Cause transcendant to itself" (Morris 1985b, 26)—meaning, of course, GOD. The ICR goes on to equate the first law with "God's 'rest' " after the biblical six days of CREATION (Morris 1985b, 212). God "enacted" the first law, we are told by ICR president Henry Morris (1984a, 194-195), after his work of creation was completed. Morris also quotes a New Testament passage (Hebrews 1:3) to explain how energy cannot now be destroyed: Jesus is "upholding all things through the word of his power."

The second law of thermodynamics basically states that the energy in any system that is left to itself will degrade into forms that are less and less useful for work. Another way of saying this is that in any closed system the *entropy,* or quantity of randomness or disorder in the system, will always increase. More simply put, things tend to become disorderly. In an open system—that is, a system in which energy can be gained from an outside source—there may be a temporary increase in order, but the total entropy of the UNIVERSE will nevertheless increase. The EARTH itself is an open system, gaining energy from the sun, and earthly LIFE, dependent on solar energy, represents an increase in order as it develops from simple into complex forms. Yet such decrease in entropy as is seen in biological organisms is more than offset by the vast quantity of energy that the sun radiates daily, energy that is largely wasted, lost into space, so that with respect to the overall universe there is a net entropy increase, a rise in disorder. Nor do we organisms long remain orderly. We age, our parts wear out, we are destined for material extinction. We must gather our rosebuds while we may, for as geologist Preston Cloud (1988, 232) says, "Entropy gets us in the end." The ICR equates this principle of decay and death with God's "Curse" upon "the ground"—that is, upon "the basic physical elements" and "all flesh constructed from those elements"—because of the sin of ADAM AND EVE (Morris 1985b, 211-212). What is the second law, asks the ICR's George Aardsma (quoted in Boxer 1987, 82), if not evidence that the world "is winding down, as God said it would?"

Creationists argue that both cosmic and biological evolution are violations of the second law. On the cosmic level, the ICR's Duane Gish (1986) claims that the BIG BANG theory posits an expanding universe going from disorder to order, a reversal of the second law. But it is actually Gish who seems to have things reversed. The hot, dense early universe was in a smoother, more orderly state than is our present, lumpy, relatively cool universe scattered across billions of light-years (Schadewald 1983, 26; Hawking 1988, 149). Order may arise locally, as in the formation of a planet or snowflake, but there is always an increase in overall entropy. Indeed, if there is insufficient mass in the universe to stop the expansion, the universe will eventually reach a state of maximum disorder, when all usable forms of energy have been expended, when all the STARS have burnt out—the *heat death* of the universe (Barrow 1988, 224-226; Spielberg and Anderson 1985, 154-155).

On the biological level, the creationists see evolution as an increase in order or complexity of life forms and therefore a violation of the second law (Morris 1985b, 38-46; 1987, 4-5, 204-205). They acknowledge that biological development represents a temporary increase in order—an embryo develops into a child, a seed into a tree—but they argue that "two essential criteria" must be satisfied for such growth to occur: There must be a "program" or "code" to direct the growth, and a "power converter" to energize it (Morris 1985b, 43-45). Life has such a program, the genetic code (see GENETICS), as well as a power converter, PLANT photosynthesis. But such a program, says Henry Morris (1982b, 100, 126), "requires a programmer"; it could not have evolved by chance, and evolution needs more than photosynthesis to energize it. So where, Morris (1982b, 100) asks, is "the remarkable cosmic converter" needed to transform "solar energy into evolutionary growth?"

Now a funny thing has happened here. The creationists have rewritten the second law! They have come up with requirements for a program or code, a programmer, and a power converter, where no such requirements exist (Freske 1981). It has been demonstrated, for example, that in far-from-equilibrium conditions (that is, where ample energy is available), new forms of chemical order—what Nobel Prize-winning thermodynamicist Ilye Prigogine (1969; Prigogine and Stengers 1984) calls "dissipative structures"—can arise spontaneously. A flow of energy is all that is required for these ordered structures to form, no code or programmer or power converter is needed.

Living organisms can be viewed as dissipative structures, having originated in the far-from-equilibrium conditions imposed on the earth by solar radiation, and requiring food or sunlight—a continuous input of energy—for their maintenance (Maynard Smith 1989, 255; Prigogine and Stengers 1984, 14). To be sure, there is still much to learn (as in all fields of science) about "the source of biological order" (Prigogine 1969, 23). But a natural occurrence of life, and the ensuing process of evolution by NATURAL SELECTION, appear to be very much in keeping with "the antientropic character of energy flow processes" (Morowitz 1985, 221). Only a miniscule amount of the sun's vast energy is needed to produce biological order on earth (Bakken 1987, 17), and all we dissipative structures can rest assured that we can continue to maintain ourselves and our species for as long as we can without violating any natural law.

TRANSITIONAL FORM

Any past LIFE form that is intermediate between, or has mixed characteristics of, two groups of organisms in the FOSSIL RECORD, thus constituting evidence of one group evolving from another. Creationists persistently claim that there are no transitional forms in the fossil record (see Gish 1985, 249-250; 1986; Moore 1976, 51-53; Morris 1977, 29-32; 1984a, 337; Morris and Parker 1987, 2, 11, 225). It is true that transitional forms are comparatively rare, partly because the odds are strong against *any* dead organism becoming fossilized. It is also a widely held view that many if not most new species arise in small, geographically isolated populations; the new species then appear suddenly in the fossil record upon extending their ranges, while the short-lived intermediate forms are unlikely to be preserved as fossils (Futuyma 1982, 83; see PUNCTUATED EQUILIBRIA). It should also be noted that it is the practice of taxonomists—those who classify fossils (see TAXONOMY)—to place a fossil in one distinct group or another, there being no transitional group in between. This is done for convenience and does not deny (though unfortunately it may hide) a form's transitional nature (Kitcher 1982, 114; McGowan 1984, 97; Raup 1983, 157).

There are nevertheless all sorts of transitional forms in the fossil record to belie the creationist argument that they do not exist. They exist not only at the species level (creationists consider these only "variant forms of the same basic kind" [Morris 1974, 267]) but between major groups: There are intermediates between FISH and AMPHIBIAN (*Ichthyostega*), amphibian and REPTILE (*Seymouria*), reptile and MAMMAL (the mammal-like reptiles), reptile and BIRD (see ARCHAEOPTERYX), extinct ape forms and MAN (see AUSTRALOPITHECINES). But creationists quibble to no end, their basic argument, as paraphrased by biologist Kenneth Miller (1984, 50), being that "the intermediates are not intermediate enough." The creationists consider the reptile-bird intermediate *Archaeopteryx*, for example, to be "100 percent bird" (Morris 1985b, 85) because it had wings and feathers and flew, when in fact *Archaeopteryx* was basically a flying, feathered reptile. What creationists challenge evolutionists to show them, it seems, is a "perfect 10" transitional form, exactly halfway between, say, fish and amphibian. But no such "fishibian," says the INSTITUTE FOR CREATION RESEARCH (ICR), has ever been found in the fossils (Morris 1985b, 82).

The creationists through such arguments exhibit no understanding of the nature of transitional forms. There is no general conversion of all parts of a transitional form at the same time; GENETICS would not produce a smooth gradation of all features of an intermediate such as the creationists with their fishibian require; rather, it is to be expected that the characteristics of an intermediate will be mixed, a pattern called *mosaic evolution* (Dodson 1985, 993; Eldredge 1982, 122; Mayr 1988, 544). Nor does a fossil form need to be in the direct line of descent between two groups to be considered transitional. *Archaeopteryx*, for example, was doubtless not the direct ancestor of birds but rather one of that ancestor's cousins. Similarly the fishlike amphibian *Ichthyostega* was probably a dead end collateral branch of the fish-to-amphibian transition (Panchen 1979). The point is that a cousin of an ancestor is the more likely paleontological find, given the multiple splitting off of species and the general spottiness of the fossil record, and is evidence enough that a transition occurred (Godfrey 1983a, 202).

The fact is, however, that not even a direct ancestral "10" would make any difference to creationists. No such form could be accommodated to their preconceived belief system. Thus creationist leader Henry Morris (1978, 44) states that even the discovery of a fossil intermediate between men and apes—Morris believes that no such intermediate has been found, the australopithecines being "merely extinct species of apes" (1978, 46)—would not be proof of human EVOLUTION. "An extinct ape," says Morris, "could have certain manlike features and still be an ape," and a man could have some apelike features and "still be a man." In other words, no conceivable ape-man transitional form could be anything other than either true ape or true man. Creationists simply cannot allow transitional forms to exist, for to do so would be to admit that evolution has occurred.

TWO-MODEL APPROACH

See INSTITUTE FOR CREATION RESEARCH; *McLEAN v. ARKANSAS*; SCIENCE; WORLD VIEW.

UNIDENTIFIED FLYING OBJECTS (UFOs)

See SATAN.

UNIFORMITARIANISM

The principle in GEOLOGY (and more broadly in all of SCIENCE) that the known laws of nature do not change, hence they have acted uniformly over time. "The present," as the saying goes, "is the key to the past." Championed by Charles Lyell (1797-1875) in his *Principles of Geology*, uniformitarianism won out over the CATASTROPHISM of early naturalists who considered the EARTH too young (based on biblical chronology) for gradual processes to have produced all the geologic changes evident in earth history (Stokes 1982, 41-46). Since the days of Lyell and the acceptance of an ancient earth, however, uniformitarianism and catastrophism have ironically become something of a blend. While the uniformity or constancy of natural laws is the "methodological assumption" that makes science practicable (Gould 1984b, 11), modern uniformitarians recognize that the earth has seen many catastrophes, and that the rates and intensity of geologic processes can vary. As examples, earthquakes and volcanoes must have been much more frequent and severe on the primitive earth (due to the intensity of its interior heat) than at present, and the young earth was heavily bombarded by planetesimals and other debris left over from the solar nebula (Kutter 1987, 307; see SOLAR SYSTEM). Uniformitarians (in its broad sense, all modern scientists) simply hold that the natural laws that underlie all geologic processes, whatever their rates and intensity, do not change.

The fact that "scientific" creationists do not agree with this principle of uniformity says a lot about their strange notion of science. According to the INSTITUTE FOR CREATION RESEARCH (ICR), America's leading "scientific" creationist organization, "present laws and processes are *not* sufficient to explain the phenomena found in the present world" (Morris 1985b, 92). ICR creationists are biblical literalists (see BIBLE) who reject the evidence from modern ASTRONOMY, geology, and PHYSICS that the earth is billions of years old. They offer as science instead a concept called *flood geology*, which rests ultimately on a literal interpretation of the biblical book of Genesis and the belief that all of the earth's layers of sedimentary rock—as much as 12 miles thick—could have been laid down by one catastrophic Deluge (see GEOLOGY and FLOOD, NOAH'S). Thus the ICR sees the Genesis Flood as "the real crux" of the creation/evolution conflict (Morris 1985b, 251). And "uniformitarian" is used pejoratively—like "secular humanist" (see HUMANISM)—in creationist parlance. ICR president Henry Morris (1984a, 130) and vice president Duane Gish (1985, 51) interpret a prophecy (2 Peter 3:3-4) by the Apostle Peter as referring specifically to uniformitarians: "There shall come in the last days scoffers, walking after their own lusts, and saying 'Where is the promise of his coming? . . . All things continue as they were from the beginning of the creation.' " That, of course, misrepresents the uniformitarian view (nature's *laws* continue as they were, not "all things")—but who can argue with the Apostle Peter? Perhaps one can sense, though, that what we are dealing with here—a miraculous Flood, biblical quotations, scientist-bashing (uniformitarians are "latter-day scoffing intellectuals" who exhibit "willful ignorance" [Morris 1984a, 130])—is not science. Indeed, it is safe to say that the ICR's "scientific" CREATIONISM is pure pseudoscience or—to borrow a phrase from the Apostle Paul (1 Timothy 6:20)—"science falsely so called."

UNIVERSE

All that exists. The study of the origin, evolution, and structure of the universe is *cosmology*. (*Cosmogony* refers specifically to ideas about origin.) Most early cosmological models were *geocentric* or EARTH-centered, including the flat, domed earth of the biblical Hebrews and Ptolemy's (second century A.D.) concept of a spherical earth encircled by spheres containing the sun, moon, planets, and STARS. The Ptolemaic view was the cosmological orthodoxy for 1,400 years, until finally displaced by the *heliocentric* or sun-centered system proposed by Copernicus (1473-1543) (see SOLAR SYSTEM). With the invention of the telescope and subsequent advances in the SCIENCE of ASTRONOMY, MAN was to learn that the sun is only one of 100 to 200 billion stars in the Milky Way Galaxy, itself only one of billions of *galaxies* or star systems in the observable universe. In the early twentieth century came Albert Einstein's theory of RELATIVITY and astronomer Edwin Hubble's discovery by observation of something that Einstein had not accepted from his own equations: The universe appears to be expanding. Hubble found that the galaxies are receding from each other at speeds roughly proportional to the distances between them—what is now called *Hubble's law.* This law is based on the *cosmological redshift,* the shift in the spectrum of light from receding stars toward the red end of the electromagnetic spectrum (see ASTRONOMY).

If the galaxies are receding from each other, it follows that in the past they were closer together. If we trace the expansion ever backward, there must have been a time—by current estimates somewhere between 10 and 20 billion years ago—when "the universe was infinitesimally small and infinitely dense," a point (called a *singularity*) of infinite space-time curvature and zero volume (Hawking 1988, 9, 46-49). Such an infinitely hot state is the basis for the BIG BANG theory of how the expanding universe began: "In the beginning there was an explosion" (Weinberg 1977, 5). In 1948, the physicists Ralph Alpher and Robert Herman proposed that if such an explosion occurred there should still be an echo of it in the form of microwave radiation coming from all directions of space and at a certain present temperature (Weinberg 1977, 124). That radiation was discovered in 1964, at almost the exact predicted temperature, by radio astronomers Arno Penzias and Robert Wilson (1979). This *cosmic background radiation* was a striking argument in favor of the big bang theory. The discovery won a

Nobel Prize for Penzias and Wilson and dealt probably a mortal blow to the *steady state theory* according to which new matter is continuously emerging from nothing as the universe expands (Eichhorn 1989; Henry 1980, 939).

The most credible cosmological theory today thus states that there were billions of years of cosmic evolution, beginning with the explosion of a singularity from which matter emerged, with stars and galaxies eventually evolving from clouds of dust and gas, and finally LIFE evolving on at least one tiny speck of the cosmos. (For discussion of the creationist argument that this theory violates the principle of *entropy*, see BIG BANG and THERMODYNAMICS.) In the early 1980s physicist Alan Guth and others supplemented the big bang scenario with a model known as the *inflationary universe:* For a fraction of a second after the explosion the universe went through an "extraordinarily rapid inflation" before the slower present stage of expansion (Guth and Steinhardt 1984; Guth 1988a). The inflationary model helps explain how the big bang could produce a universe as uniform or *isotropic* as ours appears to be. A question still to be answered by cosmologists is whether the universe is "open" or "closed"—that is, will the universe continue to expand forever, or is there enough density of matter that gravitational attraction will eventually halt the expansion and cause the universe to contract, collapsing back toward its original state? At present the density of known matter in the universe is only about 10 percent of that needed to halt the expansion (Hawking 1988, 45-46), so either there is a lot of *dark matter* or *hidden mass* yet to be discovered or the universe will simply continue to expand, eventually suffering *heat death* when all of its stars have burned out (Barrow 1988, 224-226; Spielberg and Anderson 1985, 154-155).

The leaders of the creation "science" movement are Christian fundamentalists who naturally reject most of modern cosmology since they insist upon a literal interpretation of the CREATION account in the biblical book of Genesis. They cling to a static, antiquated view of the cosmos in which the earth, in the words of creationist leader Henry Morris, is "the center of God's interest in the universe" (1984a, 162), with the stars "only of incidental significance as they serve the earth 'for signs and for seasons' (Genesis 1:14) and 'to give light upon the earth' (Genesis 1:17)" (1974, 234).

To defend this view, creationists use a variety of arguments against modern cosmological theory. Morris (1984a, 172) states that the recessional velocities of *quasars* are so high that the usual interpretation of redshift is "very questionable." Quasars ("quasi-stellar radio sources") are generally believed to be galaxies with highly energetic nuclei. (Morris, however, calls them "stars.") The brightness of these objects has fueled much discussion between astronomers and leads some of them to believe that quasars cannot be as distant as their redshifts would otherwise indicate. It has been suggested that gravitation or some other phenomena (see Amato 1989a and Kunzig 1988) may be affecting the shift. But this does not mean, as Morris seems to suggest, that astronomers are about to chuck Hubble's law and, with it, all of big bang cosmology. Most astronomers accept the quasars' great distances and speeds of recession and attribute the tremendous amounts of energy that must account for their brightness to *black holes* or other intensely radiating processes at their cores (Hartmann 1985, 438-442). There is independent evidence, from study of various radioactive isotopes (see RADIOACTIVE DATING) and of stellar evolution, for the age of the universe that the cosmological redshift implies (Weinberg 1977, 29). The theory of universal expansion is also supported by the fact that the universe cannot be static, for if it were, the influence of gravity would have caused it to contract long ago (Hawking 1988, 39; Parker 1988, 38).

Creationists have an ace in the hole, though, about the age of the cosmos. They argue that the universe was "completely functional immediately" when GOD created it; therefore it had to be created with an APPEARANCE OF AGE (Moore 1976, 61). This explains why some galaxies *appear* to be so old and far away that it would take their light (traveling about 6 trillion miles a year) several billion years to reach us. God could have created the light en route (Morris 1978, 61-62). Such an argument allows creationists to have a universe as young as they want it, and they want it, based on biblical interpretation, to be only about 10,000 years old (Aardsma 1988, iv). But by the same logic, says astronomer William Hartmann (1985, 51), "one might imagine that all 'ancient' artifacts and history books were fabricated and placed in museums in, say, 1836." The appearance-of-age argument is completely untestable, unfalsifiable, and thus unscientific.

Stars, says Morris (1985b, 24-25, 35), never change, they do not evolve. But they most certainly do. Stars go through stages, structural changes in their composition, dependent on the successive elements being burned in the nuclear reactions that produce their light. There are stars that are billions of years old and stars that are "younger than the species *Homo sapiens*" (Hartmann 1985, 291). Certainly we cannot watch any one star go through its various changes—it could take billions of years. But we can observe different stars in the various stages of stellar evolution. There are newborn stars, for example, in the Orion Nebula. Our sun is an example of a star in the hydrogen-burning *main-sequence* phase. When stars run out of consumable elements, they die, the more massive ones exploding as *supernovas*. In the case of the star Sanduleak, which exploded in 1987, astronomers have actually seen evolution occur: The star had been observed before the explosion, became a supernova, and left behind a remnant *pulsar* or spinning *neutron star* (see STAR).

But what about cosmogony, the ultimate question of origin? Here, to be sure, creationists should have their strongest case. If the big bang theory is correct, from where, asks creationist John N. Moore (1976, 63), came "the dense particle that exploded" to start the universal expansion? As yet there is no scientific answer. We have no way mathematically to describe what is called the singularity. When we try to trace the universal expansion backward all the way, we are stymied at the very last instant (known as the *Planck time*), for we have approached what theoretical physicist Stephen Hawking (1988, 133) describes as "a point of infinite density and infinite curvature of space-time. All the known laws of science would break down at such a point." One may therefore be tempted to agree with scientists Robert Jastrow (1978), Joseph Silk (1980, 104), and James Trefil (1983), that here is "the moment of creation." But what exactly do these scientists mean by "creation"? If they mean to imply a Creator, are they not departing from science to indulge in religious speculation? (Trefil offers no definition of "creation" even while using the word in his book title; Jastrow—who calls himself an agnostic—indeed means "creation" in a religious sense, for which he has been accused of duplicitously pandering to theists [Schafersman 1987, 6]; see CREATION.) What light, then, can be shed on the mystery? Hawking and other theoretical physicists continue to work toward the dream of a *unified field theory*, in which general relativity (dealing with gravity and large-scale structure) and *quantum mechanics* (dealing with elementary particles) would be unified in a single theory of *quantum gravity* describing the universe as a whole, including its early stages—thus helping us, perhaps, in Hawking's words, (1988, 175) to "know the mind of God."

When creationist Duane Gish (1986) equates the inflationary theory with belief in "outright miracles," he no doubt has in mind the oft-quoted view of inflationary theorist Alan Guth that the universe may have "evolved from literally nothing" (Guth and Steinhardt 1984, 128) and is thus "the ultimate free lunch" (quoted in Bartusiak 1987, 81). But when Guth speaks of inflation and nothingness he does so with reference not to miracles but to quantum mechanics, a branch of physics far removed from everyday, "common-sense" phenomena, a particle-antiparticle realm in which it is indeed possible for matter briefly to appear as "vacuum fluctuations" as if out of "empty space" without violating the conservation of energy (Bartusiak 1987, 79-80; Adair 1987, 223-224). Such quantum phenomena have led some physicists to speculate that the universe itself began as a vacuum fluctuation. (The quantum vacuum is a state of least energy [Adair 1987, 359]; it is not empty space but a "boiling soup" of ghostly *virtual particles* [Crease and Mann 1986, 83].) It is possible, these physicists argue, that all the positive and negative energy in the universe is perfectly balanced, so that the universe's net energy is zero (Bartusiak 1987, 79-80; Ferris 1988, 354-355; Hartmann 1985, 468; Parker 1988, 190-192; Tryon 1989, 156). As Isaac Asimov (1971, 69) has noted in a similar context, "If 0 = +1 + (-1), then something which is 0 might just as well become +1 and -1." Put another way, "Our universe," says physicist Edward Tryon (quoted in Trefil 1984, 101), "is simply one of those things which happen from time to time." It is the strange, fascinating world of quantum mechanics that Hawking and others wish to unify with relativity, hopefully to help answer scientifically the question asked by astronomer Allan Sandage (quoted in Ferris 1988, 351) and that others have asked before him: "Why is there something instead of nothing?"

Morris (1978, 57) has called cosmogony a seeming "tongue-in-cheek charade" that astronomers play. Believing that we can know about cosmic origin only "through divine revelation," Morris characterizes speculation by finite man about the universe's origin as "presumptuous and arrogant" (1984a, 138). Such a characterization is not only antiscientific but is an irrational denial of man's natural curiosity, of the quest for knowledge that has made possible man's intellectual and technological progress throughout his brief time in the cosmos. Man's search for ultimate answers was memorably characterized by Hubble in his last paper (quoted in Sandage 1956, 11): "The search will continue. The urge is older than history. It is not satisfied and it will not be suppressed."

VARIATION

See GENETICS; NATURAL SELECTION.

VESTIGIAL ORGAN

An anatomical structure that is not functional or useful—that bears, as Darwin (1859, 480) expressed it, "the plain stamp of inutility"—but is an apparent vestige or remnant of an organ that functioned in an ancestral species. Examples of vestigial organs are the rudimentary hind limbs that have been found on some whales (Edwords 1983, 5), the useless extra toes that sometimes develop on horses (Gould 1983, 177-178), and the tails that human beings occasionally are born with (Gonzalez-Cruzzi 1985, 41-43; Gould 1982). These are explainable phenomena in terms of evolutionary BIOLOGY but raise an obvious question for creationists. The question, as phrased by Douglas

Futuyma (1982, 48), is simply this: "Why should the Creator have bestowed useless, rudimentary structures on his creatures?"

The standard creationist answer is that almost all organs that were once considered vestigial are now known to be functional. The INSTITUTE FOR CREATION RESEARCH (ICR) states, for example, that "the thyroid gland, the thymus, the coccyx, the pineal gland, the ear muscles, the tonsils, and the appendix" were once thought by evolutionists to be vestigial but "are now known to have useful, and often essential, functions" (Morris 1985b, 76). The statement may be questionable with respect to, say, the appendix. But there is no point in arguing, because the statement may be considered irrelevant. None of the organs that the ICR lists are vestigial organs if one uses the term in the strict sense proposed by the Russian zoologist Alexy Yablokov (1966, as cited in Conrad 1983 and Strahler 1987, 442). In discussing variability in MAMMALS, Yablokov seeks to eliminate vague definitions of vestigial organs by restricting the term to organs that develop in some individuals but are not characteristic of the whole population (Conrad 1983, 9). Vestigial organs would thus not include the appendix and other organs that come as standard equipment (however defective) in humans. Nor do they include organs in a population that are vestigial with respect to original functions but have since acquired other functions. The gill arches that develop in human and other mammalian embryos are certainly evidence of fishy ancestors, but the arches now function as integral parts of the mammalian developmental system, contributing to the production not of gills but of the lower jaw, tongue, and other structures (Mayr 1988, 152; Wallace, King, and Sanders 1981, 888-889). Similarly, the pelvic bones and whiskers of whales, while clearly throwbacks to an earlier evolutionary stage, have important present functions and thus are not, strictly speaking, vestigial (Conrad 1983, 8-9).

There are other organs commonly called vestigial that do not meet Yablokov's definition because they are characteristic of the population. However, these organs also are clearly throwbacks to earlier evolutionary stages. They include the embryonic teeth that disappear before birth in the baleen whale (Newell 1985, 178), the wings of the flightless ostrich (Dodson 1985, 983), the rudimentary hind limbs inside of pythons (Newell 1985, 178), and the teeth of fetal calves that never cut through the gums (Futuyma 1982, 49). All living BIRDS are toothless, yet researchers have been able to grow reptilian teeth from chick embryos because chicks still retain genes for tooth formation (Newell 1985, 178).

Of all truly vestigial organs, the human tail or "caudal appendage" is no doubt the one that for humans hits closest to home. Most mammals have tails, and all normal human embryos have them temporarily (Gould 1982, 41). There have been occasional cases of human newborns retaining the embryonic structure. Creationist Duane Gish (1985, 216) would apparently have us believe that the appendages are only anomalous growths coincidentally located in the caudal region—one possible explanation (quoted in italics by Gish) given by a doctor for a Boston case reported in the *New England Journal of Medicine*. But twenty-three true human tails, capable of spontaneous motion, have been reported in the literature on caudal appendages (Dao and Netsky 1984, as cited in Gonzalez-Crussi 1985, 132). Though surgical removal is without complication, treatment was refused in one case because the parents made money exhibiting their tailed child (Gonzalez-Crussi 1985, 132).

The scientific explanation for truly vestigial organs is apparent in the chicks with the tooth genes. Genes that are normally inactive, retained from a previous stage of a species' evolution, are occasionally reactivated in some individuals, giving rise to vestigial structures (Strahler 1987, 442). The best that creationists can do with truly vestigial organs is to say that they are "degenerative changes within a species" (Frair and Davis 1983, 29). But as geologist Arthur N. Strahler (1987, 442) cogently asks, "Degenerative from what?" One simply would not expect to find hind limbs on a divinely created whale, or tails on humans created "in the image of God" (Gen. 1:27). "Is the Creator," asked the late Christian geneticist Theodosius Dobzhansky (1973, 128), "playing practical jokes?" The question was rhetorical, of course, for Dobzhansky (1955, 242) had long before expressed a logical conclusion: "There is, indeed, no doubt that vestigial rudimentary organs silently proclaim the fact of evolution."

WORLD VIEW

The philosophy of LIFE (from German *Weltanschauung*, "world view") of an individual or community. The INSTITUTE FOR CREATION RESEARCH (ICR), the flagship organization of the "scientific" creationist movement, is fond of describing the CREATION/EVOLUTION controversy in terms of two opposing "world views" (Gish 1988; Morris 1985b; Morris and Parker 1987, xii). "Evolution and creation," says ICR president Henry Morris, "are the only two comprehensive worldviews" (1987, 12); each is "a philosophy of life and meaning, of origins and destiny" (1982a, 9), and the conflict between them "comes down to Biblical revelatory creationism versus evolutionary humanism" (1988a). According to Morris, belief in creation is a great stimulus to responsible behavior, honesty, and consideration for others (1985b, 14), while belief in evolution leads normally to selfishness, aggressiveness, fighting between groups, and animalistic attitudes and behavior (1978, viii).

In logic there is a fallacy known as the *false dilemma*, which is the idea that there are only two possible choices or courses of action in a given situation (Machina 1982, 45). The either/or choice of world view that is posed by the creationists would appear to be a false dilemma. There are times in life when we must make either/or choices, but choosing a *Weltanschaunng* would not seem to be one of them. While there is overwhelming scientific evidence that evolution has occurred, it cannot be said that people who accept this evidence build their whole outlook on life around it or start acting like animals. The notion that creationists are more moral or responsible people than are evolutionists has no empirical basis whatsoever. And even assuming that there were scientific evidence for creation, to present creation and evolution to students in an either/or context would be to mislead the students about the nature of SCIENCE. As geneticist Francisco Ayala (quoted in Gilkey 1985, 141) testified in the Arkansas CREATIONISM trial (see *McLEAN v. ARKANSAS*), "In science it is impossible ever to say there are only two models or theories. Everything is always open; . . . and never are there only two possibilities."

The so-called two-model approach—creation versus evolution—that the ICR wishes to impose on the teachers and students of the public school system is a false dilemma and false science (pseudoscience) too. U.S. District Judge William Overton (1982, 317), in his *McLean* decision, aptly described the two-model approach as "a contrived dualism which has no scientific factual basis or legitimate educational purpose." Its only purpose is the same as that of the unconstitutional Arkansas statute that incorporated it: "the advancement of religion" (Overton 1982, 324).

One must not lose sight of the fact that the leaders of the creation "science" movement are Christian fundamentalists (see BIBLE and CREATIONISM). To fundamentalists the world is indeed very much either/or: light versus darkness, good versus evil, GOD versus SATAN. And they are convinced that no one can be truly religious and be an evolutionist too. In their eyes such compromise raises the ugly head of *theistic evolution.*

Theistic evolutionists are those who believe in God and accept evolution. They comprise a majority of Protestants, Catholics, and Jews in America (Frye 1983a). To creationists this is downright disgraceful. "Away with your silly drivel about theistic evolution," says creationist Homer Duncan (cited in Mattill 1982, 18). A person who must believe in evolution, says Morris (1982, 44), should "leave God out of it." Morris no doubt has in mind such persons as the late Christian geneticist Theodosius Dobzhansky, one of the giants of modern evolutionary theory. Dobzhansky (1973, 127) described himself as "a creationist *and* an evolutionist." (Needless to say, he used "creationist" in a nonfundamentalist sense.) "Evolution," said Dobzhansky, "is God's, or Nature's, method of Creation." If one wishes to believe, for example, that the first living cell, our "Universal Ancestor" (Woese 1983), was divinely created, then left to evolve, there is nothing to disprove it (although origin-of-life research does not include divine intervention [see ABIOGENESIS]). Not all theists, of course, will accept the evolutionary view. It especially leaves creationists (in the fundamentalist sense) "disturbed in their devotions" (Passmore 1983, 570). But if a Creator were to choose evolution as a method of creation, it would certainly seem to be a Creator's prerogative to do so. Could not evolution, compared with fiat creation, even be "the greater miracle" (Midgley 1978, xix)? One need not be a creationist to share the view of the poet Walt Whitman (1855)—no fundamentalist, he—that "a mouse is miracle enough to stagger sextillions of infidels."

YOUNG-EARTH ARGUMENT

See EARTH.

ZOOLOGY

See ANIMAL.

References

Aardsma, George E. 1988. "Has the Speed of Light Decayed?" *Impact* 179.

Abell, George O. 1983. "The Ages of the Earth and the Universe." Pp. 33-47 in Godfrey 1983b.

Ackerman, Paul D. 1986. *It's a Young World After All*. Grand Rapids, Mich.: Baker Book House.

Achtemeier, Paul J., ed. 1985. *Harper's Bible Dictionary*. San Francisco: Harper & Row.

Adair, Robert K. 1987. *The Great Design: Particles, Fields, and Creation*. New York: Oxford University Press.

Albert, Leon H. 1985. "Lucy out of Context." *Skeptical Inquirer* 9(4):364-372.

Alcock, James E. 1984. "Parapsychology's Past Eight Years: A Lack-of-Progress Report." *Skeptical Inquirer* 8(4):312-320.

Allen, Gina. 1981. "Humanism and Diversity of Opinion." *Free Inquiry* 1(2):9.

Amato, Ivan. 1989a. "Expanding a theory for shifting starlight." *Science News* 136:326.

———. 1989b. "RNA Offers Clue to Life's Start." *Science News* 135:372.

Amici Curiae. 1986. *Amicus Curiae Brief of 72 Nobel Laureates, 17 State Academies of Science, and 7 Other Scientific Organizations, in Surport of Appellees*. Edwin W. Edwards et al. v. Don Aguillard et al., No. 85-1513, U.S. Supreme Court.

Anderson, Bernhard W. 1966. *Understanding the Old Testament*. 2d ed. Englewood Cliffs, N.J.: Prentice-Hall.

Anderson, David E. 1987. "Creationism Ruling Hailed, Denounced." *Tampa Tribune*. June 20.

Asimov, Isaac. 1971. "What is Beyond the Universe?" *Science Digest* 69(4):69-70.

———. 1979. *Extraterrestrial Civilizations*. New York: Crown.

———. 1981. *In the Beginning*. New York: Crown.

Asimov, Isaac. 1982. *Asimov's Biographical Encyclopedia of Science and Technology*. 2d rev. ed. New York: Doubleday.

———. 1984. *Asimov's New Guide to Science*. New York: Basic Books.

———. 1989. "Why Should the General Public Have a Better Understanding of Science?" *NCSE Reports* 9(3):17.

Awbrey, Frank T. 1983. "Space Dust, the Moon's Surface, and the Age of the Cosmos." *Creation/Evolution* 13:21-29.

Ayala, Francisco J. 1977. "Phylogenies and Macromolecules." Pp. 262-313 in Dobzhansky et al. 1977.

Ayala, Francisco J., and Valentine, James W. 1979. *Evolving: The Theory and Process of Organic Evolution*. Menlo Park, Calif.: Benjamin/Cummings.

Baier, Kurt. 1988. "Threats of Futility: Is Life Worth Living?" *Free Inquiry* 8(3):47-52.

Bailey, Lloyd R. 1978. *Where is Noah's Ark?* Nashville: Abingdon.

Bakken, George S. 1987. "Creation or Evolution?" *Creation/Evolution Newsletter* 7(6):15-17.

Banach, Michael. 1988. "Henry Morris Visits His Old Haunts." *Creation/Evolution Newsletter* 8(4):17-18.

Barnes, Thomas G. 1983. *The Origin and Destiny of the Earth's Magnetic Field*. 2d ed. El Cajon, Calif.: Institute for Creation Research.

Barrow, John D. 1988. *The World within the World*. Oxford: Clarendon Press.

Bartusiak, Marcia. 1987. "Before the Big Bang: The Big Foam." *Discover* 8(9):76-83.

Bates, Vernon Lee. 1976. *Christian Fundamentalism and the Theory of Evolution in Public School Education: A Study of the Creation Science Movement*. Ph.D. Dissertation, University of California, Davis.

Beattie, Paul H. 1985. "The Religion of Secular Humanism." *Free Inquiry* 6(1):12-17.

Begley, Sharon; Rogers, Michael; and Springen, Karen. 1988. "Where the Wild Things Are." *Newsweek*, June 13, pp. 60-65.

Bendall, D. S., ed. 1983. *Evolution from Molecules to Man*. Cambridge: Cambridge University Press.

Bennetta, William J. 1987. "The Meaning of 'Balanced Treatment.' " *Creation/Evolution Newsletter* 7(5):6-7.

———. 1988a. "It's a Bird! It's a Plane! It's Satan!" *Creation/Evolution Newsletter* 8(2):21.

———. 1988b. "The Rise and Fall of the Louisiana Creationism Law, Part 1: A Bold Trick." *Terra* 26(6):20-27.

———. 1988c. "The Rise and Fall of the Louisiana Creationism Law, Part 2: 'Nonsense on Stilts.' " *Terra* 27(1):16-23.

Berggren, W. A., and Van Couvering, John A., ed. 1984. *Catastrophes and Earth History: The New Uniformitarianism.* Princeton, N.J.: Princeton University Press.

Beyerstein, Barry L. 1985. "Neuropathology and the Legacy of Spiritual Possession." *Skeptical Inquirer* 12(3): 248-262.

Bird, Phyllis A. 1985. "Shem." Page 939 in Achtemeier 1985.

Bird, Wendell. 1987. "Evaluation." Pp. i-iii in Institute for Creation Research 1987b.

Bisacre, Michael; Carlisle, Richard; Robertson, Deborah; and Ruck, John, eds. 1984. *The Illustrated Encyclopedia of Plants.* New York: Exeter Books.

Blinderman, Charles. 1986. *The Piltdown Inquest.* Buffalo, N.Y.: Prometheus Books.

Bliss, Richard B. 1988. "Good Science: A K-6 Plan for Excellence." *Impact* 182.

Bogue, Donald J. 1985. "Population." *Encyclopedia Americana,* v. 22, pp. 402-408. Danbury, Conn.: Grolier.

Boles, Donald E. 1983. "Religion in the Schools: A Historical and Legal Perspective." Pp. 170-188 in Wilson 1983.

Bollier, David. 1984. "The Witch Hunt Against 'Secular Humanism.' " *The Humanist,* Sept./Oct. 1984, 11-19, 50.

Bower, Bruce. 1986. "People in Americas Before Last Ice Age?" *Science News* 129:405-406.

Bowler, Peter J. 1989. *Evolution: The History of an Idea.* Rev. ed. Berkeley: University of California Press.

Boxer, Sarah. 1987. "Will Creationism Rise Again?" *Discover* 8(10):80-85.

Brace, C. Loring. 1983. "Humans in Space and Time." Pp. 245-82 in Godfrey 1983b.

Brauman, John L. 1988. "Frontiers in Chemistry." *Science* 240:373.

Briggs, D. E. G. 1979. "Evolution." Pp. 74-77 in Steel and Harvey 1979.

Brooks, Alison S. 1988. "What's New in Human Evolution." *Creation/Evolution Newsletter* 8(2):15-18.

Brush, Stephen G. 1983. "Ghosts from the Nineteenth Century: Creationist Arguments for a Young Earth." Pp. 49-84 in Godfrey 1983b.

Budge, E. A. Wallis. 1895. *The Book of the Dead: The Papyrus of Ani in the British Museum.* Repub. of British Museum Trustees ed. New York: Dover, 1967.

Bullough, Vern L. 1986. "The Need for Friendship Centers." *Free Inquiry* 6(4):14.

Burke, Richard J. 1986. "Is Secularism Neutral?" *Free Inquiry* 6(4):9.

Byrne, Gregory. 1989. "U.S. Students Flunk Math, Science." *Science* 243:729.

Cairns-Smith, A. G. 1985. *Seven Clues to the Origin of Life: A Scientific Detective Story.* New York: Cambridge University Press.

Calder, Nigel. 1979. *Einstein's Universe.* New York: Viking.

———. 1983. *Timescale: An Atlas of the Fourth Dimension.* New York: Viking Press.

Cavendish, Richard. 1983. "Devil." *Man, Myth and Magic: The Illustrated Encyclopedia of Mythology, Religion, and the Unknown,* ed. Richard Cavendish, v. 3, pp. 625-629. New York: Marshall Cavendish.

Cazeau, Charles. 1982. "Geology and the Bible." *Free Inquiry* 2(3):32-34.

Chaisson, Eric. 1981. *Cosmic Dawn: The Origins of Matter and Life.* Boston: Atlantic Monthly Press.

Chang, Sherwood; DesMarais, David; Mack, Ruth; Miller, Stanley L.; and Strathearn, Gary E. 1983. "Prebiotic Organic Synthesis and the Origin of Life." Pp. 53-92 in Schopf 1983.

Chaplin, J. P. 1985. *Dictionary of Psychology.* 2d rev. ed. New York: Laurel.

Charig, A. J.; Greenaway, F.; Milner, A. C.; Walker, C. A.; and Whybrow, P. J. 1986. "*Archaeopteryx* is Not a Forgery." *Science* 232:622-626.

Cloud, Preston. 1977. "Evolution Theory and Creation Mythology." In *Evolution vs. Creationism: The Schools as Battleground,* ed. Frederick Edwords, pp. 27-29. Amherst, NY: American Humanist Association, 1986.

———. 1983. " 'Scientific Creationism'—A New Inquisition Brewing?" Pp. 134-149 in Zetterberg 1983.

———. 1988. *Oasis in Space: Earth History from the Beginning.* New York: Norton.

Cockrum, E. Lendell. 1985. "Mammal." *Encyclopedia Americana,* v. 18, pp. 189-205. Danbury, Conn.: Grolier.

Cohen, Eugene N., and Eames, Edwin. 1982. *Cultural Anthropology.* Boston: Little, Brown and Co.

Cohen, Martin. 1988. *In Darkness Born: The Story of Star Formation.* Cambridge: Cambridge University Press.

Colbert, Edwin H. 1980. *Evolution of the Vertebrates.* 3d ed. New York: Wiley & Sons.

Cole, John R. 1981. "Misquoted Scientists Respond." *Creation/Evolution* 6:34-44.

———. 1983. "Scopes and Beyond: Antievolutionism and American Culture." Pp. 13-32 in Godfrey 1983b.

———. 1989. "Welcome to New Members." *NCSE Reports* 9(3):3.

Cole, John R., and Godfrey, Laurie R., eds. 1985. "The Paluxy River Footprint Mystery—Solved." Special Issue. *Creation/Evolution* 15.

Cole, John R.; Godfrey, Laurie R.; and Schafersman, Steven D. 1985. "Mantracks? The Fossils Say *No!*" Pp. 37-45 in Cole and Godfrey 1985.

Coleman, James C.; Butcher, James N.; and Carson, Robert C. 1980. *Abnormal Psychology and Modern Life.* 6th ed. Glenview, Ill.: Scott, Foresman and Co.

Connell, Christopher. 1988. "Bush Pursuing Elusive Goals for Education." *Gainesville (Fla.) Sun.* December 28.

Conrad, Ernest C. 1981. "Tripping over a Trilobite: A Study of the Meister Tracks." *Creation/Evolution* 6:30-33.

———. 1982. "True Vestigial Structures in Whales and Dolphins." *Creation/Evolution* 10:8-13.

Conway Morris, Simon. 1989. "Burgess Shale Faunas and the Cambrian Explosion." *Science* 246:339-346.

Cooke, Alistair, ed. 1955. *The Vintage Mencken*. New York: Vintage Books.

Cornell, George W. 1987. "Abrupt-Origin Advocates Say Theories Scientific, Not Religious." *Gainesville (Fla.) Sun*. February 14.

Crease, Robert P., and Mann, Charles C. 1986. *The Second Creation: Makers of the Revolution in Twentieth-Century Physics*. New York: Macmillan.

Crick, Francis. 1981. *Life Itself: Its Origin and Nature*. New York: Simon and Schuster.

Cuffey, Roger J. 1984. "Paleontologic Evidence and Organic Evolution." Pp. 255-81 in Montagu 1984.

Culliton, Barbara J. 1989. "The Dismal State of Scientific Literacy." *Science* 243:600.

Culver, Roger B., and Ianna, Philip A. 1988. *Astrology: True or False?* New ed. Buffalo, N.Y.: Prometheus Books.

Dalrymple, G. Brent. 1984a. "How Old is the Earth? A Reply to 'Scientific' Creationism." In *Evolutionists Confront Creationists*, eds. Frank Awbrey and William M. Thwaites, v. 1, part 3, pp. 66-131. Proceedings of the 63rd Annual Meeting of the Pacific Div., American Assn. for the Advancement of Science, San Francisco, 1984.

———. 1984b. Review of Barnes 1983. Pp. 3-4 in Weinberg 1984.

Dao, A. H., and Netsky, M. G. 1984. "Human Tails and Pseudotails." *Human Pathology* 15:449-53.

Darwin, Charles. 1859. *On the Origin of Species by Means of Natural Selection, or the Preservation of Favoured Races in the Struggle for Life*. London: John Murray. Facs. of 1st ed. Cambridge, Mass.: Harvard University Press, 1964.

———. 1874. *The Descent of Man and Selection in Relation to Sex*. Chicago: Rand, McNally and Co. Repub. of illus. rev. ed. Detroit: Gale Research, 1974.

Davies, Paul. 1983. *God and the New Physics*. New York: Simon and Schuster.

Davis, Horance G. 1986. "Don't Fault the Lord for Taking Time." *Gainesville (Fla.) Sun*, December 18.

Dawkins, Richard. 1986. *The Blind Watchmaker*. New York: W. W. Norton.

Diamond, Jared. 1985a. "If the Creationists Are Right, God is a Squid." *Discover* 6(6):91.

———. 1985b. "Voyage of the Overloaded Ark." *Discover* 6(6):82-92.

Dickerson, Richard E. 1986. "Letter to Dr. Charles B. Thaxton." *Creation/Evolution Newsletter* 6(3):17-18.

Dixon, Dougal; Cox, Barry; Savage, R. J. G.; and Gardiner, Brian. 1988. *The Macmillan Illustrated Encyclopedia of Dinosaurs and Prehistoric Animals*. New York: Macmillan.

Dobzhansky, Theodosius. 1955. *Evolution, Genetics, and Man*. New York: Wiley.

———. 1967. *The Biology of Ultimate Concern*. New York: New American Library.

———. 1973. "Nothing in Biology Makes Sense Except in the Light of Evolution." *American Biology Teacher* 35:125-129.

———. 1985. "Evolution." *Encyclopedia Americana*, v. 10, pp. 734-748. Danbury, Conn.: Grolier.

Dobzhansky, Theodosius; Ayala, Francisco J.; Stebbins, G. Ledyard; and Valentine, James W. 1977. *Evolution.* San Francisco: W. H. Freeman and Co.

Dodson, Edward O. 1985. "The Theory of Evolution." *Encyclopaedia Britannica,* v. 18, pp. 981-1011. Chicago: Encyclopaedia Britannica, Inc.

Dolphin, Warren D. 1983. "A Brief Critical Analysis of Scientific Creationism." Pp. 19-36 in Wilson 1983.

Dulbecco, Renato. 1987. *The Design of Life.* New Haven: Yale University Press.

Eberhart, Jonathan. 1987. "Signs of 'Something' Circling a Star." *Science News* 132:327.

———. 1988. "Seeking New Worlds: More from 'Beta Pic.' " *Science News* 133:311.

Edey, Maitland A., and Johanson, Donald C. 1989. *Blueprints: Solving the Mystery of Evolution.* Boston: Little, Brown and Co.

Edwords, Frederick. 1980. "Why Creationism Should Not Be Taught as Science. Part I: The Legal Issues." *Creation/Evolution* 1:2-23.

———. 1981. "Why Creationism Should Not Be Taught as Science. Part II: The Educational Issues." *Creation/Evolution* 3:6-36.

———. 1982. "Those Amazing Animals: The Whales and the Dolphins." *Creation/Evolution* 10:1-7.

———. 1983. "Decide: Evolution or Creation?" Pp. 163-72 in Zetterberg 1983.

Eicher, Don L. 1976. *Geologic Time.* 2d ed. Englewood Cliffs, N.J.: Prentice-Hall.

Eichhorn, Heinrich K. 1989. Personal communication.

Einstein, Albert. 1952. *Relativity: The Special and the General Theory.* Translated by Robert W. Lawson. 15th ed. New York: Crown.

———. 1956. *Out of My Later Years.* Secaucus, N.J.: Citadel Press.

Eldredge, Niles. 1981. "Do Gaps in the Fossil Record Disprove Descent with Modification?" *Creation/Evolution* 4:17-19.

———. 1982. *The Monkey Business: A Scientist Looks at Creationism.* New York: Washington Square Press.

———. 1985. *Time Frames: The Rethinking of Darwinian Evolution and the Theory of Punctuated Equilibria.* New York: Simon and Schuster.

———. 1987. *Life Pulse: Episodes from the Story of the Fossil Record.* New York: Facts on File.

Eldredge, Niles, and Gould, Stephen Jay. 1972. "Punctuated Equilibria: An Alternative to Phyletic Gradualism." Pp. 193-223 in Eldredge 1985.

Elmer-Dewitt, Philip. 1989. "The Perils of Treading on Heredity." *Time* 133(12):70-71.

Epstein, Aaron. 1987. "Court Strikes Down Law on Creationism." *Miami Herald.* June 20.

Ericson, Edward L. 1973. "Ethical Humanism." Pp. 56-57 in Kurtz 1973.

Fenton, Carroll Lane, and Fenton, Mildred Adams. 1989. *The Fossil Book: A Record of Prehistoric Life.* Revised and expanded by Patricia Vickers Rich, Thomas Hewitt Rich, and Mildred Adams Fenton. New York: Doubleday.

Ferre, Frederick. 1973. "Design Argument." Pp. 670-77 in v. 1, *Dictionary of the History of Ideas,* ed. Philip P. Wiener. New York: Charles Scribner's Sons, 1973.

Ferris, Timothy. 1988. *Coming of Age in the Milky Way.* New York: William Morrow.

Fezer, Karl D. 1988. "Paul Ellwanger Strikes Again." *Creation/Evolution Newsletter* 8(1):5-6.

Fisher, David E. 1987. *The Birth of the Earth: A Wanderlied Through Space, Time, and the Human Imagination.* New York: Columbia University Press.

Flew, Antony. 1982. "Darwin, Evolution and Creationism." *Free Inguiry* 2(3):46-49.

Fox, Sidney. 1988. *The Emergence of Life: Darwinian Evolution from the Inside.* New York: Basic Books.

Frair, Wayne, and Davis, Percival. 1983. *A Case for Creation.* 3rd ed. Chicago: Moody Press.

Franks, John. 1979. "Plants." Page 163 in Steel and Harvey 1979.

Frauenfelder, Hans. 1988. "Biomolecules." In *Emerging Syntheses in Science,* ed. David Pines. Redwood City, Calif.: Addison-Wesley.

French, Bevan M. 1981. "The Moon." In *The New Solar System,* eds. Beatty, J. Kelly; O'Leary, Brian; and Chaikin, Andrew, pp. 71-82. Cambridge, Mass.: Sky.

Freske, Stanley. 1981. "Creationist Misunderstanding, Misrepresentation, and Misuse of the Second Law of Thermodynamics." *Creation/Evolution* 4:8-16.

Fricke, Hans. 1988. "Coelecanths: The Fish that Time Forgot." *National Geographic* 173(6):824-838.

Friedman, Richard Elliott. 1987. *Who Wrote the Bible?* New York: Summit Books.

Frye, Roland M., ed. 1983a. *Is God a Creationist? The Religious Case Against Creation-Science.* New York: Scribner's.

———. 1983b. "Creation-Science Against the Religious Background." Pp. 1-28 in Frye 1983a.

———. 1983c. "The Two Books of God." Pp. 199-205 in Frye 1983a.

Futuyma, Douglas J. 1979. *Evolutionary Biology.* Sunderland, Mass.: Sinauer Associates.

———. 1982. *Science on Trial: The Case for Evolution.* New York: Pantheon Books.

Gallant, Roy A. 1984. "To Hell With Evolution." Pp. 282-305 in Montagu 1984.

Galston, Arthur W., and Slayman, Clifford L. 1979. "The Not-So-Secret Life of Plants." *American Scientist* 67:337-344.

Gardner, Martin. 1981. *Science: Good, Bad and Bogus.* Buffalo, N.Y.: Prometheus Books.

———. 1988. *The New Age: Notes of a Fringe-Watcher.* Buffalo, N.Y.: Prometheus Books.

Geisler, Norman L., and Anderson, J. Kerby. 1987. *Origin Science: A Proposal for the Creation-Evolution Controversy.* Grand Rapids: Baker Book House.

Ghiselin, Michael T. 1986. "We Are All Contraptions." *New York Times Book Review,* December 14, pp. 18-19.

Gier, Nicholas F. 1982. "Humanism as an American Heritage." *Free Inquiry* 2(2):27-29.

Gilkey, Langdon. 1985. *Creationism on Trial: Evolution and God at Little Rock.* Minneapolis, Minn.: Winston Press.

Ginsberg, H. L., tr. 1969. "Ugaritic Myths, Epics, and Legends." Pp. 129-155 in Pritchard 1969.

Gillespie, Neal C. 1979. *Charles Darwin and the Problem of Creation.* Chicago: University of Chicago Press.

Gish, Duane T. 1973. "Creation, Evolution, and the Historical Evidence." Pp. 266-282 in Ruse 1988.

———. 1977. *Dinosaurs: Those Terrible Lizards.* El Cajon, Calif.: Master Books.

———. 1981. Letter to the Editors. *Discover* 2(7):6.

———. 1985. *Evolution: The Challenge of the Fossil Record.* El Cajon, Calif.: Creation-Life Publishers.

———. 1986. "It's Evolutionists, Not Creationists, Who Advocate Blind Dogmatism." *Miami Herald,* October 12.

———. 1987. "Startling Discoveries Support Creation." *Impact* 171.

———. 1988. Debate with Ian Plimer. Videotape.

Glenister, Brian F., and Witzke, Brian J. 1983. "Interpreting Earth History." Pp. 55-84 in Wilson 1983.

Godfrey, Laurie R. 1983a. "Creationism and Gaps in the Fossil Record." Pp. 193-218 in Godfrey 1983b.

———, ed. 1983b. *Scientists Confront Creationism.* New York: Norton.

———. 1984. "Scientific Creationism: The Art of Distortion." Pp. 167-181 in Montagu 1984.

———. 1985. "Foot Notes of an Anatomist." Pp. 16-36 in Cole and Godfrey 1985.

Goldberg, Robert B. 1988. "Plants: Novel Developmental Processes." *Science* 240: 1460-1467.

Gonzalez-Crussi, F. 1985. *Notes of an Anatomist.* New York: Harcourt Brace Janovich.

Goodgame, Dan. 1989. "Calling for an Overhaul." *Time* 134 (15):60, 69.

Gore, Rick. 1983. "The Once and Future Universe." *National Geographic* 163(6):704-748.

Gould, Stephen Jay. 1980. *The Panda's Thumb.* New York: Norton.

———. 1982."Fascinating Tails." *Discover* 3(9):40-41.

———. 1983. *Hen's Teeth and Horse's Toes.* New York: Norton.

———. 1984a. "Evolution as Fact and Theory." Pp. 117-25 in Montagu 1984.

Gould, Stephen Jay. 1984b. "Toward the Vindication of Punctuational Change." Pp. 9-34 in Berggren and Van Couvering 1984.

———. 1987. "Darwinism Defined: The Difference Between Fact and Theory." *Discover* 8(1):64-70.

———. 1989. *Wonderful Life: The Burgess Shale and the Nature of History.* New York: W. W. Norton.

Greene, John C. 1959. *The Death of Adam: Evolution and its Impact on Western Thought.* Ames, Iowa: Iowa State University Press.

Greenspahn, Frederick E. 1983. "Biblical Views of Creation." *Creation/Evolution* 13:30-38.

Greenwood, P. Humphrey. 1985. "Fish." *Encyclopedia Americana,* v. 11, pp. 289-306. Danbury, Conn.: Grolier.

Gretener, Peter E. 1984. "Reflections on the 'Rare Event' and Related Concepts in Geology." Pp. 77-89 in Berggren and Van Couvering 1984.

Gribbin, John, and Cherfas, Jeremy. 1982. *The Monkey Puzzle: Reshaping the Evolutionary Tree.* New York: McGraw-Hill.

Gross, Richard E. 1985. "Social Sciences." *Encyclopedia Americana,* v. 25, pp. 130-131. Danbury, Conn.: Grolier.

Guth, Alan H. 1988a. "The Birth of the Cosmos." Pp. 1-41 in Osterbrock and Raven 1988.

———. 1988b. Interview. *Omni* 11(2):75-79, 94-96.

Guth, Alan H., and Steinhardt, Paul J. 1984. "The Inflationary Universe." *Scientific American* 250(5):116-128.

Halstead, L. Beverly. 1984. "Evolution—the Fossils Say Yes!" Pp. 240-54 in Montagu 1984.

Ham, Ken. 1987. *The Lie: Evolution.* El Cajon, Calif.: Master Books.

———. 1989a. "Bishop or Bible? A Question of Authority." *Acts & Facts* 18(1):5-6.

———. 1989b. "Five Vital Questions to Ask Your Church or School." *Acts & Facts* 18(5):a-c.

———. 1989c. "Is God an Evolutionist?" *Acts & Facts* 18(3):a-b.

Hammond, Allen, and Margulis, Lynn. 1981. "Farewell to Newton, Einstein, Darwin . . ." *Science 81* 2(10):55-57.

Hansel, C. E. M. 1984. "The Evidence for ESP: A Critique." *Skeptical Inquirer* 8(4):322-328.

Hanson, Robert W., ed. 1986. *Science and Creation: Geological, Theological, and Educational Perspectives.* New York: Macmillan.

Hartmann, William K. 1985. *Astronomy: The Cosmic Journey.* 3rd ed. Belmont, Calif.: Wadsworth.

Hartmann, William K., and Davis, Donald R. 1975. "Satellite-Sized Planetesimals and Lunar Origin." *Icarus* 24:504-515.

Hastey, Stan. 1987. "High Court Strikes Down Creation Science Law." *Florida Baptist Witness* 73(173):31.

Hastings, Ronnie J. 1985. "Tracking Those Incredible Creationists." Pp. 5-15 in Cole and Godfrey 1985.

———. 1987. "Creationists' Tooth Claims Evolve into a New 'Fish Story.' " *Creation/ Evolution Newsletter* 7(5):18-20.

Hastings, Ronnie J. 1989. "Creationists' 'Glen Rose Man' Proves to be a Fish Tooth (as Expected)." *NCSE Reports* 9(3):14-15.

Hawking, Stephen W. 1988. *A Brief History of Time: From the Big Bang to Black Holes*. New York: Bantam.

Hechinger, Fred M. 1986. "Fundamentalists Turn to Courts, Ballot Box for Control of Schools." *Gainesville (Fla.) Sun*, November 8.

Heidel, Alexander. 1951. *The Babylonian Genesis: The Story of Creation*. Chicago: University of Chicago Press.

Heinze, Thomas F. 1973. *Creation vs. Evolution*. 2d rev. ed. Grand Rapids, Mich.: Baker Book House.

Henry, Paul S. 1980. "A Simple Description of the 3 K Cosmic Microwave Background." *Science* 207:939-42.

Hiers, Richard H. 1974. "Satan, Demons, and the Kingdom of God." *Scottish Journal of Theology* 27:35-47.

———. 1988. *Reading the Bible Book by Book: An Introductory Study Guide to the Books of the Bible with Apocrypha*. Philadelphia: Fortress Press.

———. 1989. Personal communication.

Hill, Harold. 1976. *How Did It All Begin?* Plainfield, N.J.: Logos International.

Hollingsworth, Thomas H. 1983. "Population." *Collier's Encyclopedia*, v. 19, pp. 248-253. New York: Macmillan.

Hooke, S. H. 1947. *In the Beginning*. Oxford: Clarendon Press.

———. 1963. *Middle Eastern Mythology*. Baltimore, Md.: Penguin.

Horner, John R., and Gorman, James. 1988. *Digging Dinosaurs*. New York: Workman.

Hoyle, Fred. 1956. "The Steady-State Universe." *Scientific American*, September, pp. 157-166.

Huchingson, James E. 1982. "Science and Religion: Uneasy Armistice." *Miami Herald*, January 10.

Hume, David. 1779. *Dialogues Concerning Natural Religion*. Edited by Norman Kemp Smith. 2d ed. London: Thomas Nelson and Sons, 1947.

Humphreys, Russell. 1989. "The Mystery of the Earth's Magnetic Field." *Impact* 188.

Institute for Creation Research. 1987a. "Creationism and the Supreme Court." *Acts & Facts* 16(8):1, 3.

———. 1987b. "The Supreme Court Decision and its Meaning." *Impact* 170.

———. 1988a. "Radio Debate on the Age of the Earth." *Acts & Facts* 17(2):2-3, 7.

——. 1988b. "Search for Noah' s Ark Continues. " *Acts & Facts* 17(11):4.

Jackson, Francis, and Moore, Patrick. 1987. *Life in the Universe.* New York: Norton.

Jacob, Francois. 1977. "Evolution and Tinkering." *Science* 196:1161-1166.

Jaroff, Leon. 1989. "The Gene Hunt." *Time* 133(12):62-67.

Jastrow, Robert. 1978. *God and the Astronomers.* New York: Norton.

———. 1979. *Red Giants and White Dwarfs.* New ed. New York: Norton.

Johanson, Donald C. and Edey, Maitland A. 1981. *Lucy: The Beginnings of Humankind.* New York: Simon and Schuster.

Johanson, Donald C. and White, Tim D. 1979. "A Systematic Assessment of Early African Hominids." *Science* 203:320-330.

Jukes, Thomas H. 1983. "Molecular Evidence for Evolution." Pp. 117-38 in Godfrey 1983b.

———. 1988. "Molecular Evolution and Ancestry of Living Organisms." *Creation/Evolution Newsletter* 8(4):5-7.

Kehoe, Alice B. 1983. "The Word of God." Pp. 1-12 in Godfrey 1983b.

Keith, Bill. 1982. *Scopes II: The Great Debate.* Shreveport, La.: Huntington House.

Kitcher, Philip. 1982. *Abusing Science: The Case Against Creationism.* Cambridge, Mass.: MIT Press.

Klotz, John W. 1985. *Studies in Creation: A General Introduction to the Creation/Evolution Debate.* St. Louis, Mo.: Concordia Publishing House.

Kramer, S. N., tr. 1969. "Sumerian Myths and Epic Tales." Pp. 37-59 in Pritchard 1969.

Kritsky, Gene. 1987. "Fossil Insects: Pests of Creation." *Creation/Evolution* 20:13-19.

Kuban, Glen J. 1986. "A Summary of the Taylor Site Evidence." *Creation/Evolution* 17:10-18.

Kunzig, Robert. 1988. "The Wolf Effect." *Discover* 9(8):18-20.

Kurtz, Paul, ed. 1973. *The Humanist Alternative.* Buffalo, N.Y.: Prometheus Books.

———. 1980. "A Secular Humanist Declaration." *Free Inquiry* 1(1):3-6.

———. 1981. "The State Should be Neutral." *Free Inquiry* 1(2):11-12.

———. 1985. "Homer Duncan's Crusade Against Secular Humanism." *Free Inquiry* 6(1):37-42.

———. 1986. "The New Inquisition in the Schools." *Free Inquiry* 7(1):4-5.

———. 1987. "Breaking with the Old Humanism." *Free Inquiry* 8(1):5.

Kutter, G. Siegfried. 1987. *The Universe and Life: Origins and Evolution.* Boston: Jones and Bartlett.

LaHaye, Tim. 1975. "Introduction." Pp. 5-6 in Morris 1982b.

———. 1980. *The Battle for the Mind.* Old Tappan, N.J.: Fleming H. Revell Co.

LaHaye, Tim, and Morris, John. 1976. *The Ark on Ararat.* San Diego, Calif.: Creation-Life Publishers.

Lambert, W. G. 1965. "A New Look at the Babylonian Background of Genesis." *Journal of Theological Studies* 16(Pt.2):288-300.

Lamont, Corliss. 1957. *The Philosophy of Humanism.* 4th ed. New York: Philosophical Library.

Landau, Matthew. 1982. "Whales: Can Evolution Account for Them?" *Creation/Evolution* 10:14-19.

Lawrence, Jill. 1989. "Schools Show Deficiencies in High-Level Skills." *Gainesville (Fla.) Sun.* February 15.

Leakey, Richard E. 1981. *The Making of Mankind.* New York: E. P. Dutton.

Lemaitre, Georges. 1950. *The Primeval Atom.* New York: Van Nostrand.

Lemonick, Michael D. 1989. "Wormholes in the Heavens." *Time* 133(3):55.

Lewin, Roger. 1987a. *Bones of Contention: Controversies in the Search for Human Origins.* New York: Simon and Schuster.

———. 1987b. "Creationism Case Argued Before Supreme Court." *Science* 235:22-23.

———. 1988a. "Conflict over DNA Clock Results." *Science* 241:1598-1600.

———. 1988b. "Family Relationships are a Biological Conundrum." *Science* 242:671.

———. 1988c. *In the Age of Mankind: A Smithsonian Book of Human Evolution.* Washington: Smithsonian Books.

———. 1988d. "Linguists Search for the Mother Tongue." *Science* 242:1128-1129.

Lieberman, Philip. 1984. *The Biology and Evolution of Language.* Cambridge, Mass.: Harvard University Press.

Longstaff, Thomas R. W. 1985. "God." Pp. 350-51 in Achtemeier 1985.

Lorenz, Konrad. 1966. *On Aggression.* Translated by Marjorie Kerr Wilson. New York: Harcourt, Brace, and World.

MacDonald, David. 1988. "The Flood: Mesopotamian Archaeological Evidence." *Creation/Evolution* 23:14-20.

Machina, Kenton F. 1982. *Basic Applied Logic.* Dallas, Tex.: Scott, Foresman and Co.

Mallove, Eugene F. 1987. *The Quickening Universe: Cosmic Evolution and Human Destiny.* New York: St. Martin's.

Margulis, Lynn, and Schwartz, Karlene. 1988. *Five Kingdoms: An Illustrated Guide to the Phyla of Life on Earth.* 2d ed. New York: W. H. Freeman.

Marsden, George M. 1984. "Understanding Fundamentalist Views of Science." Pp. 95-116 in Montagu 1984.

Martz, Larry, and McDaniel, Ann. 1987. "Keeping God out of the Classroom." *Newsweek,* June 29, 23-24.

Marx, Jean L. 1988. "The AIDS Virus Can Take on Many Guises." *Science* 241:1039-1040.

Mattill, A. J. 1982. "Three Cheers for the Creationists!" *Free Inquiry* 2(2):17-18.

Max, Edward E. 1986. "Plagiarized Errors and Molecular Genetics: Another Argument in the Evolution-Creation Controversy." *Creation/Evolution* 19:34-46.

May, Herbert G., and Metzger, Bruce M., ed. 1973. *The New Oxford Annotated Bible with the Apocrypha.* Revised Standard Version. New York: Oxford University Press.

Maynard Smith, John. 1975. *The Theory of Evolution.* 3rd ed. New York: Penguin.

———. 1986. *The Problems of Biology.* New York: Oxford University Press.

———. 1988. *Did Darwin Get It Right? Essays on Games, Sex, and Evolution.* New York: Chapman and Hall.

Mayr, Ernst. 1954. "Change of Genetic Environment and Evolution." In Julian Huxley, ed., *Evolution as a Process,* pp. 157-80. London: Allen and Unwin.

———. 1964. "Introduction." Pp. vii-xxvii in Darwin 1859.

———. 1970. *Populations, Species, and Evolution.* Cambridge, Mass.: Harvard University Press.

———. 1983. "Darwin, Intellectual Revolutionary." Pp. 23-41 in Bendall 1983.

———. 1988. *Toward a New Philosophy of Biology: Observations of an Evolutionist.* Cambridge, Mass.: Belknap Press.

McGowan, Chris. 1984. *In the Beginning: A Scientist Shows the Creationists are Wrong.* Buffalo, N.Y.: Prometheus Books.

McIver, Tom. 1987. "Nebraska Man Strikes Again and Again." *Creation/Evolution Newsletter* 7(4):13-14.

———. 1988a. "Catholic Anti-Evolutionists and Historical Revisionists." *Creation/Evolution Newsletter* 8(3):15-16.

———. 1988b. "Creationist Misquotation of Darrow." *Creation/Evolution* 23:1-13.

———. 1988c. "Formless and Void: Gap Theory Creationism." *Creation/ Evolution* 24:1-24.

McKean, Kevin. 1983. "Life on a Young Planet." *Discover* 4(3):39-42.

McKenzie, John L. 1980. *The Old Testament without Illusion.* Garden City, N.Y.: Image Books.

McKinney, Joan. 1987. "Court Hears Creationism Arguments." *Creation/Evolution Newsletter* 6(6):11-12.

McKown, Delos B. 1986. "Accuracy in Academia, or What to Do About Humbug." *The Humanist* 46(6):5-7, 34.

McQueen, David R. 1988. "Days of Noah." *Days of Praise* (June-July-August), July 24.

Medawar, P. B. and Medawar, J. S. 1983. *Aristotle to Zoos: A Philosophical Dictionary of Biology*. Cambridge, Mass.: Harvard University Press.

Meisler, Stanley. 1989. "6-Nation Study Finds U.S. Teens Worst in Math." *Gainesville (Fla.) Sun*. February 1.

Mencken, H. L. 1925a. "The Hills of Zion." Pp. 153-61 in Cooke 1955.

———. 1925b. "In Memoriam: W. J. B." Pp. 161-67 in Cooke 1955.

Mereson, Amy. 1988. "Monkeying Around with the Relatives." *Discover* 9(3):26-27.

Mettinger, Tryggve N. D. 1988. *In Search of God: The Meaning and Message of the Everlasting Names*. Translated by Frederick H. Cryer. Philadelphia, Pa.: Fortress Press.

Meyers, Robert A., ed. 1989. *Encyclopedia of Astronomy and Astrophysics*. San Diego, Calif.: Academic Press.

Midgley, Mary. 1978. *Beast and Man: The Roots of Human Nature*. Ithaca, N.Y.: Cornell University Press.

Miller, Kenneth R. 1982. "Answers to the Standard Creationist Arguments." *Creation/Evolution* 7:1-13.

———. 1984. "Scientific Creationism versus Evolution: The Mislabeled Debate." Pp. 18-63 in Montagu 1984.

Miller, Madeleine S. and Miller, J. Lane. 1973. *Harper's Bible Dictionary*. 8th ed. New York: Harper and Row.

Miller, Stanley L. 1953. "A Production of Amino Acids Under Possible Primitive Earth Conditions." *Science* 117:528-529.

Miller, Stanley L. and Orgel, Leslie E. 1974. *The Origins of Life on the Earth*. Englewood Cliffs, N.J.: Prentice Hall.

Monastersky, Richard. 1988. "Vents Would Scald a Primordial Soup." *Science News* 134:117.

———. 1989. "New Record for World's Oldest Rocks." *Science News* 136:228.

Montagu, Ashley, ed. 1984. *Science and Creationism*. New York: Oxford University Press.

Moore, John A. 1984. "Science as a Way of Knowing: Evolutionary Biology." *American Zoologist* 24:467-534.

Moore, John N. 1976. *Questions and Answers on Creation/Evolution*. Grand Rapids, Mich.: Baker Book House.

Moore, John N., and Slusher, Harold S. 1970. *Biology: A Search for Order in Complexity*. Grand Rapids, Mich.: Zondervan.

Moore, Robert A. 1981. "Arkeology: A New Science in Support of Creation?" *Creation/Evolution* 6:6-15.

———. 1983. "The Impossible Voyage of Noah's Ark." *Creation/Evolution* 11:1-43.

Morowitz, Harold J. 1985. *Mayonnaise and the Origin of Life: Thoughts of Minds and Molecules*. New York: Charles Scribner's Sons.

Morris, Henry M. 1963. *The Twilight of Evolution*. Grand Rapids, Mich.: Baker Book House.

———. 1967. *Evolution and the Modern Christian*. Grand Rapids, Mich.: Baker Book House.

———. 1970. *Biblical Cosmology and Modern Science*. Nutley, N.Y.: Craig Press.

———. 1974. *Many Infallible Proofs*. San Diego, Calif.: Creation-Life Publishers.

———. 1977. *The Scientific Case for Creation*. San Diego, Calif.: Master Books.

———. 1978. *The Remarkable Birth of Planet Earth*. Minneapolis, Minn.: Bethany House.

———. 1982a. *Creation and its Critics*. San Diego, Calif.: Creation-Life Publishers.

———. 1982b. *The Troubled Waters of Evolution*. 2d ed. San Diego, Calif.: Creation-Life Publishers.

Morris, Henry M. 1983. *Science, Scripture and the Young Earth*. El Cajon, Calif.: Institute for Creation Research.

———. 1984a. *The Biblical Basis for Modern Science*. Grand Rapids, Mich.: Baker Book House.

———. 1984b. *A History of Modern Creationism*. San Diego, Calif.: Master Books.

———. 1985a. *The Religion of Evolution*. El Cajon, Calif.: Institute for Creation Research.

———. ed. 1985b. *Scientific Creationism*. 2d gen. ed. El Cajon, Calif.: Master Books.

———. 1986. *Science and the Bible*. Rev. ed. Chicago: Moody Press.

———. 1987a. "Is Creationism Scientific?" *Acts & Facts* 16(12):1, 4.

———. 1987b. "The Judging Spirit of God." *Days of Praise* (Sept.-Oct.-Nov.), Oct. 28.

———. 1987c. Letter to friends of the ICR. May.

———. 1987d. Letter to friends of the ICR. July.

———. 1987e. Letter to friends of the ICR. August.

———. 1987f. Letter to friends of the ICR. October.

———. 1987g. Letter (with *Days of Praise*) to friends of the ICR. December.

———. 1987h. "The Physical Sciences." Pp. 187-293 in Morris and Parker 1987.

———. 1988a. "The Compromise Road." *Impact* 177.

———. 1988b. "God-Hardened Hearts." *Days of Praise* (June-July-August), August 3.

———. 1988c. "Harvest is Past." *Days of Praise*, (Dec.-Jan.-Feb.), Dec. 31.

———. 1988d. "The Heritage of the Recapitulation Theory." *Impact* 183.

———. 1988e. Letter to friends of the ICR. November.

———. 1988f. Letter to friends of the ICR. December.

———. 1988g. *Men of Science, Men of God: Great Scientists of the Past who Believed in the Bible*. Rev. ed. El Cajon, Calif.: Master Books.

———. 1989a. "Evolution: A House Divided." *Impact* 194.

———. 1989b. "The Fire of God." *Days of Praise* (June-July-August), June 7.

———. 1989c. "How a Christian Dies." *Impact* 193.

Morris, Henry M. 1989d. Letter to friends of the ICR. February.

———. 1989e. "1988 a Great Year! Annual Report of ICR Activities." *Acts & Facts* 18(1):2, 9.

Morris, Henry M., and Parker, Gary E. 1987. *What Is Creation Science?* Rev. ed. El Cajon, Calif.: Master Books.

Morris, John D. 1988. "A Report on the ICR Ararat Expedition, 1987." *Impact* 175.

———. 1989a. "The Allure of the Crowd." *Days of Praise* (March-April-May), March 19.

———. 1989b. "How Do the Dinosaurs Fit In?" *Acts & Facts* 18(5):d.

Moyer, Wayne A. 1986. "Science versus Revealed Truth: Meeting the Challenge of Creationism in the Classroom." Pp. 46-54 in Hanson 1986.

Murphy, Jeffrie G. 1982. *Evolution, Morality, and the Meaning of Life.* Totowa, N.J.: Rowman and Littlefield.

Murray, N. Patrick, and Buffaloe, Neal D. 1983. "Creationism and Evolution: The Real Issues." Pp. 454-476 in Zetterberg 1983.

Napier, B. Davie. 1962. *Song of the Vineyard.* New York: Harper and Brothers.

National Academy of Sciences. 1984. *Science and Creationism: A View from the National Academy of Sciences.* Washington: National Academy Press.

National Commission on Excellence in Education. 1983. "A Nation at Risk." In *The Great School Debate,* ed. Beatrice Gross and Ronald Gross, pp. 23-49. New York: Simon and Schuster, 1985.

Nelkin, Dorothy. 1982. *The Creation Controversy: Science or Scripture in the Schools.* New York: Norton.

Newell, Norman D. 1984. "Mass Extinction: Unique or Recurrent Causes?" Pp. 115-27 in Berggren and Van Couvering 1984.

———. 1985. *Creation and Evolution: Myth or Reality?* New York: Praeger.

Nickels, Martin K. 1986. "Creationists and the Australopithecines." *Creation/Evolution* 19:1-15.

Nord, Warren A. 1986. "Liberals Could Learn Something From the Religious Right." *St. Petersburg Times,* July 19.

Noss, John B. 1980. *Man's Religions.* 6th ed. New York: Macmillan.

Numbers, Ronald L. 1982. "Creationism in 20th-Century America." *Science* 218:538-544.

Oates, Joan. 1979. *Babylon.* London: Thames and Hudson.

Oldroyd, Harold. 1985. "Insect." *Encyclopedia Americana,* v. 15, pp. 196-208. Danbury, Conn.: Grolier.

Olson, Everett C. 1965. *The Evolution of Life.* New York: New American Library.

Ordovensky, Pat. 1989. "Dropout Rate Rises; 'Scary Situation.' " *USA Today*. May 4.

Osterbrock, Donald E., and Raven, Peter H., ed. 1988. *Origins and Extinctions*. New Haven, Conn.: Yale University Press.

Overton, Judge William R. 1982. "United States District Court Opinion: *McLean v. Arkansas*." Pp. 307-331 in Ruse 1988.

Ozima, Minoru. 1981. *The Earth: Its Birth and Growth*. Translated by Judy Wakahayashi. Cambridge: Cambridge University Press.

Page, Thornton, and Sagan, Carl, ed. 1972. *UFOs: A Scientific Debate*. Ithaca, N.Y.: Cornell University Press.

Palen, Kathy. 1987. "Seminary Professor Calls for 'Divorce' within SBC." *Florida Baptist Witness* 62(162):6.

Paley, William. 1802. *Natural Theology: or Evidences of the Existence and Attributes of the Deity, Collected from the Appearances of Nature*. Reprint. Houston, Tx.: St. Thomas Press, 1972.

Panchen, A. L. 1979. "Ichthyostegids." Page 103 in Steel and Harvey 1979.

Parker, Barry. 1988. *Creation: The Story of the Origin and Evolution of the Universe*. New York: Plenum.

Parker, Gary E. 1987. "The Life Sciences." Pp. 31-184 in Morris and Parker 1987.

Passmore, J. 1983. "Epilogue." Pp. 569-75 in Bendall 1983.

Patlak, Margie. 1989. "The Fickle Virus." *Discover* 10(2):24-25.

Patterson, John W. 1983. "An Engineer Looks at the Creationist Movement." Pp. 150-161 in Zetterberg 1983.

Perdue, Leo G. 1985. "Names of God in the Old Testament." Pp. 685-687 in Achtemeier 1985.

Peterson, Ivars. 1988. "Hints of Planets Circling Nearby Stars." *Science News* 134:103.

———. 1989. "Astronomers Glimpse Birth of a Pulsar." *Science News* 135:100.

Pettersson, Hans. 1960. "Cosmic Spherules and Meteoritic Dust." *Scientific American* 2:123-132.

Popper, Karl R. 1968. *The Logic of Scientific Discovery*. 3d ed. London: Hutchinson.

Prigogine, Ilye. 1969. "Structure, Dissipation, and Life." In *Theoretical Physics and Biology*, ed. M. Marois, pp. 23-52. New York: American Elsevier.

Prigogine, Ilye, and Stengers, Isabelle. 1984. *Order Out of Chaos: Man's New Dialogue with Nature*. New York: Bantam Books.

Pritchard, James B., ed. 1969. *Ancient Near Eastern Texts Relating to the Old Testament*. 3d ed. Princeton, N.J.: Princeton University Press.

Rad, Gerhard von. 1961. *Genesis*. Philadelphia, Pa.: Westminster Press.

Raloff, Janet. 1986. "Is There a Cosmic Chemistry of Life?" *Science News* 130:182.

———. 1987. "High Court Rejects Creationism Law." *Science News* 131:404.

Raup, David M. 1983. "The Geological and Paleontological Arguments of Creationism." Pp. 147-162 in Godfrey 1983b.

Raup, David M., and Stanley, Steven M. 1971. *Principles of Paleontology*. San Francisco, Calif.: Freeman.

Reber, Arthur S. 1985. *The Penguin Dictionary of Psychology*. New York: Penguin.

Richards, Graham. 1987. *Human Evolution: An Introduction for the Behavioural Sciences.* London: Routledge & Kegan Paul.

Roberts, Leslie. 1988. "Hard Choices Ahead on Biodiversity." *Science* 241:1759-1761.

Roeder, Martin. 1989. Personal communication.

Romer, Alfred Sherwood. 1966. *Vertebrate Paleontology*. 3d ed. Chicago: University of Chicago Press.

Roux, Georges. 1966. *Ancient Iraq*. Baltimore, Md.: Penguin.

Rubin, Gerald M. 1988. "*Drosophila melanogaster* as an Experimental Organism." *Science* 240:1453-1459.

Ruse, Michael. 1982. *Darwinism Defended: A Guide to the Evolution Controversies.* Reading, Mass.: Addison-Wesley.

———. 1986. *Taking Darwin Seriously: A Naturalistic Approach to Philosophy.* Oxford: Basil Blackwell.

———, ed. 1988. *But Is It Science? The Philosophical Question in the Creation/Evolution Controversy.* Buffalo, N.Y.: Prometheus Books.

Russell, Bertrand. 1957. *Why I Am Not a Christian.* New York: Simon and Schuster.

———. 1961. *Religion and Science.* New York: Oxford University Press.

Russell, Cristine. 1986. "Survey Finds Half in U.S. Reject Evolution Theory." *Creation/Evolution Newsletter* 6(3):4.

Russell, Jane L. 1983. "Astronomical Creation: The Evolution of Stars and Planets." Pp. 46-54 in Wilson 1983.

Russell, Jeffrey Burton. 1977. *The Devil: Perceptions of Evil from Antiquity to Primitive Christianity.* Ithaca, N.Y.: Cornell University Press.

Sagan, Carl. 1980. *Cosmos*. New York: Random House.

———. 1989. "Why We Need to Understand Science." *Parade,* Sept. 10, pp. 6-13.

Sagan, Carl, and Druyan, Ann. 1985. *Comet.* New York: Random House.

Saladin, Kenneth S. 1980. "Creationist Bill Dies in Georgia Legislature." *The Humanist,* May/June 1980, 59-60.

———. 1988. "Saladin-Gish Debate." *Creation/Evolution Newsletter* 8(6):11, 14.

Sandage, Allan R. 1956. "The Red-Shift." In *Cosmology +1: Readings from Scientific American.* San Francisco, Calif.: W. H. Freeman, 1977.

Sarich, Vincent, and Wilson, Allan. 1967. "Immunological Time Scale for Hominid Evolution." *Science* 158:1200-1203.

Schadewald, Robert J. 1982. "Six 'Flood' Arguments Creationists Can't Answer." *Creation/Evolution* 9:12-17.

———. 1983a. "Creation Pseudoscience." *Skeptical Inquirer* 8(1):22-35.

———. 1983b. "The Evolution of Bible-Science." Pp. 283-299 in Godfrey 1983b.

———. 1986. "The 1986 International Conference on Creationism." *Creation/Evolution Newsletter* 6(5):8-14.

———. 1988. "The ICR Summer Institute, July 11-15, 1988." *Creation/Evolution Newsletter* 8(5):14-16.

Schaeffer, Francis A. 1982. *A Christian Manifesto.* Rev. ed. Westchester, Ill.: Crossway Books.

Schafersman, Steven D. 1987. "Review of ASA Booklet." *Creation/Evolution Newsletter* 7(2&3):5-7.

Schlafly, Phyllis. 1981. "What is Humanism?" *Free Inquiry* 1(2):8.

Schopf, J. William, ed. 1983. *Earth's Earliest Biosphere: Its Origin and Evolution.* Princeton, N.J.: Princeton University Press.

Schopf, J. William; Hayes, J. M.; and Walter, Malcolm R. 1983. "Evolution of Earth's Earliest Ecosystems: Recent Progress and Unsolved Problems." Pp. 361-384 in Schopf 1983.

Scott, Andrew. 1986. *The Creation of Life: Past, Future, Alien.* New York: Basil Blackwell.

Scott, Eugenie C. 1987. "Louisiana Decision Announced." *Creation/Evolution Newsletter* 7(4):1, 5-8.

———. 1988. "ICR Denied State Approval to Grant Degrees." *Creation/Evolution Newsletter* 8(6):4-5.

Segraves, Kelly L. 1975. *Sons of God Return.* New York: Pyramid Books.

Seldes, George, comp. 1967. *The Great Quotations.* New York: Pocket Books.

Shapiro, Robert. 1986. *Origins: A Skeptic's Guide to the Creation of Life on Earth.* New York: Summit Books.

Shklovskii, I. S., and Sagan, Carl. 1966. *Intelligent Life in the Universe.* San Francisco, Calif.: Holden-Day.

Sick, Helmut. 1985. "Birds." *Encyclopaedia Britannica,* v. 15, pp. 1-13. Chicago: Encyclopaedia Britannica.

Silk, Joseph. 1980. *The Big Bang: The Creation and Evolution of the Universe.* New York: W. H. Freeman.

Simpson, George Gaylord. 1964. *This View of Life: The World of an Evolutionist.* New York: Harcourt, Brace, and World.

———. 1967. *The Meaning of Evolution: A Study of the History of Life and of its Significance for Man.* Rev. ed. New Haven, Conn.: Yale University Press.

Skehan, James W. 1986. "The Age of the Earth, of Life, and of Mankind: Geology and Biblical Theology versus Creationism." Pp. 10-32 in Hanson 1986.

Skinner, B. F. 1981. Letter to the editor. *Free Inquiry* 1(2):3-4.

Sloan, Robert E. 1983. "The Transition Between Reptiles and Mammals." Pp. 263-277 in Zetterberg 1983.

Slusher, Harold S. 1981. *Critique of Radiometric Dating.* 2d ed. San Diego, Calif.: Creation-Life Publishers.

Smart, J. J. C. 1962. "The Existence of God." Pp. 211-220 in *Philosophy of Religion: A Book of Readings*, eds. George L. Abernethy and Thomas A. Langford. New York: Macmillan, 1962.

Sonleitner, Frank J. 1987. "The Origin of Species by Punctuated Equilibria." *Creation/Evolution* 20:24-30.

Speiser, E. A., tr. 1969. "Akkadian Myths and Epics." Pp. 60-119 in Pritchard 1969.

Spencer, Edgar W. 1983. *Physical Geology.* Reading, Mass.: Addison-Wesley.

Spielberg, Nathan, and Anderon, Byron D. 1985. *Seven Ideas that Shook the Universe.* New York: John Wiley and Sons.

Stambaugh, James S. 1989. "Death Before Sin?" *Impact* 191.

Stanley, Steven M. 1981. *The New Evolutionary Timetable: Fossils, Genes, and the Origin of Species.* New York: Basic Books.

Starr, Cecie, and Taggart, Ralph. 1984. *Biology: The Unity and Diversity of Life.* 3d ed. Belmont, Calif.: Wadsworth.

Staunton, Lawrence P. 1984. Review of *The Origin of the Universe* by Harold S. Slusher. Page 52 in Weinberg 1984.

Stebbins, G. Ledyard. 1982. *Darwin to DNA, Molecules to Humanity.* San Francisco, Calif.: W. H. Freeman.

Steel, Rodney. 1979. "Insects." Pp. 104-105 in Steel and Harvey 1979.

Steel, Rodney, and Harvey, Anthony P., ed. 1979. *The Encyclopedia of Prehistoric Life.* New York: McGraw-Hill.

Stein, Gordon. 1987. "Implausibilities Shown to be Plausible." *Skeptical Inquirer* 11(4):407-408.

Stokes, W. Lee. 1982. *Essentials of Earth History: An Introduction to Historical Geology.* 4th ed, Englewood Cliffs, N.J.: Prentice-Hall.

Strahler, Arthur N. 1987. *Science and Earth History: The Evolution/Creation Controversy.* Buffalo, N.Y.: Prometheus Books.

Sullivan, Dean. 1988. *Papal Bull.* Deephaven, Minn.: Meadowbrook.

Suzuki, David, and Knudtson, Peter. 1989. *Genethics: The Clash Between the New Genetics and Human Values.* Cambridge, Mass.: Harvard University Press.

Tax, Sol, ed. 1960. *The Evolution of Life.* Chicago: University of Chicago Press.

Thomsen, Dietrick E. 1985. "The Quantum Universe: A Zero-Point Fluctuation?" *Science News* 128:72-74.

Trefil, James S. 1983. *The Moment of Creation: Big Bang Physics From Before the First Millisecond to the Present Universe.* New York: Scribner's.

———. 1984. "The Accidental Universe." *Science Digest*, June, pp. 53-55, 100-101.

Tryon, Edward P. 1989. "Cosmic Inflation." Pp. 123-57 in Meyers 1989.
Thwaites, William M. 1983. "An Answer to Dr. Geisler—From the Perspective of Biology." *Creation/Evolution* 13:13-20.

Valentine, James W. 1977a. "The Geological Record." Pp. 314-348 in Dobzhansky et al. 1977.
———. 1977b. "Transspecific Evolution." Pp. 233-261 in Dobzhansky et al. 1977.
Valentine, James W. and Campbell, Cathryn A. 1975. "Genetic Regulation and the Fossil Record." *American Scientist* 63:673.
Van Andel, Tjeerd H. 1985. *New Views on an Old Planet: Continental Drift and the History of Earth.* Cambridge: Cambridge University Press.
Vawter, Bruce. 1977. *On Genesis: A New Reading.* Garden City, N.Y.: Doubleday.
———. 1983. "Creationism: Creative Misuse of the Bible." Pp. 71-82 in Frye 1983a.

Wakefield, J. Richard. 1987. "Gentry's Tiny Mystery: Unsupported by Geology." *Creation/Evolution* 22:13-33.
Waldrop, M. Mitchell. 1988. "Shroud of Turin is Medieval." *Science* 242:378.
———. 1989a. "Catalytic RNA Wins Chemistry Nobel." *Science* 246:325.
———. 1989b. "How Do You Read from the Palimpset of Life?" *Science* 246:578-579.
———. 1989c. "The Supernova 1987A Pulsar: Found?" *Science* 243:892.
Walker, James C. G. 1977. *Evolution of the Atmosphere.* New York: Macmillan.
Wallace, Robert A.; King, Jack L.; and Sanders, Gerald P. 1981. *Biology: The Science of Life.* Glenview, Ill.: Scott, Foresman, and Co.
Warner, Greg. 1987. "Inerrancy Gets a Hearing." *Florida Baptist Witness* 66(166):10-11.
Watson, James D. 1968. *The Double Helix.* New York: Atheneum.
Webber, Robert E. 1982. *Secular Humanism: Threat and Challenge.* Grand Rapids, Mich.: Zondervan.
Weber, Christopher Gregory. 1980. "Common Creationist Attacks on Geology." *Creation/Evolution* 2:10-25.
Weinberg, Stan, ed. 1984. *Reviews of Thirty Creationist Books.* Syosset, N.Y.: National Center for Science Education.
———. 1986. "Creation/Evolution Literature from Australia." *Creation/Evolution Newsletter* 6(5):20-22.
Weinberg, Steven. 1977. *The First Three Minutes: A Modern View of the Origin of the Universe.* New York: Basic Books.
Weisburd, Stefi. 1984. "Mapping the Earth's Magnetic Reversals." *Science News* 126:341.
———. 1985a. "The Earth's Magnetic Hiccup. " *Science News* 128:218-220.
———. 1985b. "Modeling Magnetism: The Earth as a Dynamo." *Science News* 128:220.

Weisburd, Stefi. 1985c. " 'Seeing' Continents Drift." *Science News* 128:388.
———. 1986. "Oldest Bird and Longest Dinosaur." *Science News* 130:103.
Wellnhofer, Peter. 1988. "A New Specimen of *Archaeopteryx*." *Science* 240:1790-1792.
Wheeler, Thomas J. 1987. "More on Creationists and Meteoritic Dust." *Creation/Evolution Newsletter* 7(4):14-15.
Whitcomb, John C. 1973. *The World That Perished.* Grand Rapids, Mich.: Baker Book House.
———. 1984. *The Bible and Astronomy.* Winona Lake, Ind.: BMH Books.
Whitcomb, John C. and Morris, Henry M. 1961. *The Genesis Flood: The Biblical Record and its Scientific Implications.* Grand Rapids, Mich.: Baker Book House.
———. 1964. "Preface to the Sixth Printing." Pp. xxv-xxix in Whitcomb and Morris 1961.
Whitman, Walt. 1855. "Song of Myself." *Leaves of Grass.*
Whittaker, J. E. P. 1979. "Fossilization." Page 87 in Steel and Harvey 1979.
Wigglesworth, Sir Vincent Brian. 1985. "Insects: The Class Insecta." *Encyclopaedia Britannica,* v. 21, pp. 585-598. Chicago: Encyclopaedia Britannica.
Wilford, John Noble. 1985. *The Riddle of the Dinosaur.* New York: Random House.
Wilson, David B., ed. 1983. *Did the Devil Make Darwin Do It? Modern Perspectives on the Creation-Evolution Controversy.* Ames, Iowa: Iowa State University Press.
Wilson, E. O. 1985. *Biophilia.* Cambridge, Mass.: Harvard University Press.
———.1987. "Biology's Spiritual Products." *Free Inquiry* 7(2):13-15.
Wilson, E. O.; Carpenter, F. M.; and Brown, W. L. 1967. "The First Mesozoic Ants, with the Description of a New Subfamily." *Psyche* 74:1-19.
Wilson, Robert W. 1979. "The Cosmic Microwave Background Radiation." *Science* 205:866-874.
Woese, Carl R. 1983. "The Primary Line of Descent and the Universal Ancestor." Pp. 209-33 in Bendall 1983.
Wolf, John, and Mellett, James S. 1985. "The Role of 'Nebraska Man' in the Creation-Evolution Debate." *Creation/Evolution* 16:31-43.
Woosley, S. E., and Phillips, M. M. 1988. "Supernova 1987A!" *Science* 240:750-759.
Wright, G. Ernest. 1962. *Biblical Archaeology.* Rev. ed. Philadelphia, Pa.: Westminster Press.

Yablokov, Alexy. 1966. *Variability of Mammals.* Moscow: Nauka Publishers.
Young, Davis A. 1982. *Christianity and the Age of the Earth.* Grand Rapids, Mich.: Zondervan.

Zetterberg, Peter J., ed. 1983. *Evolution Versus Creationism: The Public Education Controversy.* Phoenix, Az.: Oryx Press.

Zimmerman, Michael. 1987. "That Court Ruling Won't Stop the Creationists." *Creation/Evolution Newsletter* 7(5):4-5.

Index

INDEX